IMAGES
of America

Greeks in Tarpon Springs

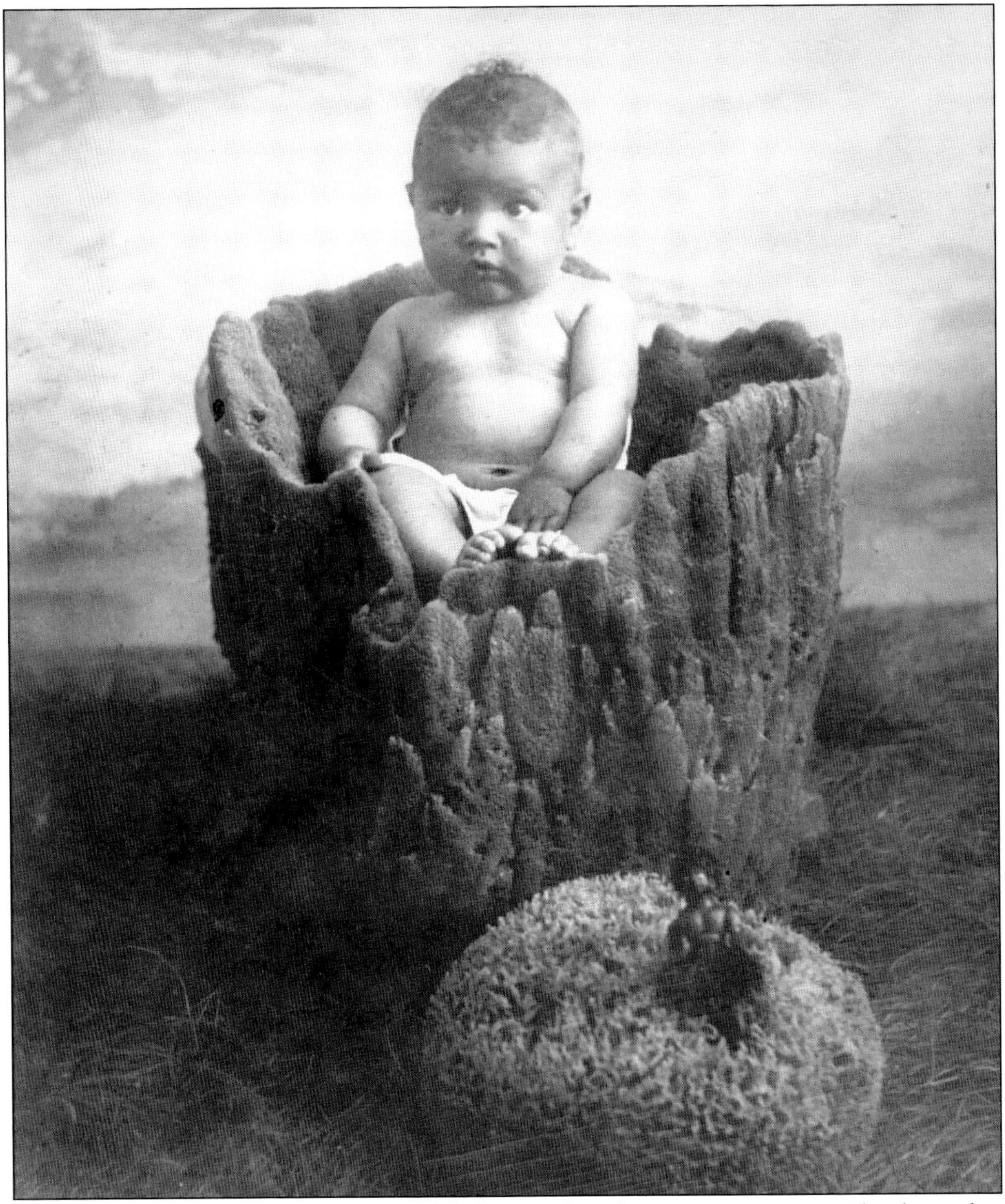

This 1920s image of an unidentified Greek baby seated in a large vase sponge provides the perfect metaphor for the birth of the Greek community of Tarpon Springs. (Courtesy of the Tarpon Springs Area Historical Society.)

On the Cover: Men string sponges on a Greek boat in the Anclote River. After cleaning the sponges, members of the crew typically sort the sponges according to type and size, then string them on twine using heavy needles about two feet long—this keeps them sorted and makes them easier to carry. The strings of sponges were then taken to the Sponge Exchange for storage and sale. (Photograph by Francis G. Wagner, courtesy of Special Collections Department, Tampa Library, University of South Florida.)

IMAGES
of America

GREEKS IN TARPON SPRINGS

Tina Bucuvalas

ARCADIA
PUBLISHING

ISBN 978-1-4671-1546-9

Published by Arcadia Publishing
Charleston, South Carolina

Printed in the United States of America

Library of Congress Control Number: 2015946386

For all general information, please contact Arcadia Publishing:
Telephone 843-853-2070
Fax 843-853-0044
E-mail sales@arcadiapublishing.com
For customer service and orders:
Toll-Free 1-888-313-2665

Visit us on the Internet at www.arcadiapublishing.com

To the remarkable members of the Tarpon Springs Greek community. In the face of many changes, they have maintained their culture and the Greek spirit for more than a century.

Contents

ACKNOWLEDGMENTS

I would like to express my gratitude to the many who provided me with generous contributions of information, images, and time: Duchess Arfaras; Kalotina Assimack; Ellen Babb, Heritage Village; City Clerk's Office, City of Tarpon Springs; Anna Tsoukalas Billiris; Frances Billiris Daskarolis; Dr. Themistocles J. Diamandis; Martha Emmanuel; Vasile Faklis; George Faklis; Michael Faklis; Florida Folklife Program, Department of State; Irene Giannaras Garner; Kaliope Lerios George; Bertha Pappas Houllis; Anna Smolios Ioannidis; Anastasios Karistinos; Scott Keeler; Katherine Alissandratos Kelly; Colleen Kindinis; George Kouskoutis; Irene Koutelas; Nick and Betty Krouskos; Barbara Lewis, Special Collections Department, Tampa Library, University of South Florida; Kaliope Lulias; John Lulias; Metropolitan Nikitas Lulias; George and Beverly Mandalou; Michele Manousos; Kathleen Monahan; Maggie Kavouklis Nichols; Jody Norman, State Archives of Florida; Joyce Pappas; Goldie Tsalichis Parr; George Patides; Yasmin Pianese; Esther Jordan Raptis; the *Tampa Tribune*; David Parsons, Tampa-Hillsborough County Public Library System; Tarpon Springs Area Historical Society; Dale Terrell, St. Nicholas Greek Orthodox Cathedral; Magdaline Peronis Tiliakos; Nellie Peronis Tiliakos; Anna Tiliakos; Mary Lerios Toth; Nicholas Toth; and Sylvia Tsongranis. Their participation and assistance made this project a joy. Alyce Diamandis and Nickollet Tsourakis Henderson made major contributions to this volume not only by contributing images and collections but also by organizing photograph collection sessions and making themselves readily available for identification and support—I cannot thank them enough. Photographer Eleni Christopoulos-Lekkas shared not only family photographs but also many of her own remarkable images that document the *horio*. Alexandra Curran provided her time and expertise in digitizing many of the images. Special thanks go to Liz Gurley of Arcadia Publishing for her patience, kindness, assistance, and persistence.

INTRODUCTION

Nestled around the bayous and Anclote River on the central coast of the Gulf of Mexico, Tarpon Springs is a unique community with a rich heritage based on its maritime history and Greek culture. First settled after the Civil War by scattered fishermen and farmers, the area had become a winter home to wealthy northerners by the early 1880s. In the 1920s, the town was a regional cultural center promoted as "the Venice of the South," but it had changed significantly because of the sponge business.

The Industrial Revolution created great demand for sponges in addition to their household, hygienic, and medical uses—generating an important international trade. Until a French merchant started exporting Bahamian sponges to Europe in the 1840s, the world supply was harvested in the Mediterranean. By 1849, Bahamian sponge fishermen had developed operations in the Florida Keys, and trade soon developed between Key West merchants and New York wholesalers. Conchs from Key West and Bahamians harvested sponges up both Florida coasts, then returned to Key West to sell them. By 1900, Key West had been established as one of the largest world markets.

In 1873, turtle fishermen near Tarpon Springs found sponges in their nets—the first sign of 9,000 square miles of untouched beds. Sponge fishing in the Gulf accelerated in the late 19th century, and by 1890, Tarpon Springs had become a market for Gulf sponges. The 1898 Spanish-American War impelled boats in the Keys sponging fleet to sell their harvest in Tarpon Springs, with the result that some Conchs and Bahamians settled there.

Around 1886, businessman and landowner John Cheyney began supplying sponges from Tarpon Springs to the US market through his Anclote and Rock Island Sponge Company. He built warehouses for processing and selling sponges and launched the first sponge fishing boat. Soon, others established sponge companies in the area, supplied by sponge fisherman who hooked sponges with long poles from dinghies.

Greek immigrants significantly changed and expanded the sponge industry. John Cocoris arrived in 1896 as a buyer for the New York–based Lembessis Company. A year later, he began working for Cheyney, who helped finance Cocoris's early efforts to make the industry more efficient. Cocoris and his three brothers surveyed the Gulf and found it full of sponges. They believed that more and better sponges could be gathered with the deep-sea diving methods used in the Aegean. Sponges had long been harvested in Greece with breath-hold diving, but in 1863, deep-sea diving utilizing a rubberized canvas suit attached to a metal helmet and hand-cranked air compressor was introduced into the Dodecanese islands. Although it dramatically increased production, many divers became paralyzed or died from decompression sickness. In 1905, the Cocoris brothers brought a crew and diving equipment from Aegina, Greece. The first diver reported, "There are enough sponges down there to supply the whole world."

In Greece, sponge diving crews from the Dodecanese islands of Kalymnos, Halki, and Symi and the Saronic Gulf islands of Aegina and Hydra learned about Tarpon Springs through letters, newspaper articles, and advertisements offering to pay travel expenses. Later in 1905, about 500 men arrived. Within a year or two, there were 100 sponge boats based in Tarpon Springs and up to 1,500 Greeks working Florida waters. With the spongers came related maritime businesses: ship chandlers, machine shops, boatbuilders, and a sail loft.

Sponge merchants established sponge warehouses with branches in their home islands and international trade centers. European buyers visited and investors came to finance sponge fishing ventures or boatbuilding. In 1908, the Sponge Exchange was founded as a cooperatively owned space and system for buying and grading sponges. The permanent structure across from the Sponge Docks consisted of iron-grilled *klouves* (storage cells) separating the catches around the perimeter, with a courtyard in the center. It hosted sponge auctions every Tuesday and Friday. Buyers and sellers paid a small percentage to maintain the exchange. In the early years, the sponge boats set aside a portion of the harvest from each trip to build a church dedicated to St. Nicholas, patron saint of mariners.

Using both deep-sea diving and hooking techniques on boats with engines and sails, the Greeks harvested four times the quantity and often better quality sponges from deeper waters than the Key West Conchs. They revolutionized the industry and shifted its center to Tarpon Springs. The combined fleets of the Greeks and Conchs made sponges Florida's most lucrative sea product during the early 20th century.

Community Development

Throughout the early 20th century, Greeks continued to settle in Tarpon Springs, seeking better opportunities in a difficult industry and escaping from deteriorating political conditions in their home islands. At first, men arrived alone, often living in boardinghouses or shacks near the Sponge Docks. As they brought families, they moved into the houses of Greektown, just south of the Sponge Docks.

The arrival of the Greeks changed Tarpon Springs forever. Since Greeks came in relatively large numbers, they were able to keep an unusually large portion of their culture intact. Greektown flourished with residences, stores, churches, restaurants, coffeehouses, and recreational facilities that stretched from the Sponge Docks to the central section of town. Sponge fishing and related activities became the economic base for the community. By 1913, some believe that as many as half of all residents were Greek. Signs at the railway station were posted in both English and Greek, and many businesses displayed Greek and American flags.

As the sponge industry ascended, the city gradually took on a Mediterranean character, and its earlier role as a resort diminished. During the years from 1905 to 1940, Greeks often constituted the numerically dominant cultural group. Although they maintained their traditional culture, they also participated in all aspects of American life. As their financial situations improved, many moved out of Greektown and into more expensive homes, often in the Fruit Salad area south of Spring Bayou.

Women played an important role, although their freedom was limited in accord with Greek culture. They not only handled the family's daily life while the men were away on the sponge boats but also frequently managed or worked in gift shops or sponge company offices.

The sponge industry grew steadily through the first half of the 20th century. The WPA's 1939 guidebook *Florida: A Guide to the Southernmost State* characterizes Tarpon Springs primarily by its sponge business and tours as well as its Greek population and festivals. At least publicly, Greek culture and sponges dominated the town's reputation. The Greeks gradually acquired greater control over municipal politics as the majority or by allying themselves with black Tarponites. Many African Americans developed close relationships with the Greeks while working on their boats and in the warehouses—often learning to speak Greek.

In 1940, there were well over 1,000 men actively engaged in the sponge industry. These men and their families constituted roughly 2,500 Greeks in a town of 3,402. With the onset of World War II and closure of the European market, the supply of sponges decreased while the demand dramatically increased—and Tarpon Springs was the world's leading sponge production center. But the prosperity of the wartime sponge industry ended with the European war.

In the 1930s, a sponge disease spread north in the Caribbean and Atlantic, destroying the rich Bahamian and Cuban sponge beds. By 1948, red tide had devastated the Florida beds, Mediterranean sponges had flooded the market, and DuPont had introduced cheap synthetic sponges. The harvest in Tarpon Springs plummeted. From a record-high production of $4 million in 1946, the total fell over $1 million in the following year. Many families left for the northern steel mills. During the decade from 1947 to 1957, the sponge industry nearly collapsed. By the time the beds recovered in the 1960s and 1970s, the children of the spongers had entered more secure occupations, and the link with the past was all but broken.

Despite the decline of the sponge industry, Tarpon Springs thrived. The emerging ethnic character of Tarpon Springs had coincided with the development of mass tourism, so businesses based on cultural tourism had developed by the 1920s. In the late 1940s and early 1950s, tourism became the city's biggest source of income. The films *16 Fathoms Deep* (1948) and *Beneath the 12-Mile Reef* (1953) created a romantic aura around the sponge industry and Tarpon Springs. In addition, the Epiphany ceremonies captured national attention and drew thousands of visitors.

By the late 1970s, an estimated one-third of residents were Greek in a town of 13,000. Sponge fishing continued on a limited basis until the mid-1980s. Due to catastrophic sponge mortalities in the eastern Mediterranean in 1986, Tarpon Springs experienced a major revival, supporting about 40 working boats. By 1996, however, cyclical red tides and other causes had leveled off the market, with 8–10 boats working regularly, a handful of others working periodically, three major sponge distributors, and a handful of smaller ones.

Tarpon Springs Today

Tarpon Springs preserves a strong ethnic and maritime character. Its Greek heritage has been reinforced with the return of many former residents who moved north for work and with a constant influx of other Greeks and Greek Americans attracted by the cultural infrastructure. Among 24,000 residents, the percentage of Greek descent has shrunk as many have moved to nearby communities for work or larger homes. Yet the city remains the epicenter of a corridor that hosts such a large ethnic population that the Greek government established a consulate in Tampa. Greeks retain significant political power at all levels. While some major US cities have a larger Greek population, none has a greater percentage of residents with Greek heritage than Tarpon Springs.

Still revolving around its Greek heritage and sponge industry, tourism is Tarpon Springs' biggest business. It is centered on Dodecanese Boulevard, along the docks where boats unload sponges or tourists take cruises. Across the street, the Sponge Exchange was demolished and replaced with boutiques. Greek restaurants, tourist stores, and community events are frequented by both locals and tourists. Some ethnic businesses cater primarily to locals, such as Athens Street's market, bakery, and the traditional *kafeneia*, where men gather to imbibe coffee and spirits, play cards, smoke cigars, and discuss politics or sports.

Today, Greek identity is expressed and reinforced through a wide array of everyday activities and special events. It is reflected in the built environment, boats, occupations, social or regional organizations, rites of passage, beliefs, family values, foodways, religious practices, and music and dance in restaurants or embedded in community events.

One

Early Days

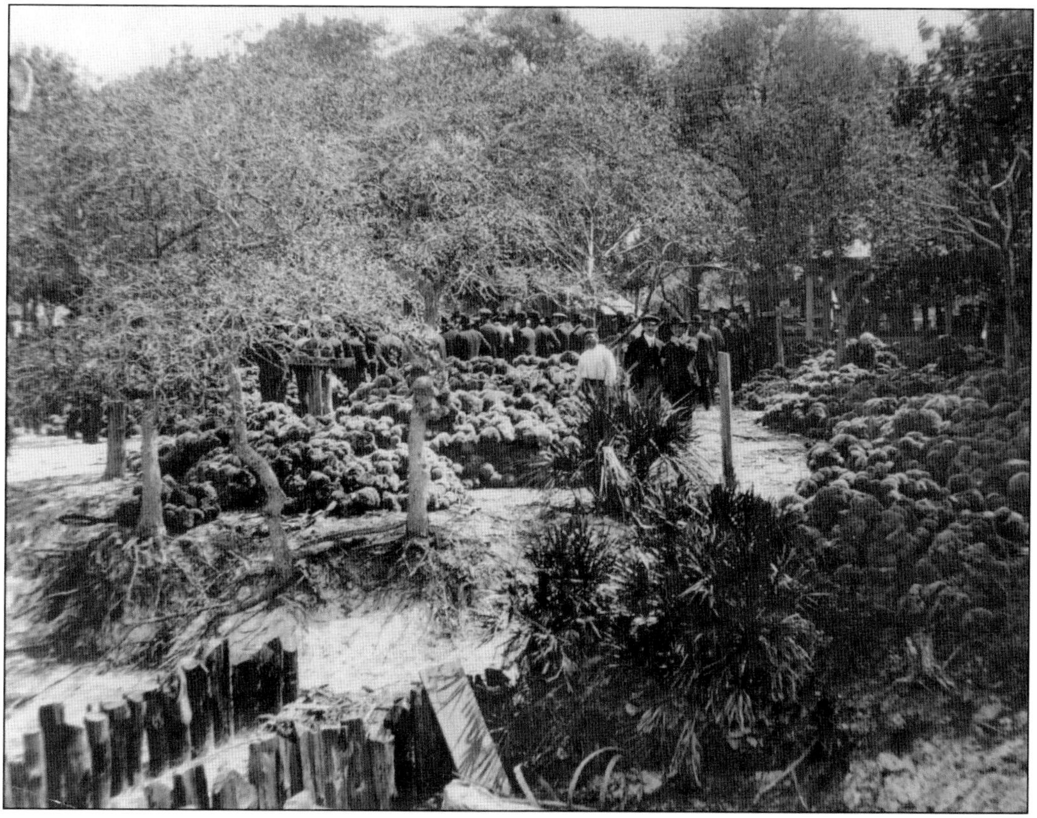

A sponge auction is held across the Anclote River at Bailey's Bluff, where most of the commerce took place before the establishment of the Sponge Exchange in Tarpon Springs. In this image from the early 20th century, the two men in the foreground appear to be Greek. With the rapid expansion of boats and sponge fishermen after the Greeks arrived, the facilities at Bailey's Bluff were not adequate for the burgeoning sponge business. (Courtesy of the Tarpon Springs Area Historical Society.)

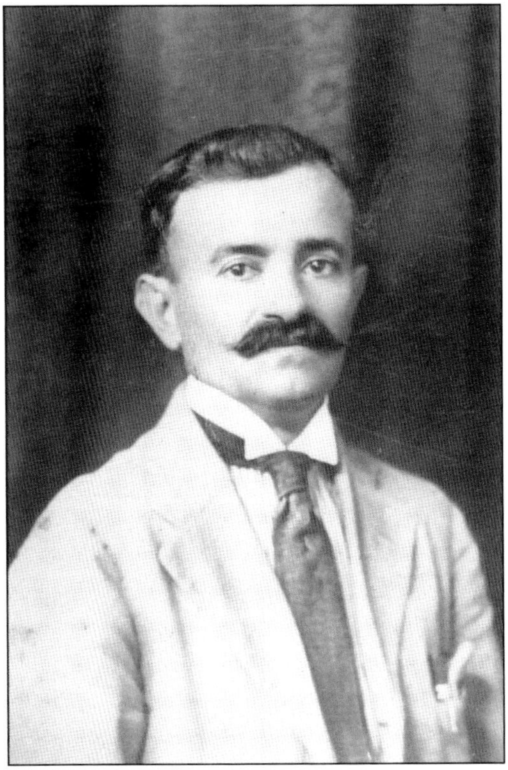

John Cocoris emigrated to the United States from Leonidion, located on the Aegean coast of the Peloponnese. In 1896, he was hired to buy and process sponges from Key West and Tarpon Springs for a New York sponge export firm, the Lembessis Company. The next year, he went to work for Tarpon Springs' leading sponge distributor, John Cheyney. Cocoris returned to Greece in 1901 to marry Anna Nicoloulia Cocoris, who became the first Greek woman in Tarpon Springs. Their daughter, Stamatina, was the first Greek child born in the city. Cocoris and his three brothers—George, Constantine, and Elias—surveyed the Gulf of Mexico for sponges, then saved and borrowed money to bring a diving crew and equipment from Greece. They bought and refurbished a sailboat for sponging, the *Elpis* (*Hope*). In 1905, they brought a captain, two divers, and two deckhands from Aegina. Cocoris's idea was the spark that brought the Greeks to Tarpon Springs. As early as 1916, he served as sheriff and became the first Greek on the city council. (Both, courtesy of the Tarpon Springs Area Historical Society.)

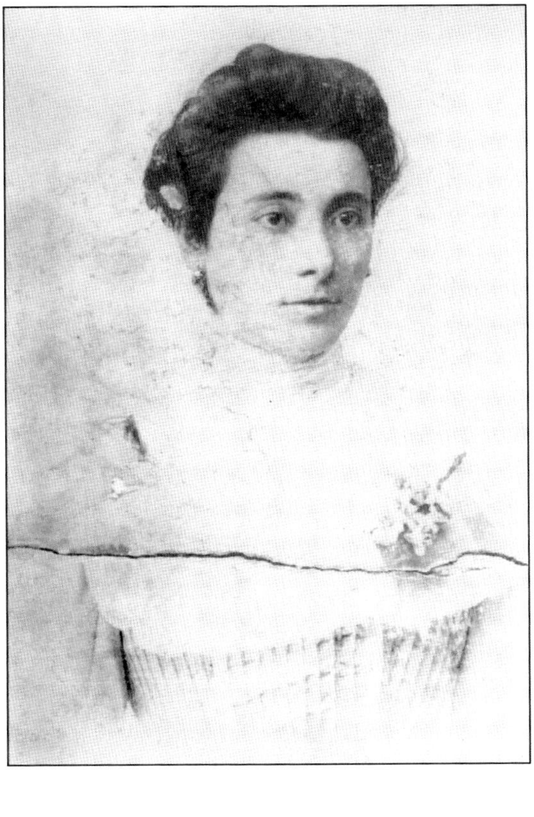

This image shows the *Anthoula*, a small Greek boat with a lateen sail, during the early days of Greek settlement. Triangular lateen sails are set on a long yard and mounted at an angle to the mast in a fore-and-aft direction. This type of sail is common in the Mediterranean and several other parts of the world. (Courtesy of the Tarpon Springs Area Historical Society.)

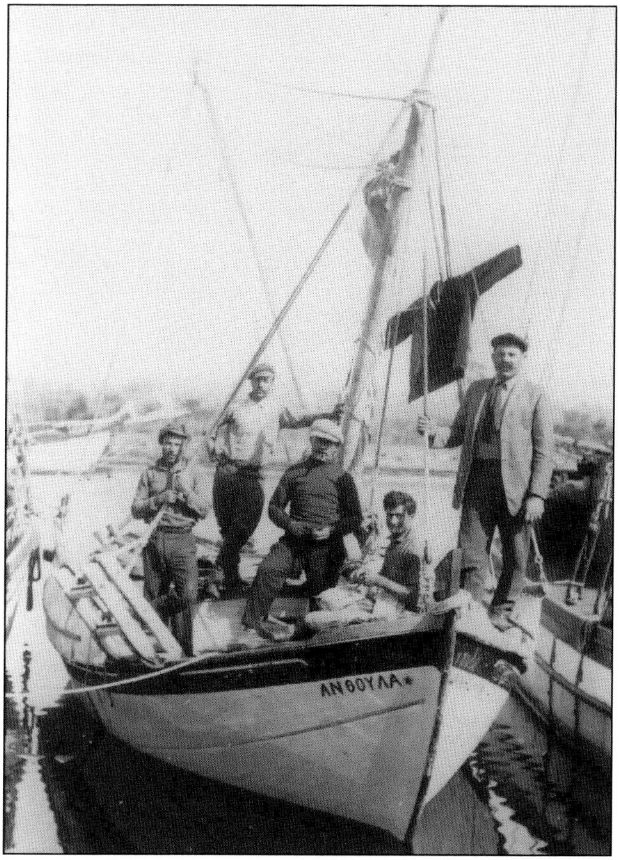

This early diving boat crew includes the diver in the *skafandro*, a diving suit of rubberized canvas with a heavy brass breastplate that attaches to the copper helmet. One crew member holds a net catch bag, which the diver loads with sponges when underwater. While the skafandro is no longer used, divers still use the same catch bag. Note that two crew members are wearing sashes, which men wore in the Greek islands during this period. (Photograph by C.C. Allen, courtesy of Dr. Themistocles J. Diamandis.)

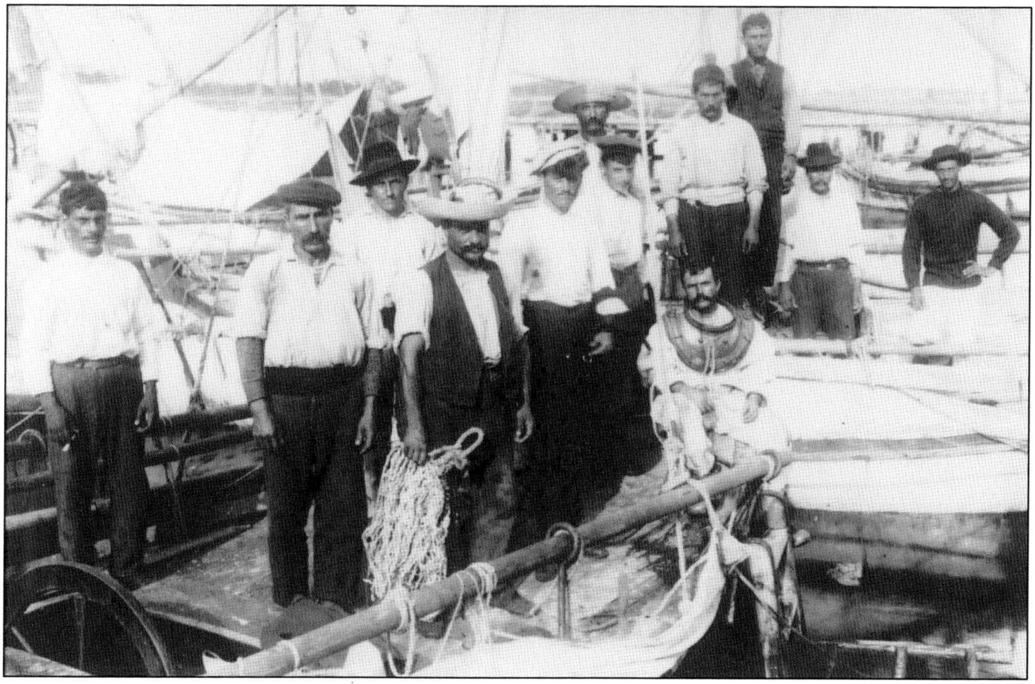

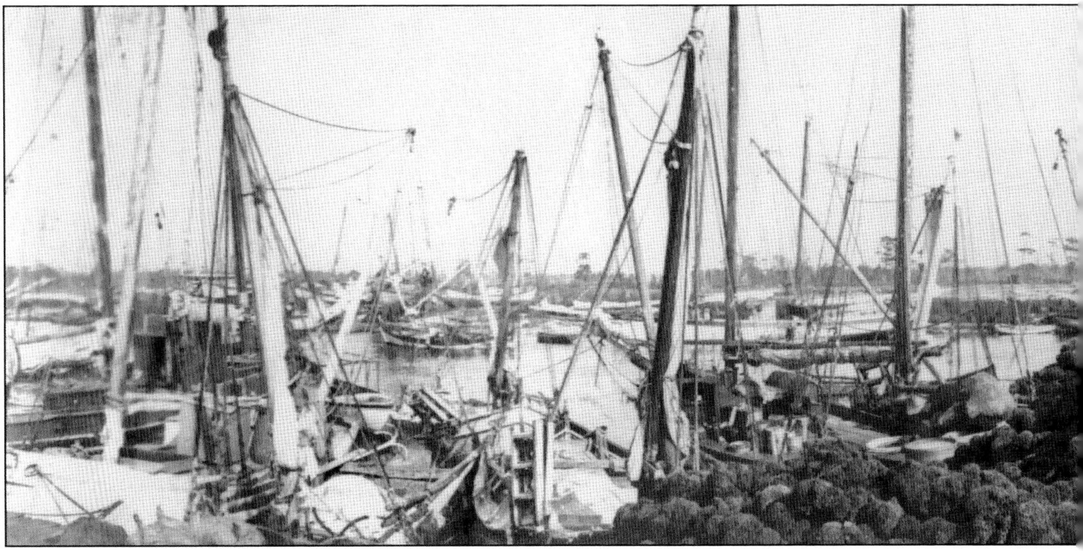

This panoramic view is one of the earliest glimpses of the Sponge Docks. The original wooden bridge across the Anclote River, faintly visible in the background, started from the point where

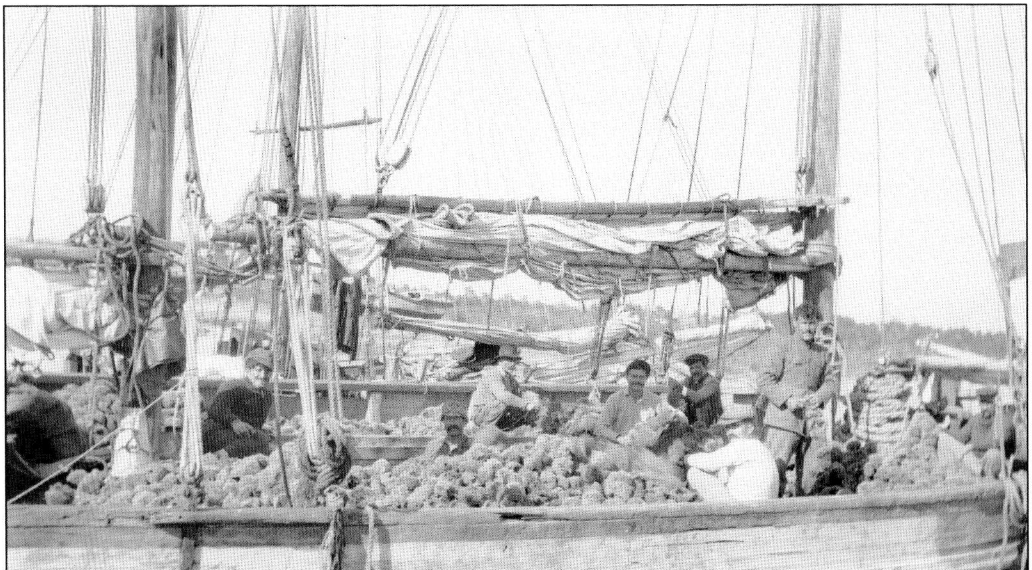

Men string sponges on a Greek boat in the Anclote River. After cleaning the sponges, members of the crew typically sort the sponges according to type and size, then string them on twine using heavy needles about two feet long—this keeps them sorted and makes them easier to carry. The strings of sponges were then taken to the Sponge Exchange for storage and sale. (Photograph by Francis G. Wagner, courtesy of Special Collections Department, Tampa Library, University of South Florida.)

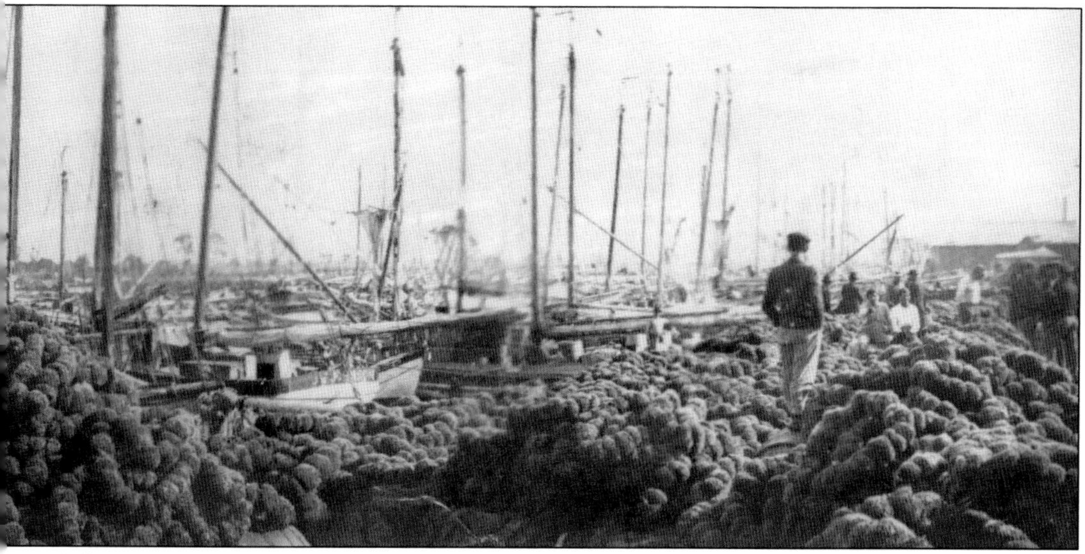

Athens Street meets the Sponge Docks today. Both diving and hooking boats (*gazerika*) are anchored wherever they can find a space. (Courtesy of the City of Tarpon Springs.)

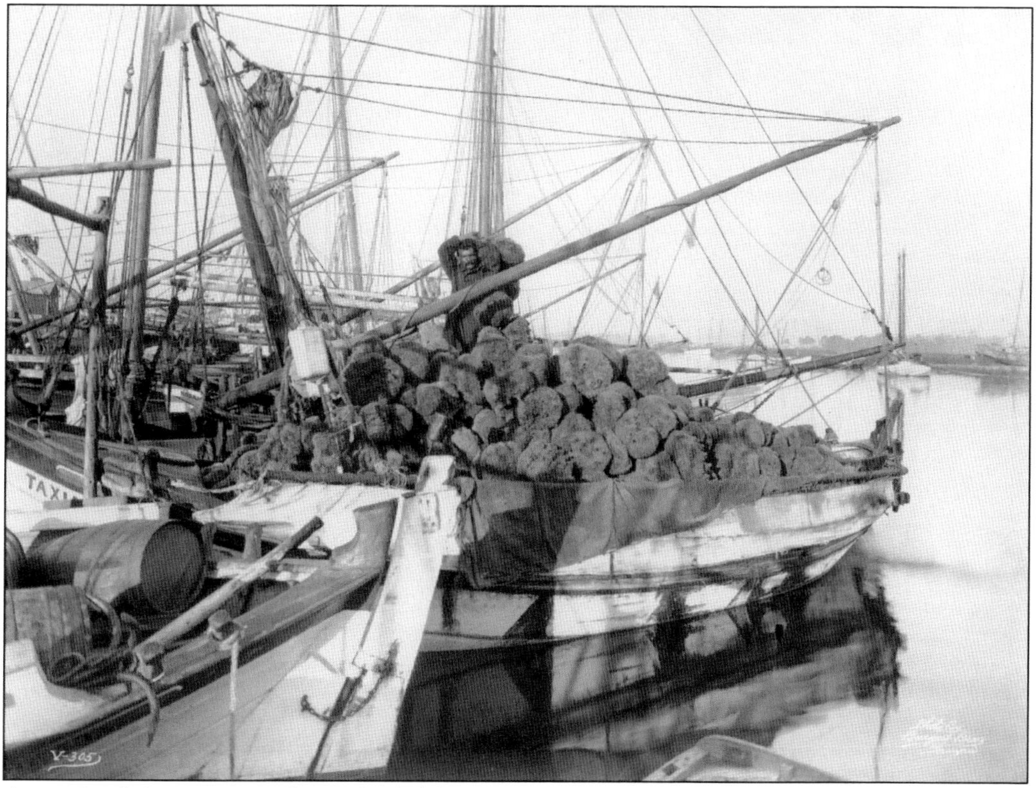

A man hauls large sponges from a loaded lateen sail sponge boat on the Anclote River in 1921. The name on the boat is barely legible, but it is probably *Taxiarchis Mihail* (St. Michael the Archangel), the patron saint of Symi. The boat in the foreground shows the rudder end of a typical Greek sponge boat. (Photograph by Burgert Brothers, courtesy of the Special Collections Department, Tampa Library, University of South Florida.)

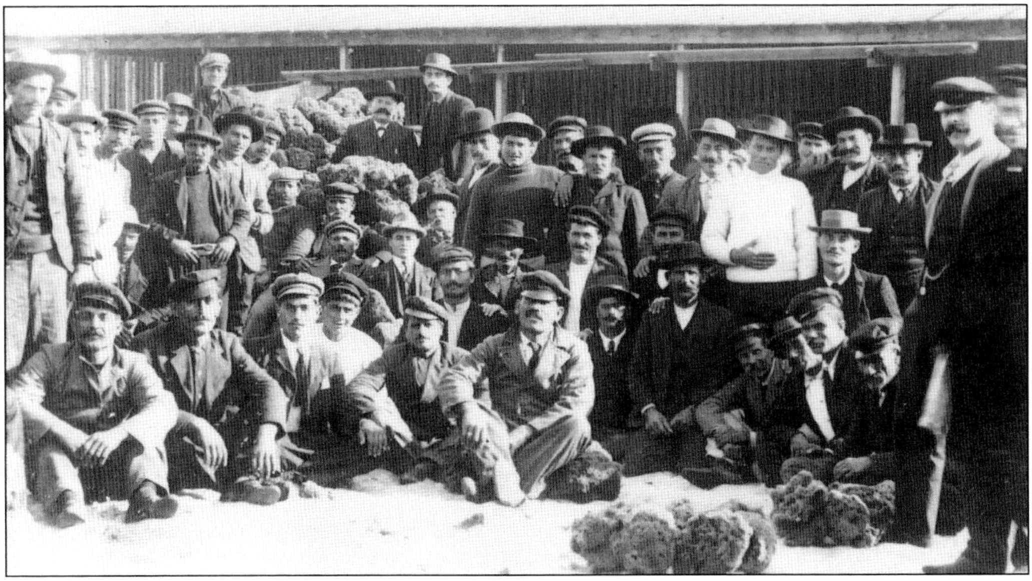

Greek men gather in the courtyard at an early version of the Sponge Exchange. The Sponge Exchange was founded around 1907 or 1908 as a nonprofit corporation with shares owned by 50 buyers. At this cooperative space across the street from the Sponge Docks, sponges were sorted, strung, stored, and finally auctioned. The buildings were replaced several times over the years. (Courtesy of Dr. Themistocles J. Diamandis.)

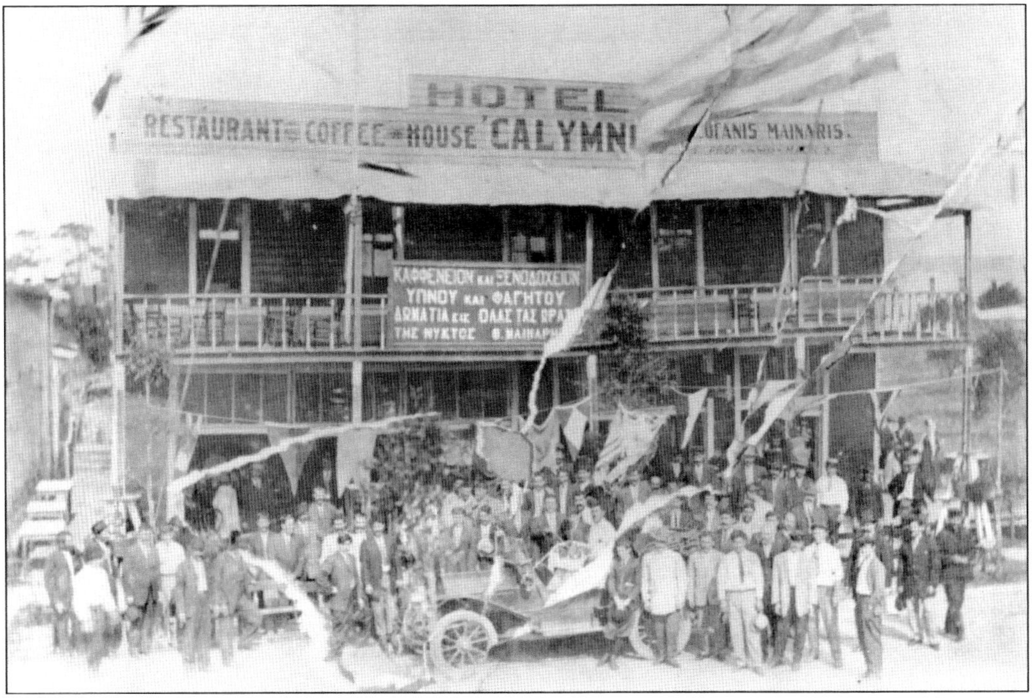

A crowd of Greek men pose in front of the Hotel Calymnos, whose proprietor was Theofanis Mainaris. This early establishment included a restaurant and coffee shop that catered to the needs of both the sponge boat crews and the visiting sponge buyers. The hotel was undoubtedly located near the Sponge Docks to facilitate business. (Courtesy of the City of Tarpon Springs.)

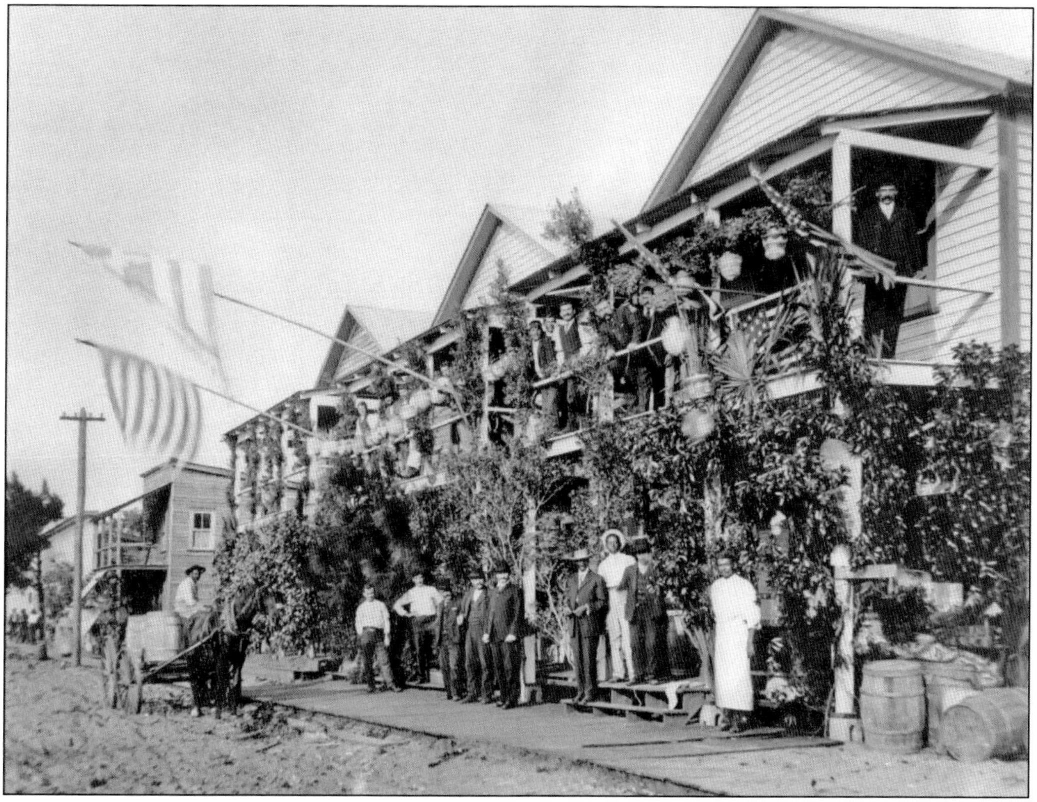

Men pose at a Greek boardinghouse with both Greek and American flags around 1910. The census from that year identifies only two men as homeowners; the others boarded with the heads of households and at rooming houses in the Greektown area just south of the Sponge Docks. Most ship carpenters, divers, and sailors were listed as residing on ships. Later, many lived in "divers' cottages," tiny houses built behind larger ones near the Sponge Docks. (Courtesy of the Tarpon Springs Area Historical Society.)

This image was probably taken at one of the *kafeneia* (men's coffeehouses) located on Athens Street. There is a long-standing tradition of Greek men spending their free time at these establishments, which offered not only coffee but also food and companionship. Indeed, the tiny divers' cottages that housed sponge crew members in the early days sometimes did without plumbing in part because the men spent all their waking moments working on the boats or at the coffeehouses. (Courtesy of Dr. Themistocles J. Diamandis.)

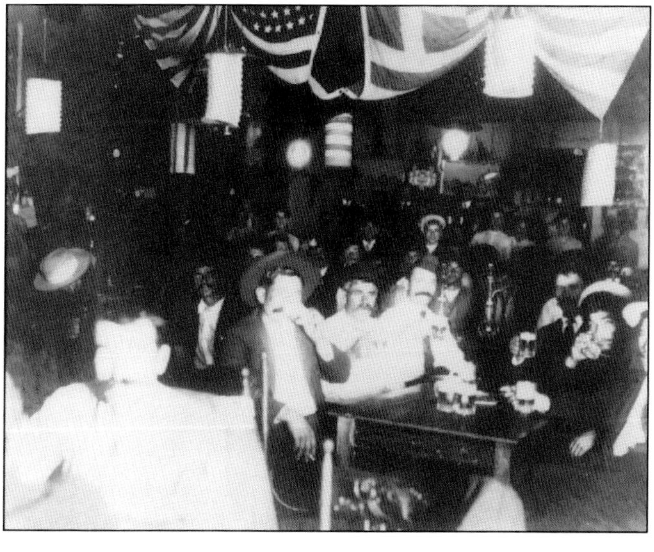

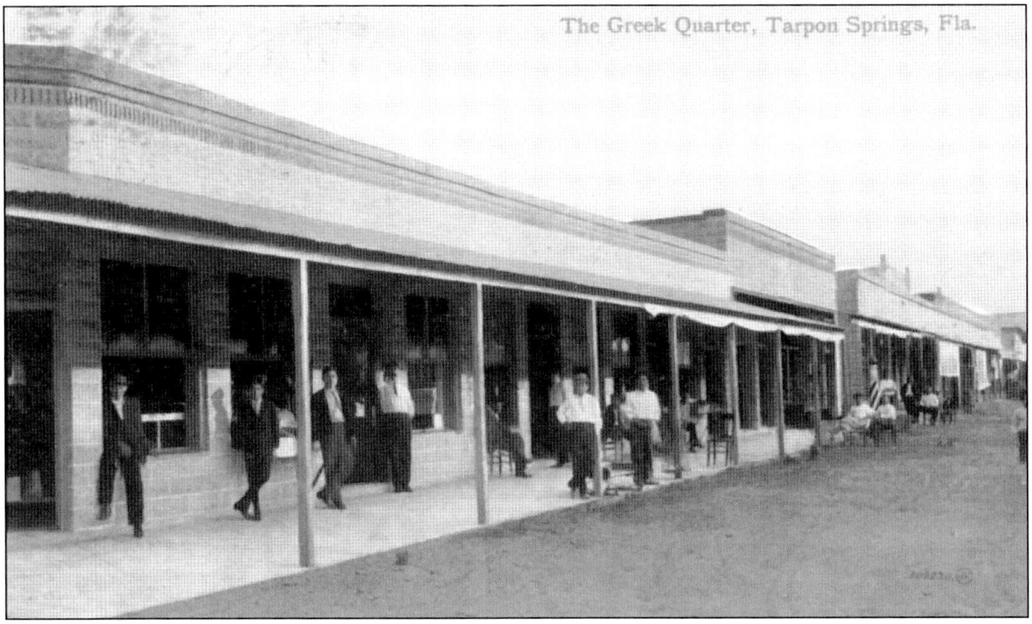

This image of the Greek Quarter from the Hampton Dunn Collection of Florida Postcards probably shows Athens Street around 1910. Not long after the Greeks arrived in large numbers, the Greektown area developed with homes, stores, churches, restaurants, coffeehouses, and recreational facilities stretching from the Sponge Docks to the central section of Tarpon Springs. According to the 1910 census, the Greektown community supported 11 house carpenters who were rarely unemployed. (Courtesy of the Special Collections Department, Tampa Library, University of South Florida.)

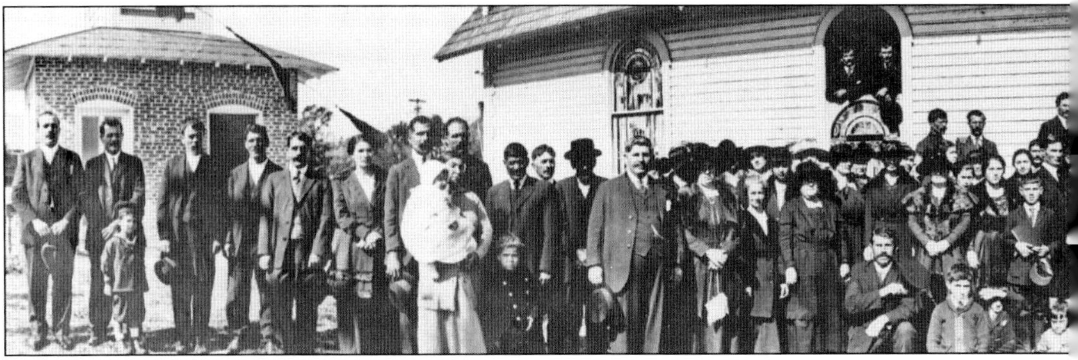

By 1907, about 800 Greeks, primarily men, were residing in Tarpon Springs. Some began sending money home to bring their families, while others brought brides. Built not long afterward in 1908, the original St. Nicholas Greek Orthodox Church held about 250 parishioners. This panoramic view in front of the church, probably taken during the 1910s, reveals a majority of men but also many women and children. St. Nicholas Greek Orthodox Church plays a pivotal role in the

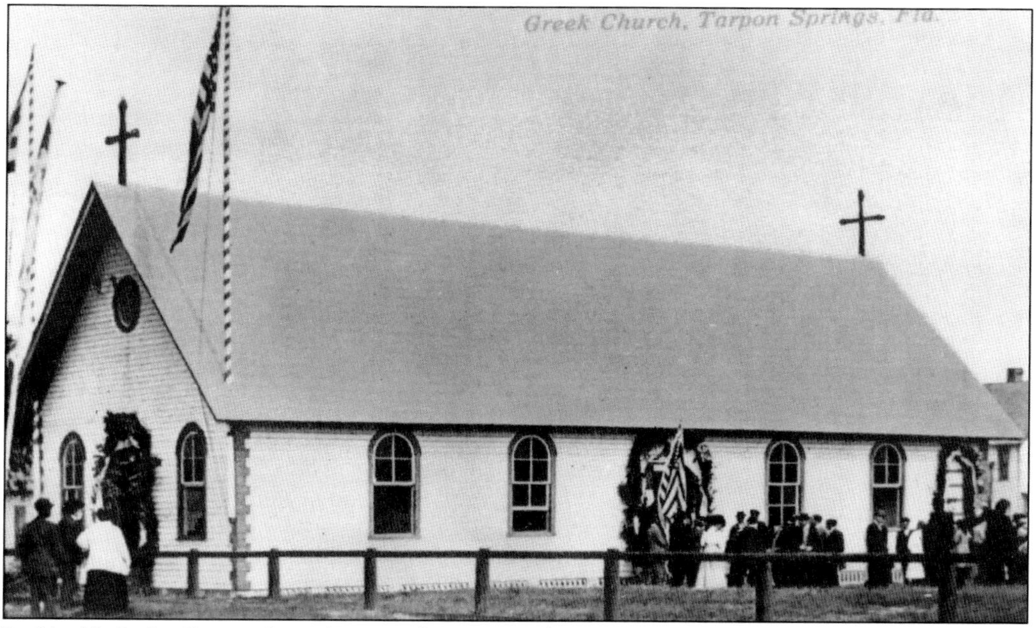

Led by Nicholas Peppas from Aegina, the men in the sponge industry organized a committee to establish a church in 1907. By 1908, the white wooden structure had been completed and named for St. Nicholas, in honor of the protector of mariners. The first priest was the Reverend Father Stamatis Koutouzis from Kalymnos. He was succeeded by several other priests who stayed for relatively short periods until the Reverend Father Theophilos Karaphillis arrived from Kalymnos in 1922. (Courtesy of the Tarpon Springs Area Historical Society.)

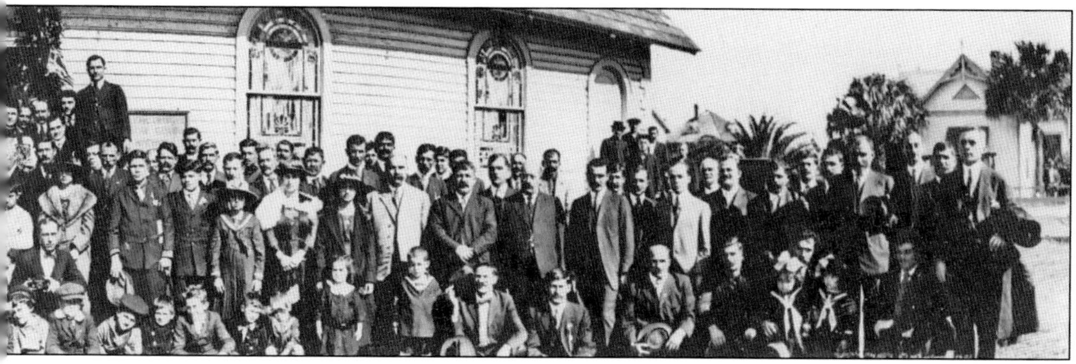

community by sustaining religious traditions. It also provides opportunities for children or adults to learn the language through Greek school and to absorb the culture through participation in church-sponsored activities. The first church fell victim to fire and was replaced in the early 1940s. (Courtesy of Dr. Themistocles J. Diamandis.)

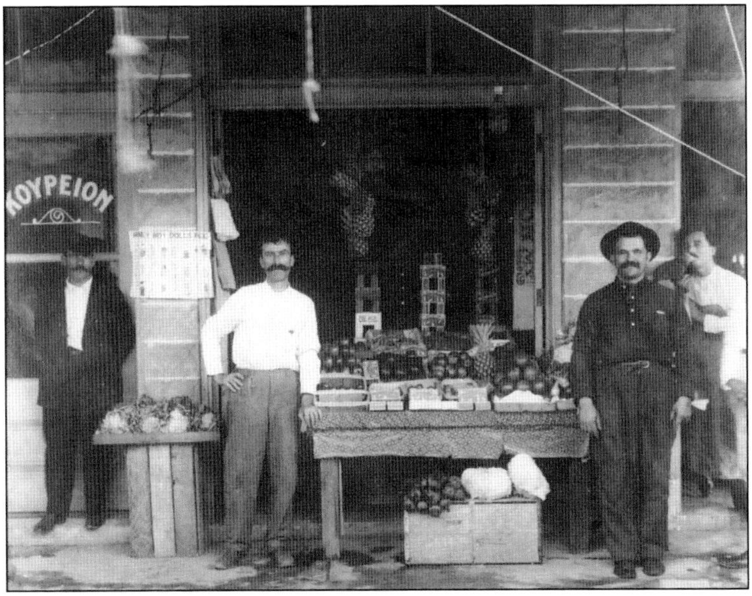

These men are pictured in front of a *koureion* (barbershop) and grocery with a beautiful display of vegetables and fruit, including pineapples that were probably grown in South Florida. Note the man at far right who is holding a pet parrot. (Courtesy of Dr. Themistocles J. Diamandis.)

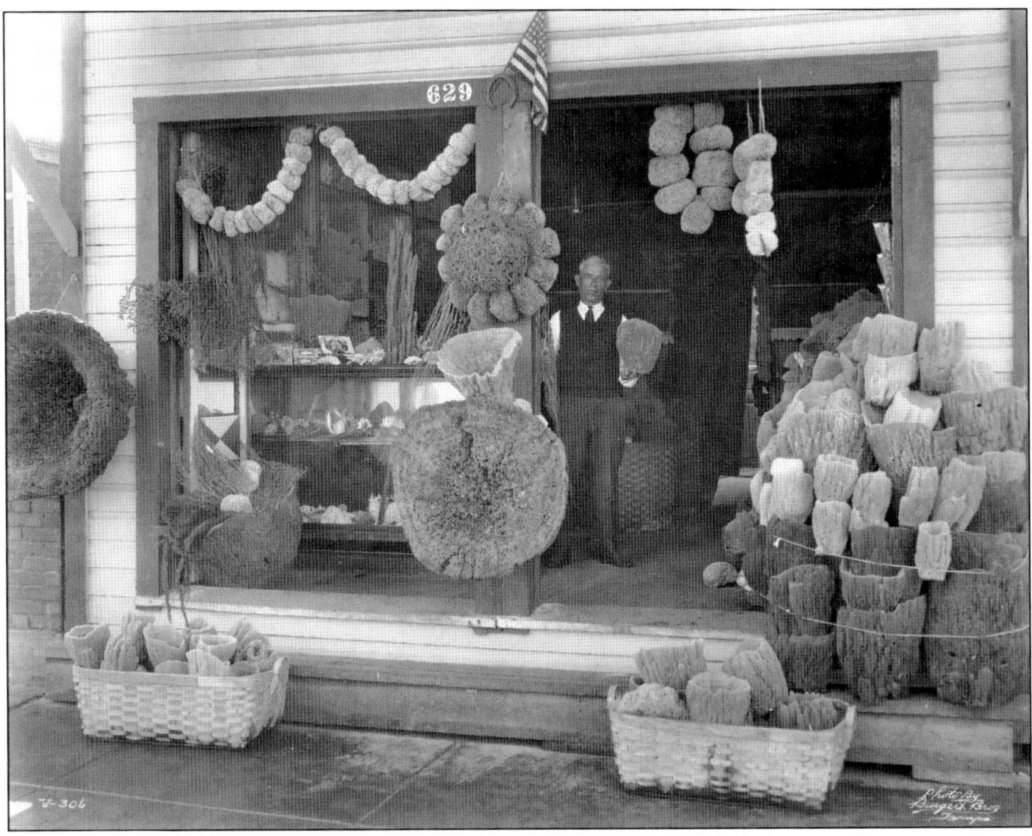

Mass tourism bloomed after World War I as the middle class expanded. As a result, tourism based on the sponge industry and Greek culture developed early in Tarpon Springs. This image shows a store selling sponges at 629 Dodecanese Boulevard in 1921. (Photograph by Burgert Brothers, courtesy of the Special Collections Department, Tampa Library, University of South Florida.)

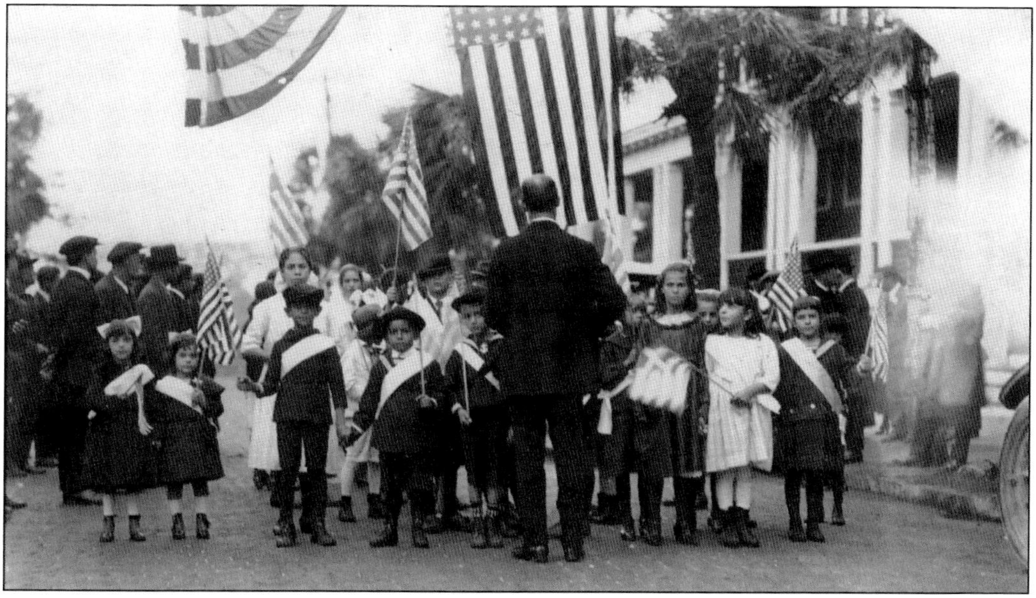

According to the Mandalou family, this is an early image documenting the celebration of American Independence Day in Tarpon Springs around July 4, 1920. The two little girls seen at front left are Katina Angel, age eight, and Maria Angel Mandalou, age six. (Courtesy of George Mandalou.)

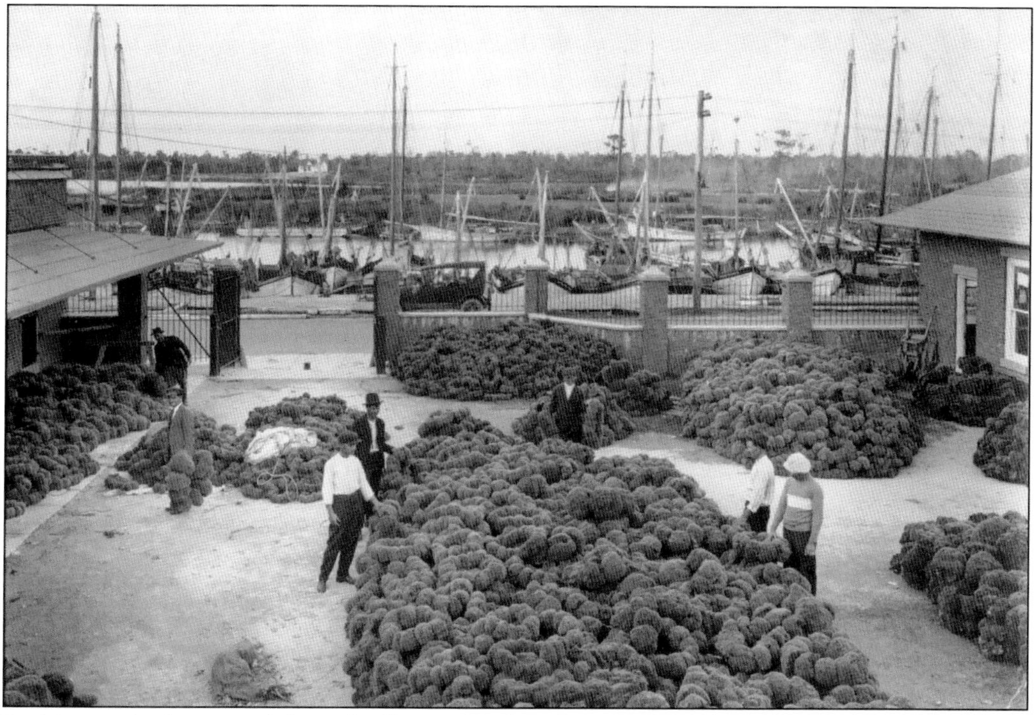

In this view looking north from the Sponge Exchange to the boats lining the Sponge Docks, men examine enormous piles of strung sponges harvested on recent trips. When the photograph was taken in 1921, the old wooden buildings had been replaced with brick structures and a brick-and-iron retaining fence faced the street. (Photograph by Burgert Brothers, courtesy of the Special Collections Department, Tampa Library, University of South Florida.)

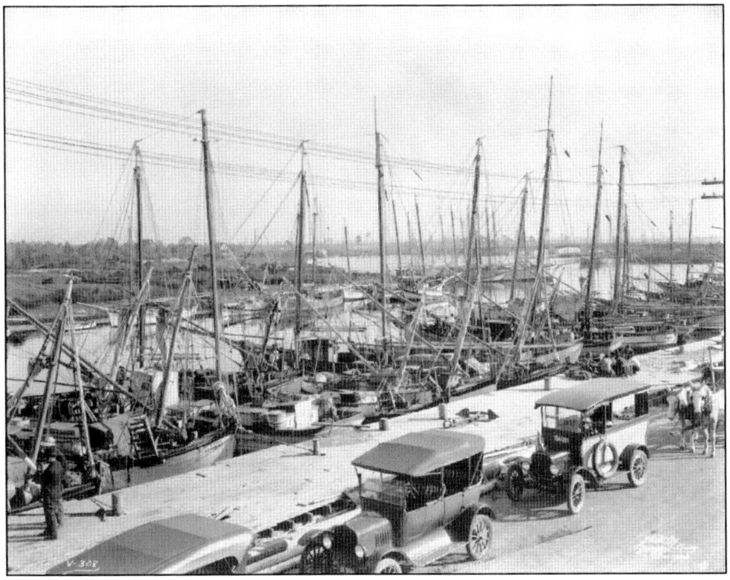

In 1921, dozens of Greek boats in the sponge fleet line the wooden docks where men work and an anchor lies. Along with the lone horse-drawn buggy are the Sponge Exchange jitney and cars that are probably owned by the more affluent sponge merchants. (Photograph by Burgert Brothers, courtesy of Special Collections Department, Tampa Library, University of South Florida.)

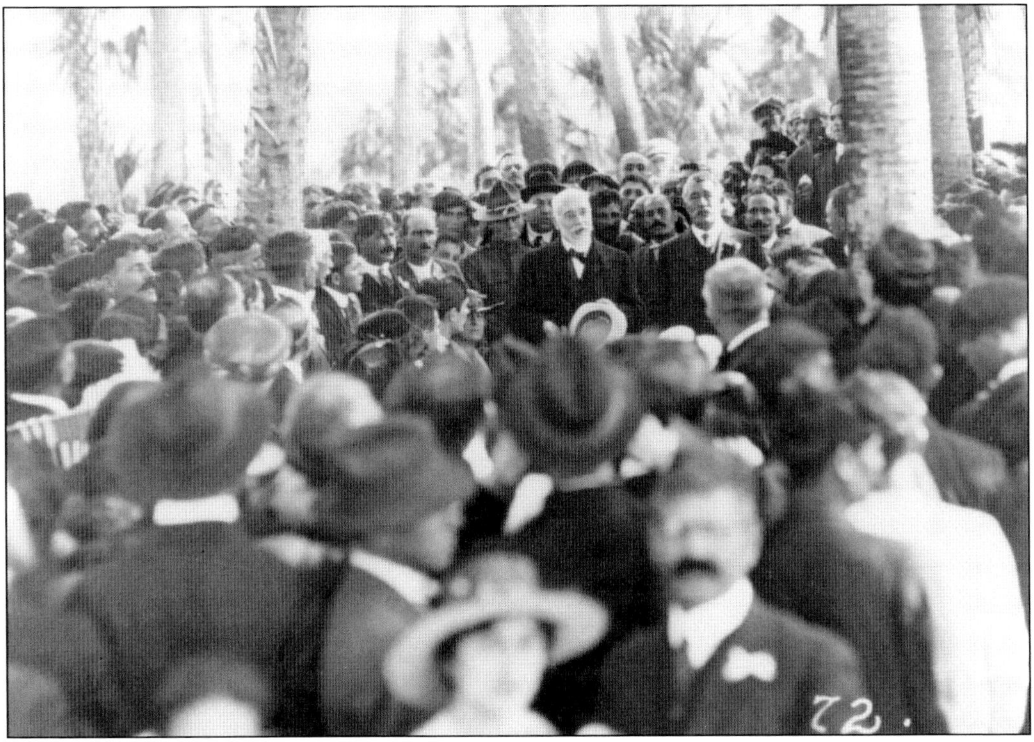

Greek prime minister Eleftherios Venizelos (1864–1936) delivers a speech at Anclote Lighthouse on January 30, 1922. One of the most respected Greek statesmen of the 20th century, Venizelos led the Greek national liberation movement and promoted liberal-democratic policies. He visited Greek diaspora communities, such as Tarpon Springs, during the periods when he was not serving as prime minister. (Photograph by H. Bigelow, courtesy of State Archives of Florida, Florida Memory.)

Two

Schools, Organizations, and Military Service

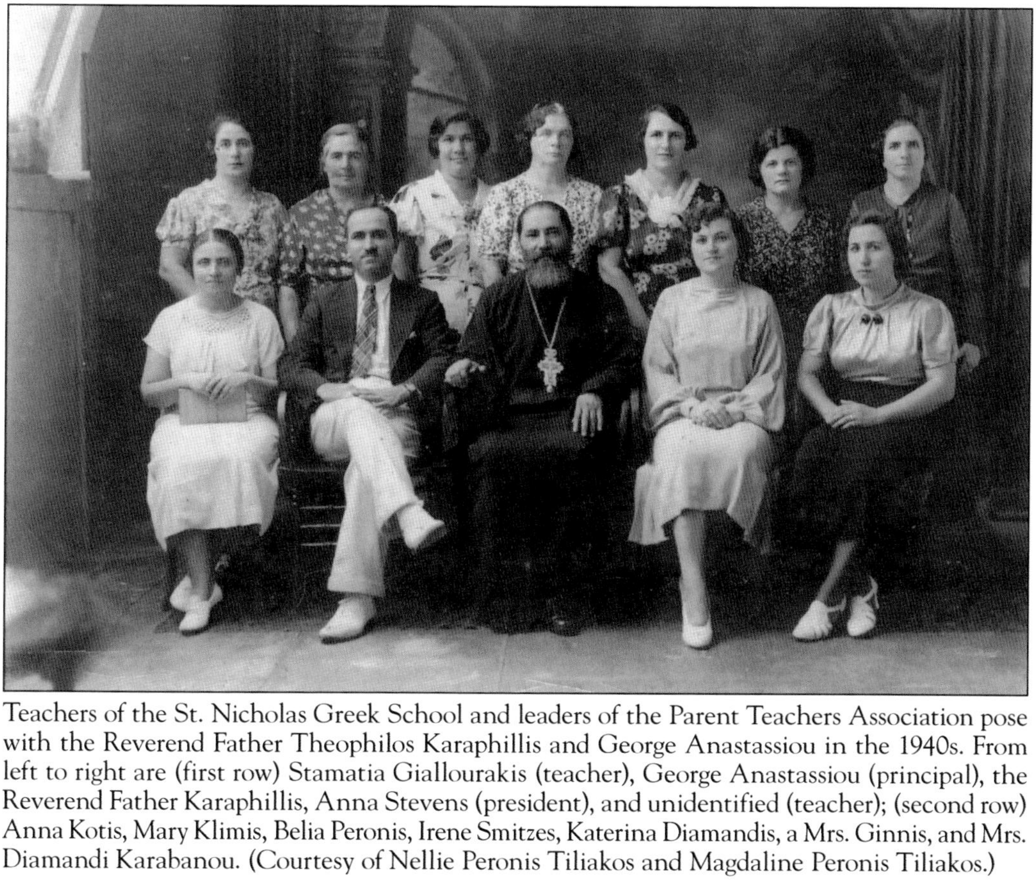

Teachers of the St. Nicholas Greek School and leaders of the Parent Teachers Association pose with the Reverend Father Theophilos Karaphillis and George Anastassiou in the 1940s. From left to right are (first row) Stamatia Giallourakis (teacher), George Anastassiou (principal), the Reverend Father Karaphillis, Anna Stevens (president), and unidentified (teacher); (second row) Anna Kotis, Mary Klimis, Belia Peronis, Irene Smitzes, Katerina Diamandis, a Mrs. Ginnis, and Mrs. Diamandi Karabanou. (Courtesy of Nellie Peronis Tiliakos and Magdaline Peronis Tiliakos.)

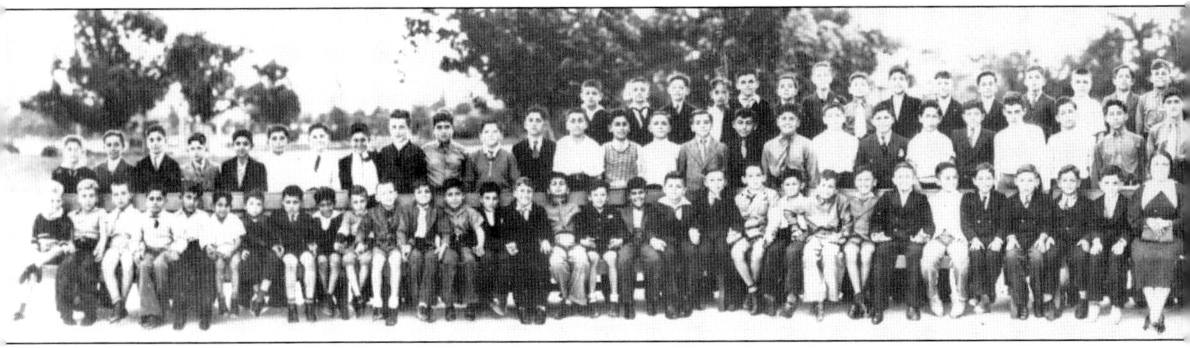

The Greek community opened its first parochial school in 1925. In the early years, 200 children attended daily classes after public school. St. Nicholas Greek School employed three teachers and assistants who taught Greek history, language, culture, writing, reading, religion, and music. This panoramic view appears to have been taken during the 1920s. During the 20th century,

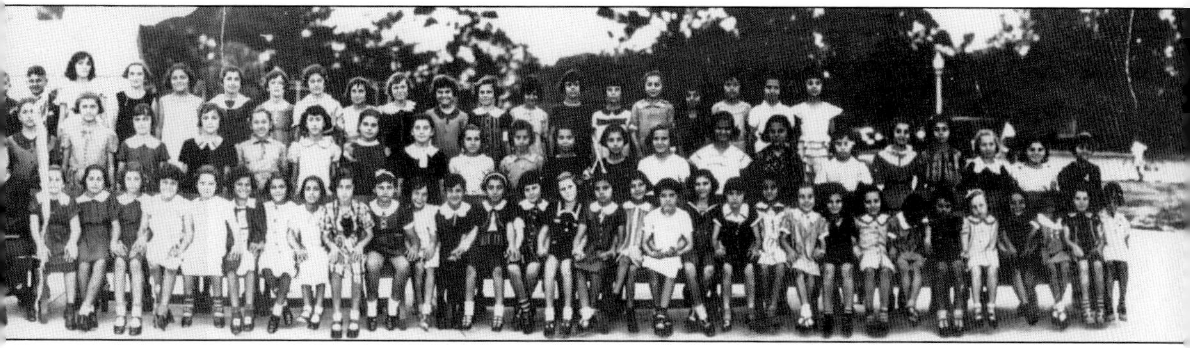

many ethnic communities established separate schools to teach children the history and language of their culture. These classes were often held after school or on Saturdays. (Courtesy of Dr. Themistocles J. Diamandis.)

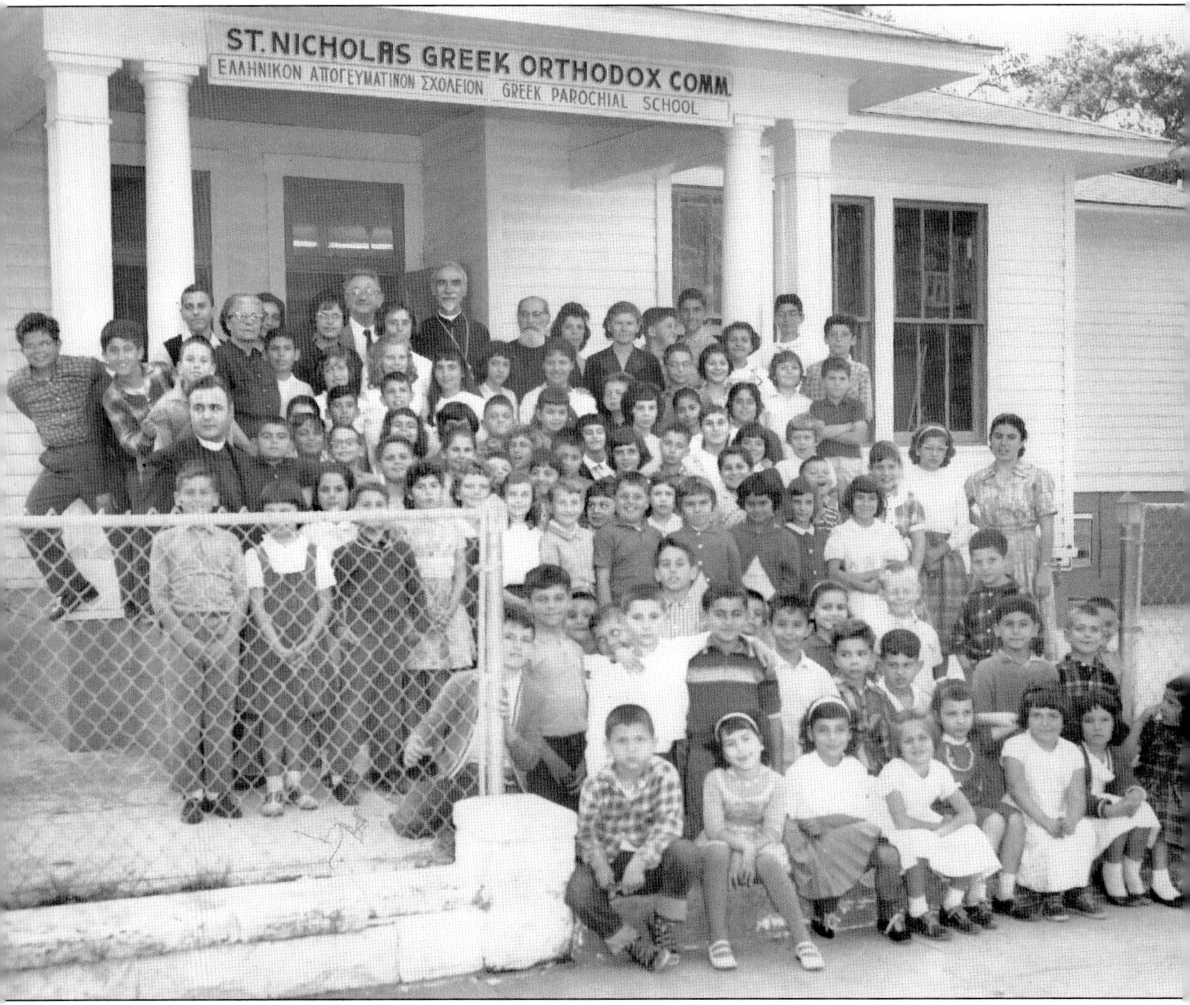

The St. Nicholas Greek Orthodox Community Greek Parochial School has endured for 90 years. Teachers, students, and visitors pose outside the school for this 1963 photograph. The adults in the image include, from left to right, the Reverend Father Constantinos Raptis, Irene Giallourakis, George Emmanuel, Metropolitan Germanos Polizoidis, the Reverend Father Theophilos Karaphillis, Stamatia Giallourakis, and Maria Pantelis. (Author's collection.)

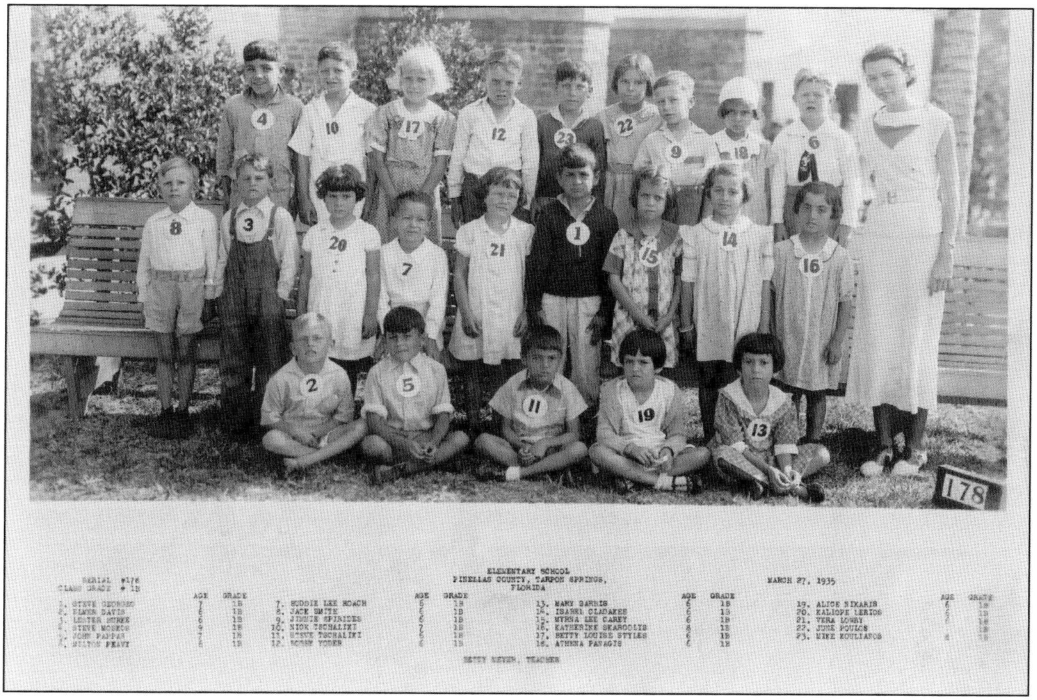

Greek children began attending Tarpon Springs Elementary School in the 1910s. According to a 1916 book by Rev. Thomas J. Lacey, the school principal told him, "There are about 40 Greek children in our school, nearly all of them in one room (for the sake of learning English). All teachers who have anything to do with them report them quite bright as a class. The teacher . . . likes the Greeks better than any other foreigners she ever had, saying that they surpass the others in nearly every respect, including the ability to learn English . . . We find them a rather noisy bunch, but not vicious. There are only two or three above the fourth grade." He also said they were especially apt in mathematics. In this March 1935 class photograph, 61 percent of the first grade students are of Greek heritage. (Courtesy of Kaliope Lerios George.)

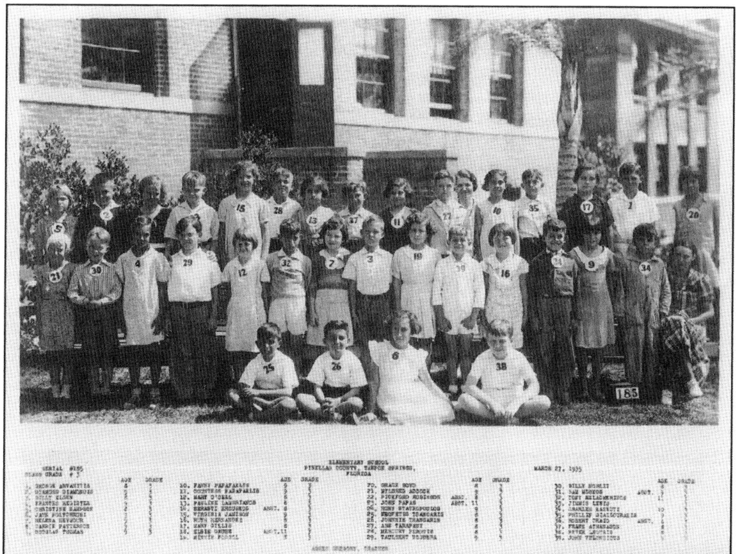

The third-grade students of the Tarpon Springs Elementary School pose for a class photograph in March 1935. Note that children of Greek heritage number almost 50 percent of the class. During this era, schools were racially segregated, so African American students attended a separate school. (Courtesy of Goldie Tsalichis Parr.)

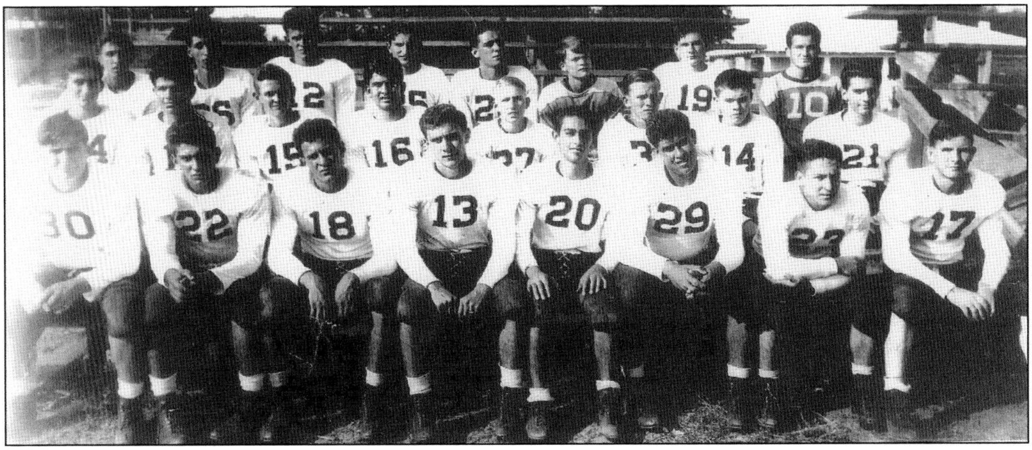

The Greeks in Tarpon Springs have taken football seriously ever since the sons and grandsons of the sponge fishermen started playing on their school teams. In fact, the Tarpon Springs High School team is named the Spongers for the brave men who faced the dangers of the Gulf. In the past, some plays were reputedly called in Greek so that opposing teams would not understand. By 1940, Greek names predominated the lineup. From left to right are (first row) unidentified, Costas Tsataros, George Tsourakis, Odge Cretekos, John Saklarides, Andrew Spanolios, Bill Walters, and Frank Manos; (second row) Lukas Pappas, unidentified, Curtis Gause, Nick Kavouklis, Jessie Burgess, William Murphy, Archie Clement, and Manuel Tsavaris; (third row) Neophitos Tsangaris, Nick Cladakis, Pete Tsourakis, George Billiris, Tony Spanolios, D.S. Lovett, Bill Ennett, and Coach Jennings. (Courtesy of Nickollet Tsourakis Henderson.)

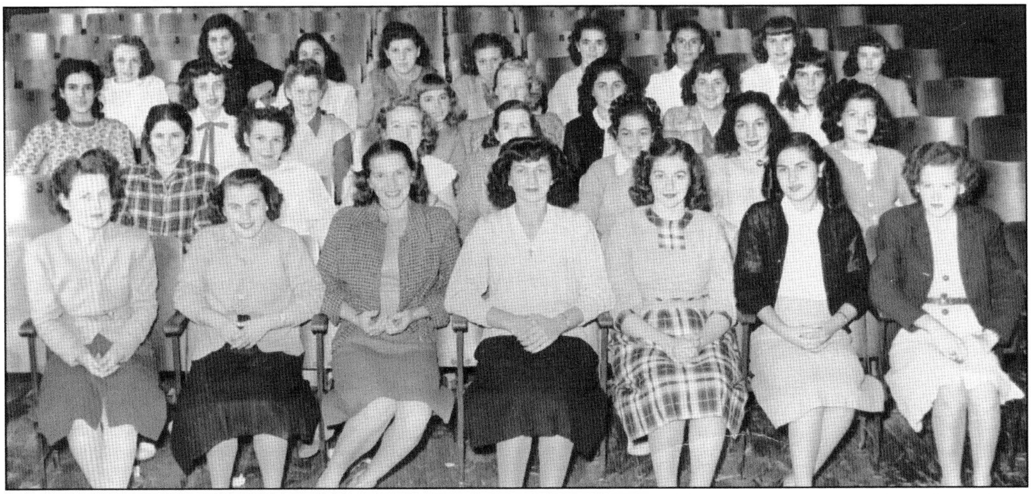

The Tarpon High School chapter of the Future Homemakers of America is pictured on March 1, 1948. From left to right are (first row) Mildred Simmons, Irene Harvey, Zula Piperis, Mary Tsalichis, Kalliope Simeon, Else Sakiotis, and unidentified; (second row) Evelyn Kotis, Bessie Johns, Mildred Croft, Frances Bailey, Urania Stavrulakis, Fannie Ypsilantis, and Thelma Vaporis; (third row) Irene Moskos, Patricia McMickle, unidentified, Dolly Drake, Dolores Deardon, Cleo Kapetanis, Nellie Peronis, and Leoni Piperis; (fourth row) unidentified, Sula Filareton, Argie Pappas, Helen Pavlos, Fayla Stavrakis, Tessie Diamandes, Anna Smolios, Barbara Bragg, and Barbara Campbell. Guided by the US Department of Education and American Home Economics Association, Future Homemakers of America clubs around the nation dedicated themselves to home economics and community leadership beginning in 1945. (Courtesy of Magdaline Peronis Tiliakos and Nellie Peronis Tiliakos.)

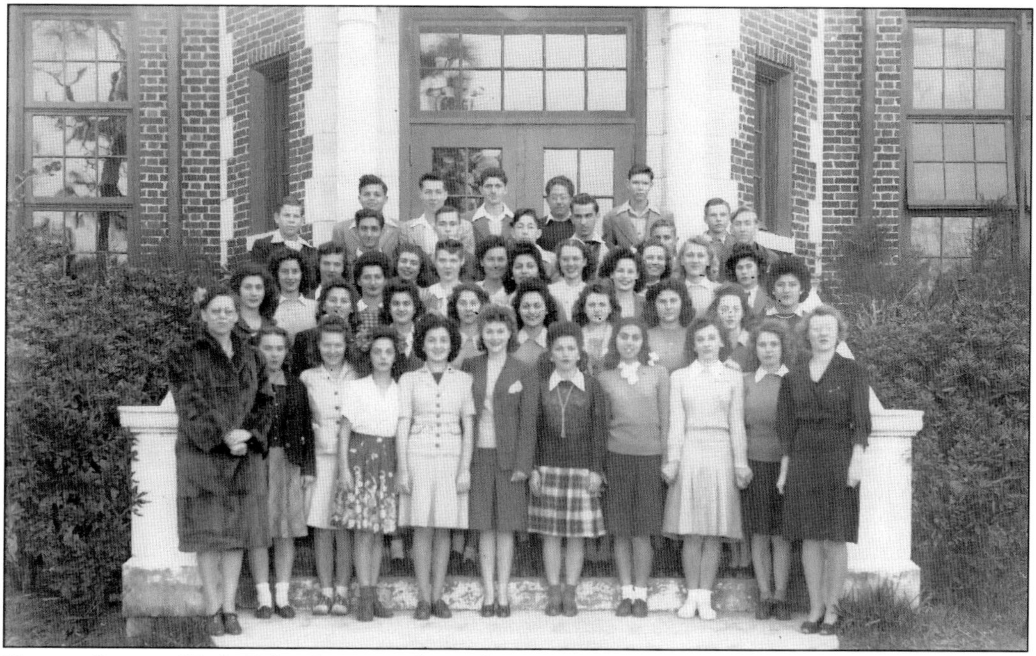

Tarpon Springs High School juniors from the 1944–1945 academic year stand in front of the school entrance with their teachers. Tarpon Springs High School operated in this building on Pine Street from 1927 until the new high school opened in 1962. The old high school is now the Tarpon Springs City Hall and Performing Arts Center. (Courtesy of Nick and Betty Krouskos.)

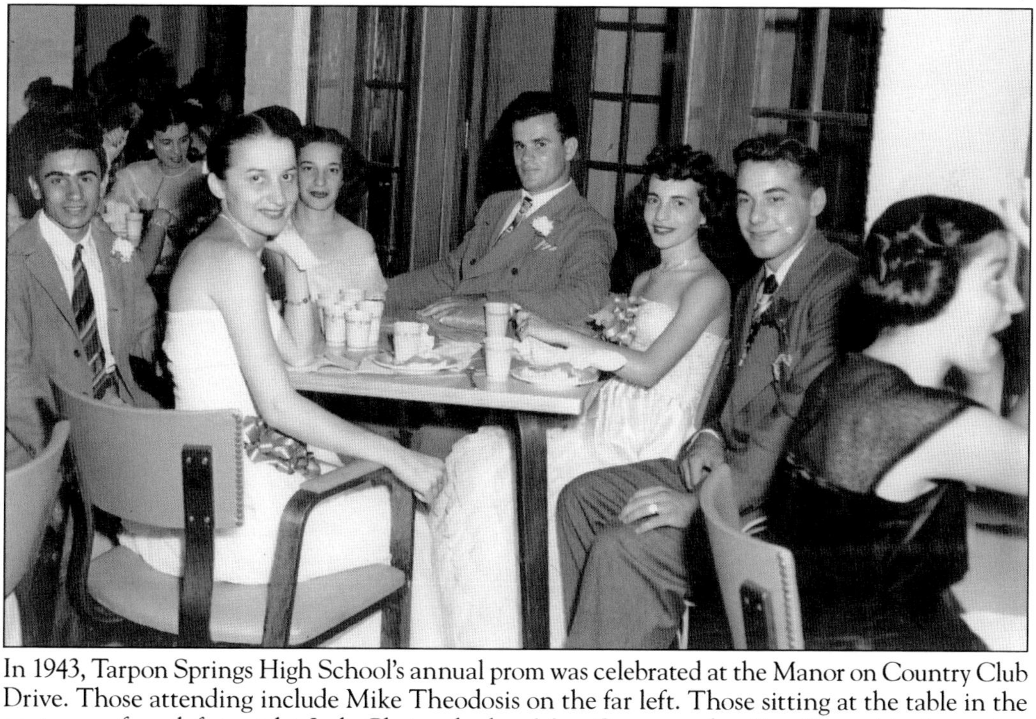

In 1943, Tarpon Springs High School's annual prom was celebrated at the Manor on Country Club Drive. Those attending include Mike Theodosis on the far left. Those sitting at the table in the center are, from left to right, Lula Christodoulou, Mary Stavropoulos, Pete Tsourakis, Augustine Paskalakis, and Steve Stavrakis. (Courtesy of Nickollet Tsourakis Henderson.)

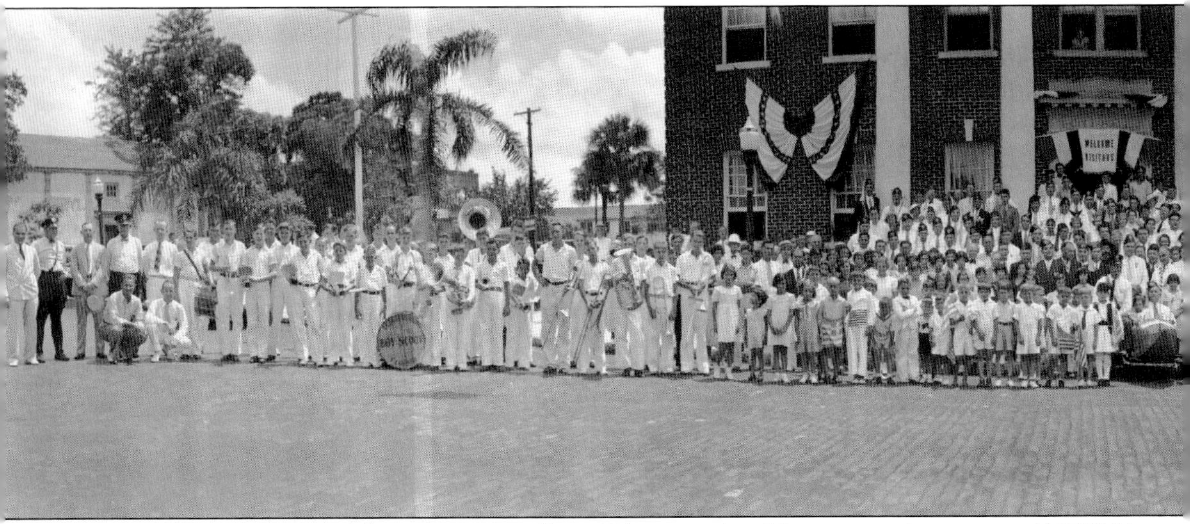

This panoramic view of the American Hellenic Educational and Progressive Association (AHEPA) convention includes both members and local residents in front of Tarpon Springs City Hall in 1928. Many AHEPA members wear a fez with the organization's acronym and logo. AHEPA remains

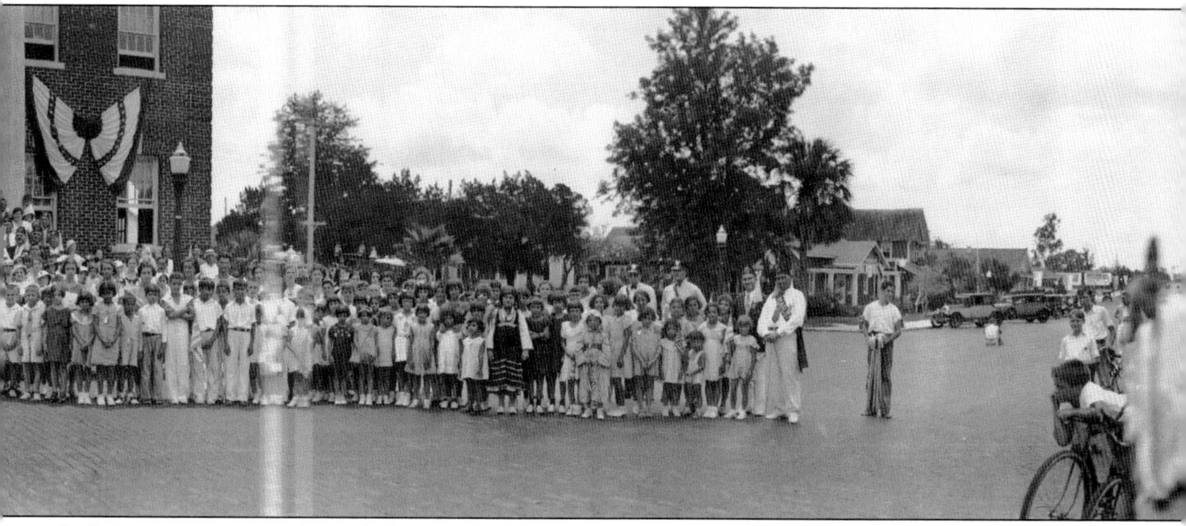

the largest non-regional Greek fraternal organization, with chapters in most Greek communities around the nation. (Photograph by Burgert Brothers, courtesy of the Tampa-Hillsborough County Public Library System.)

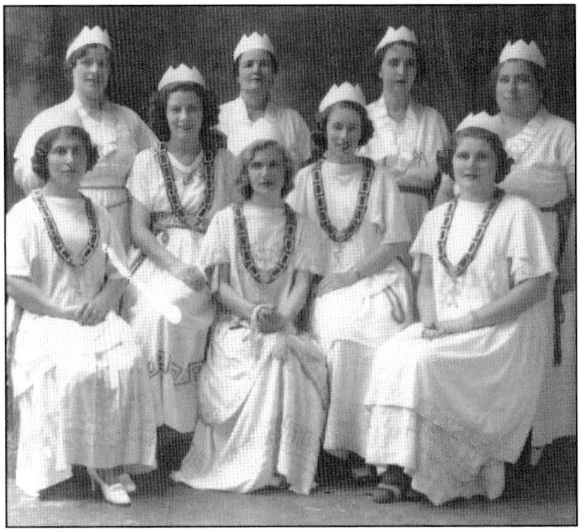

Dressed for a special event, the women of GAPA include, from left to right, (first row) Foto Lerios, Mary Gianneskis Manticos, and Catherine Gonatos Bouchlas; (second row) Sofie Stamas Athas and Despina Smirlis; (third row) Dikea Nicholas Arfaras, Assimina Velousis, Paraskevi Christou, and unidentified. The Greek American Progressive Association (GAPA) was founded in 1923 as a more conservative alternative to AHEPA. Its stated mission was to preserve Greek language and culture, and it was closely associated with the Orthodox Church. By the 1930s, however, its membership had declined. (Courtesy of Mary Lerios Toth.)

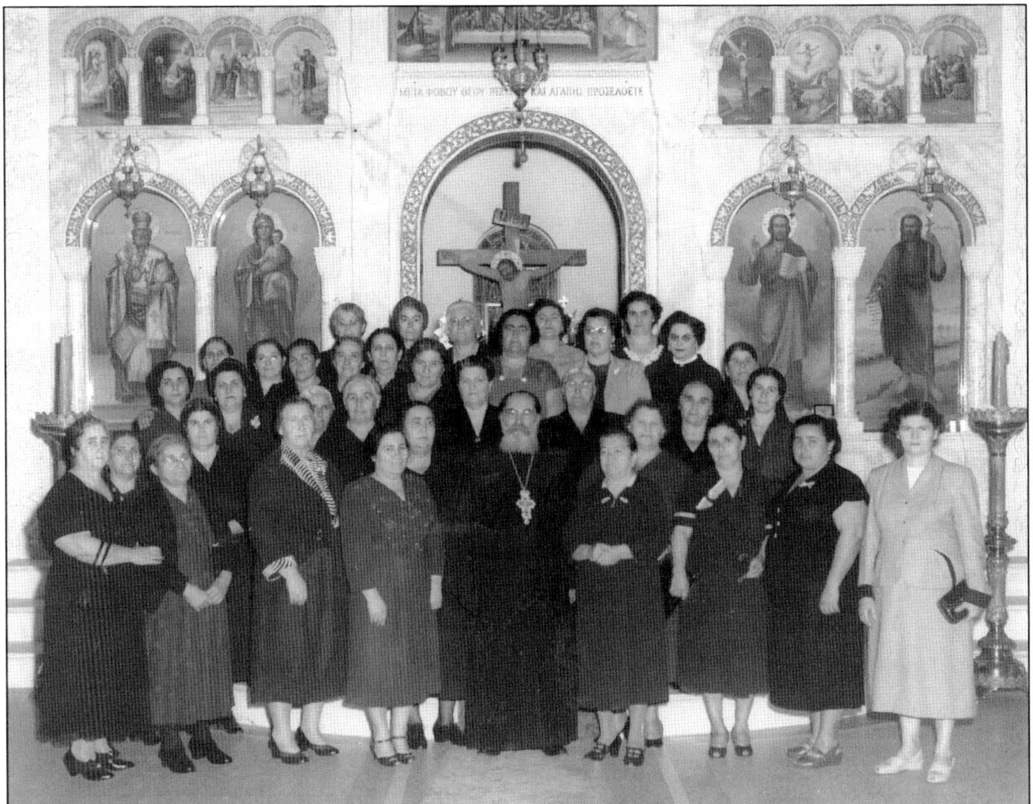

Members of the Ladies Kalymnian Society gather with the Reverend Father Theophilos Karaphillis in front of the altar inside the St. Nicholas Greek Orthodox Church in 1944. After the initial influx, Kalymnians gradually became the largest regional group within the Greek community. They have maintained an active membership that is part of the national Pan-Kalymnian Society network. As in many ethnic communities, immigrants from different islands, regions, or cities banded together to create organizations that were designed for both fellowship and mutual support in times of personal or social crisis. (Courtesy of Nickollet Tsourakis Henderson.)

Members of the Symian Society and children gather with the Reverend Father Theophilos Karaphillis in 1930. Another of the major island groups represented in the Greek community is from the island of Symi. Symians were the first to adopt the *skafandro*, or the heavy rubberized diving suit with helmet, and were known for their diving abilities. Like the islands of Kalymnos and Halki, Symi was also known for its shipyards. (Courtesy of the Faklis family.)

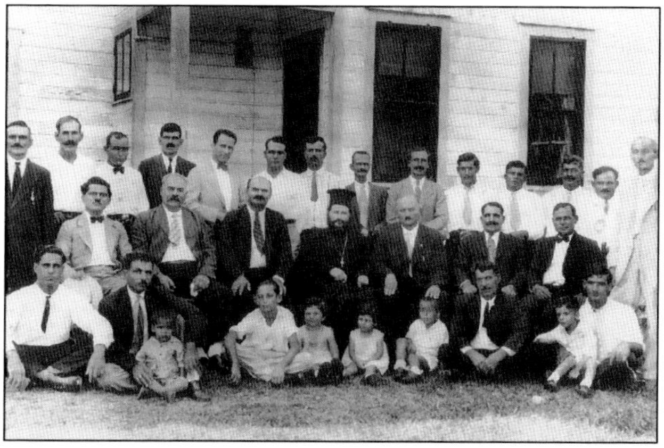

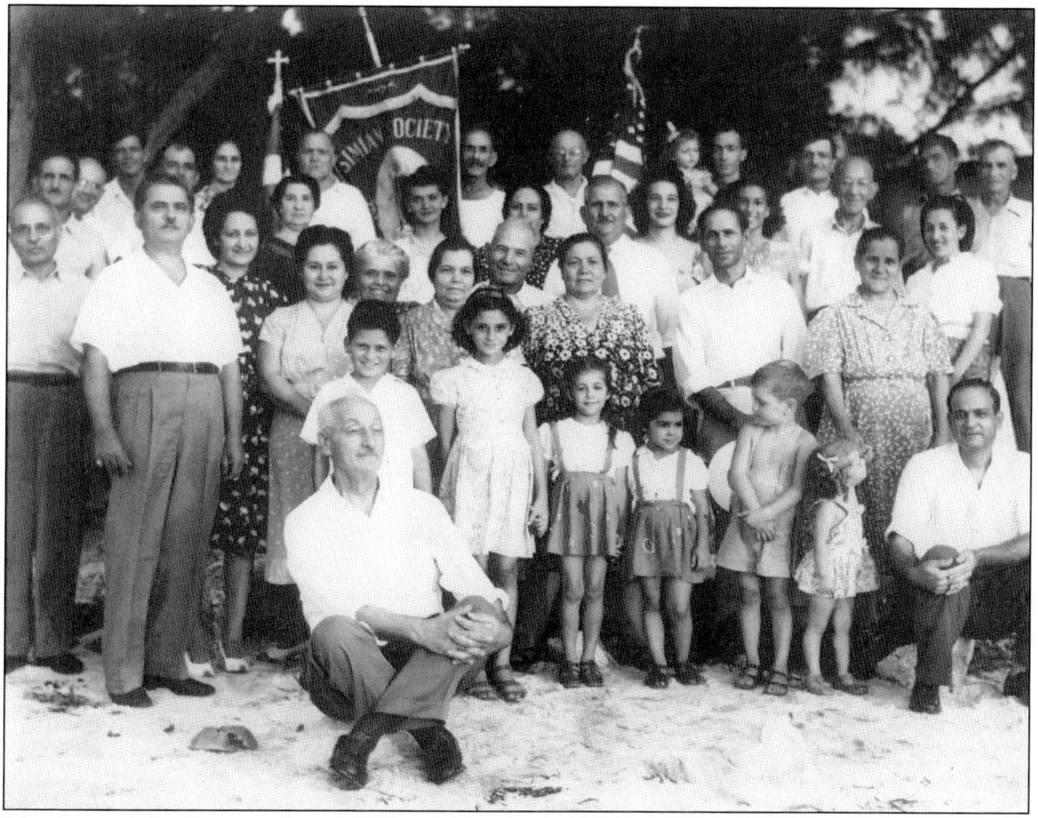

Members of the Symian Society attend a picnic at the beach in 1946. Pictured are, from left to right, (sitting) George Cladakis and Agapitos Megaloudis; (children) Michael Faklis, Sylvia Tsangranis, Irene Zouroudis, Nikki Zouroudis, George Giannaras, and Margo Filis; (second row) Nikitas Faklis, Vasile Faklis, Mina Sarris, Dikea Faklis, Ypapanti, Mr. and Mrs. George Georgiadis, Epakoy Kaladoukas, Nick Zouroudis, and Eleni Stavropoulos; (third row) Gabriel Astipolitis, Irene Sarris, a Mrs. Antoniades, unidentified, James Antonoglou, Mary Stavropoulos, Irene Sarris Tsangaris, Dimitrios Stavropoulos, and Flora Stavropoulos; (fourth row) Panayiotis Ypapandakis, Savvas Moskos, Minas Sarris, Eleni and Theodoros Antonoglou, Sotiris Makrinakis, John Palogianos, Paul Antoniades, Kyriakos Loupis, Zaharias Kastronis, and Kostas Antoniades. (Courtesy of the Faklis family.)

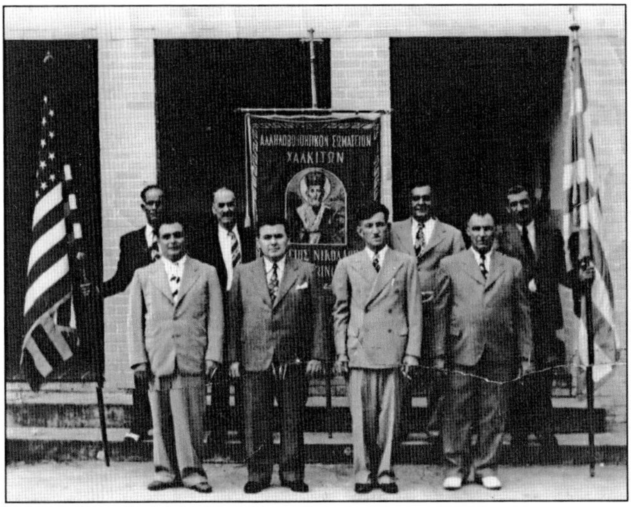

Members of the Men's Halki Society pose in front of the Philoptochos Society building on Hope Street in the early 1950s. From left to right are (first row) George Pappas, John Nefton, Costas "Dinio" Klimantos, and Diamantis Leonis; (second row) Vasilis Pokrakis, Pepos Phillippou, George Manousos, and Koukoulis Koukoulakis. Although it is a tiny island, Halki produced great divers, captains, and shipbuilders. (Courtesy of the Halki Society.)

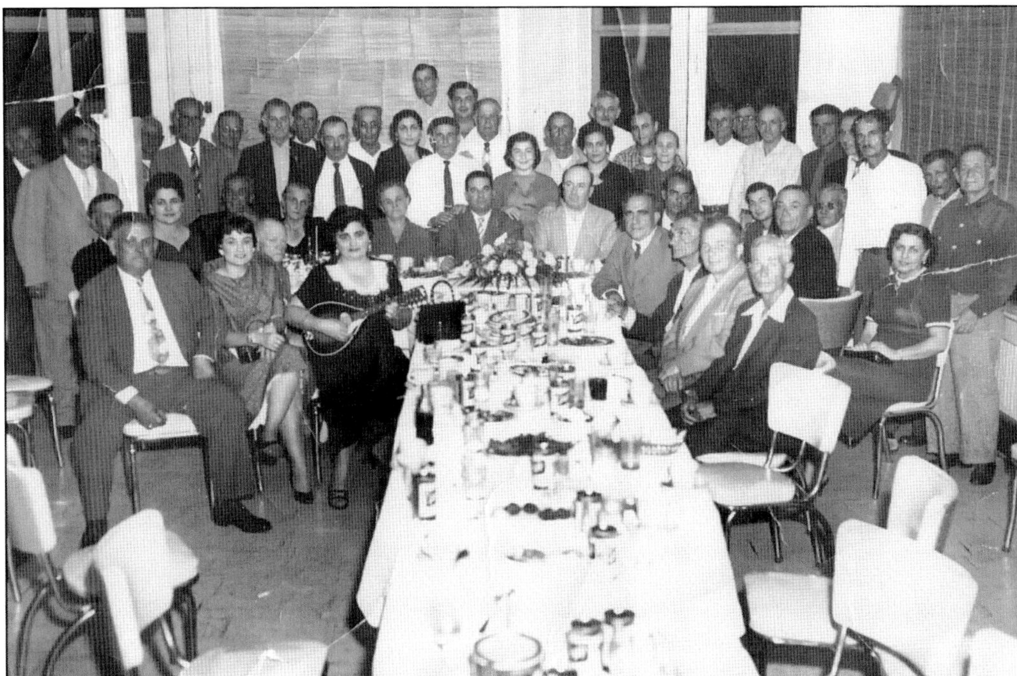

The Halki Society celebrates an occasion with dinner and music in the early 1950s. Celebrants are, from left to right, (first row) unidentified, Arvanos Christou, a Mr. Spanos, and Pasithea Christou (playing mandolin); (second row) Dinio Klimantos, Katherine Klimantos, Diamantis Leonis, Fanio Leonis, Assimina Velousis, unidentified, George Frantzis, Giorgos Manousos, Theophilos Kanannis, Perry Pipinos, and Semeone Sfyriou; (third row) George Pappas, Vasilis Pokrakis, George "Kirki" Himonetos, unidentified, Alice Giannaras, Zaharis Pappas, Fanitsa Frantzis, Zoula Frantzis, Stamatouli Theodosis, unidentified, Filarota Filaretou, Demosthenes Kananis, Simeon Filaretou, and Ourania Sfyriou; (fourth row) two unidentified, Vasilis Pokrakis, Steve John, unidentified, a Mr. Polidoros, Pharaoni Mostris, Mihalis Kelades, Yiannis Papadopoulos, Basili ?, Kelades Kelades, Themistocles Kelades, unidentified, Pavlos Kalogrides, Rally Hourdas, unidentified, "Fasaria" ?, Diogenis Papadoparolos, and Leonidas Spanos. (Courtesy of the Halki Society.)

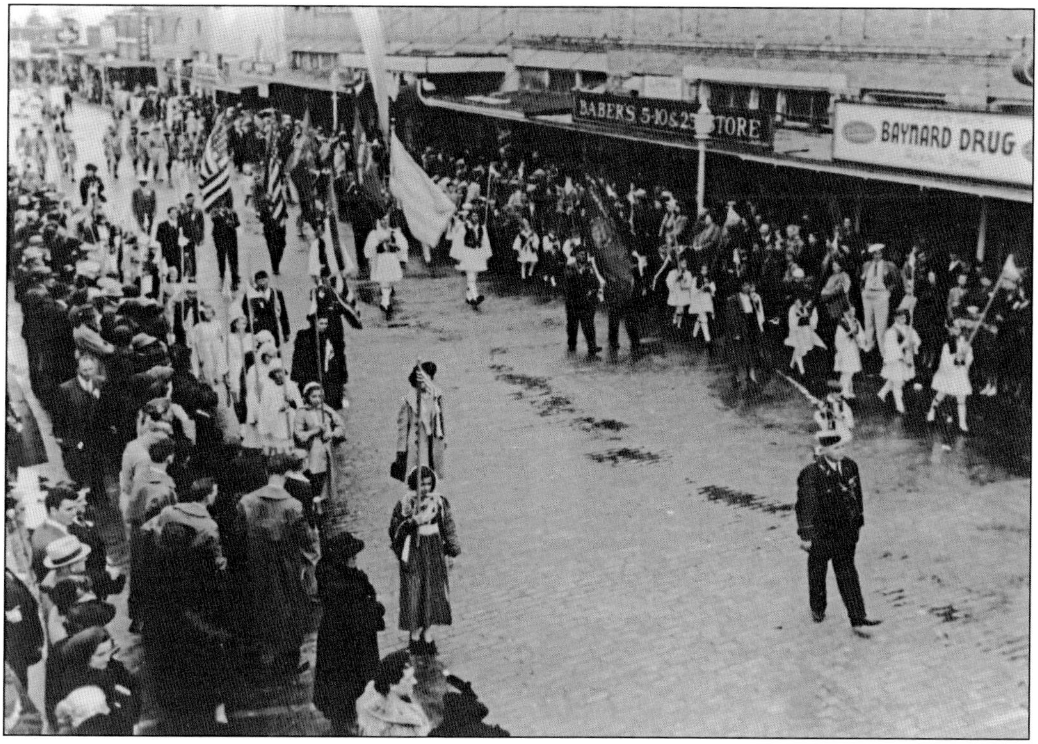

The Greek community observes many types of festive secular occasions. The successful Greek Revolution against 400 years of Ottoman rule is celebrated on March 25 throughout the Greek diaspora. In this parade down Tarpon Avenue during the 1940s, men dressed as evzones march with young women in village costumes, as well as many wearing everyday street clothes. (Courtesy of the City of Tarpon Springs.)

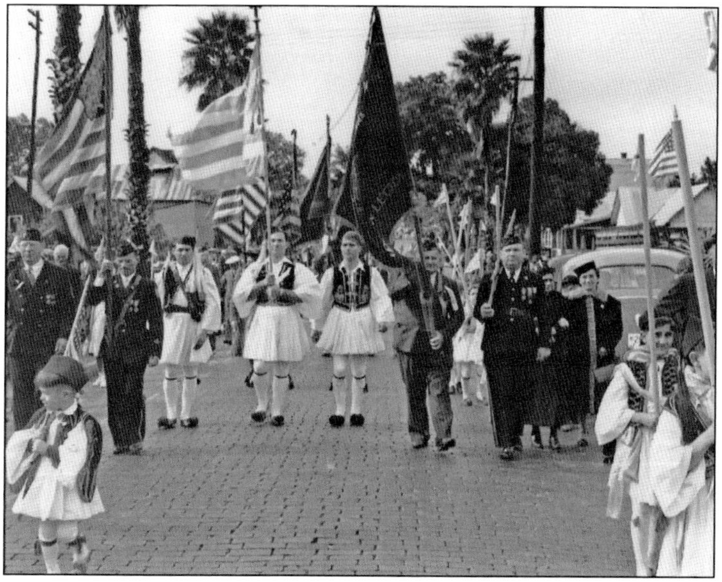

In Tarpon Springs, Greek Independence Day is usually celebrated with a parade and *glendi* (celebration) that include dance groups, children in regional costumes, community organizations, church officials, and dignitaries from Greece. This image shows Greek Independence Day around 1943, with Nicholas Kavouklis at front left. (Courtesy of Maggie Kavouklis Nichols.)

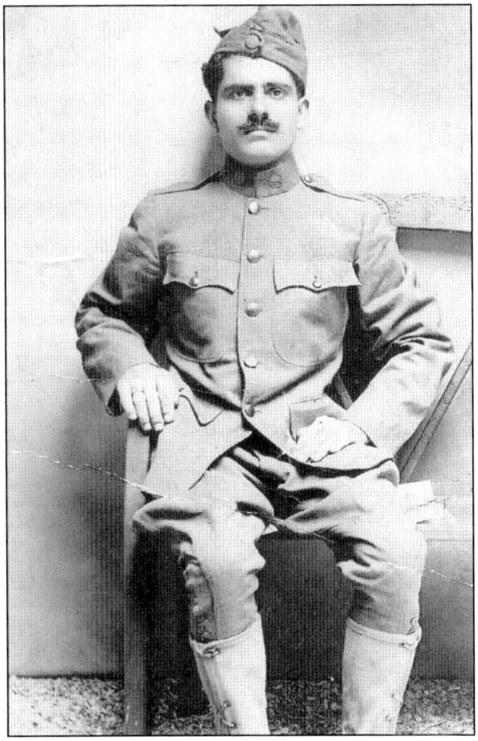

Vasile G. Faklis (1892–1982) left Symi for Tarpon Springs, where he founded Faklis' Department Store and Shoe Repair in 1912. He proudly served in the US Army during World War I and is shown here in his military uniform in 1917. His sons, George and Michael, served during World War II and continued the family business. (Courtesy of the Faklis family.)

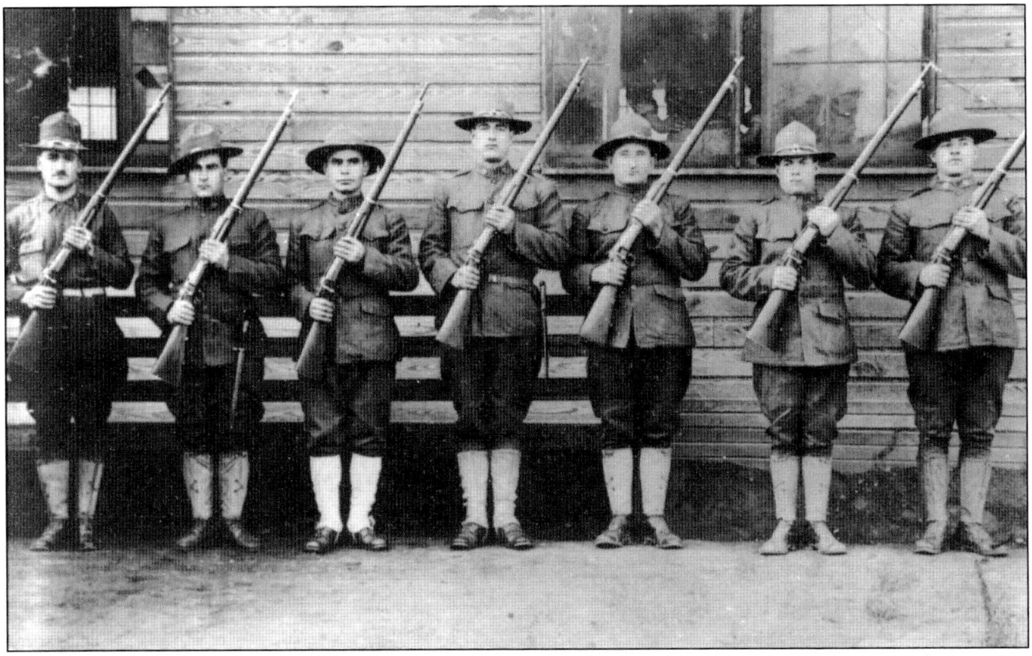

This group of Greek American soldiers served in a single unit during World War I. Pantelis Peronis (1893–1953), second from left, came to the United States before 1910. In Tarpon Springs, he worked as a sponge diver and raised a family of six children with his wife, Belia. He had to cease his dangerous job as a diver and turn to other work after he fell victim to decompression sickness, also known as the bends. (Courtesy of Magdaline Peronis Tiliakos and Nellie Peronis Tiliakos.)

Shown here in his military uniform during World War I, Nick Karavokiros (1892–1945) worked as a cook on a sponge boat owned by the Samarkos family. The family lived in Indiana before moving to Tarpon Springs. (Courtesy of Nickollet Tsourakis Henderson.)

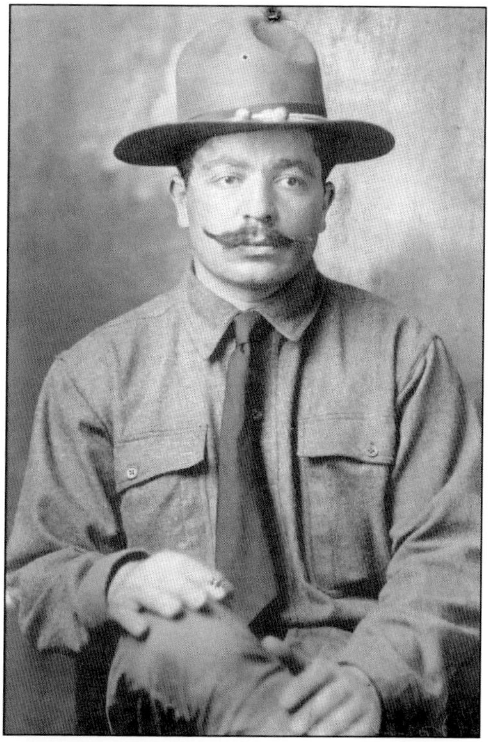

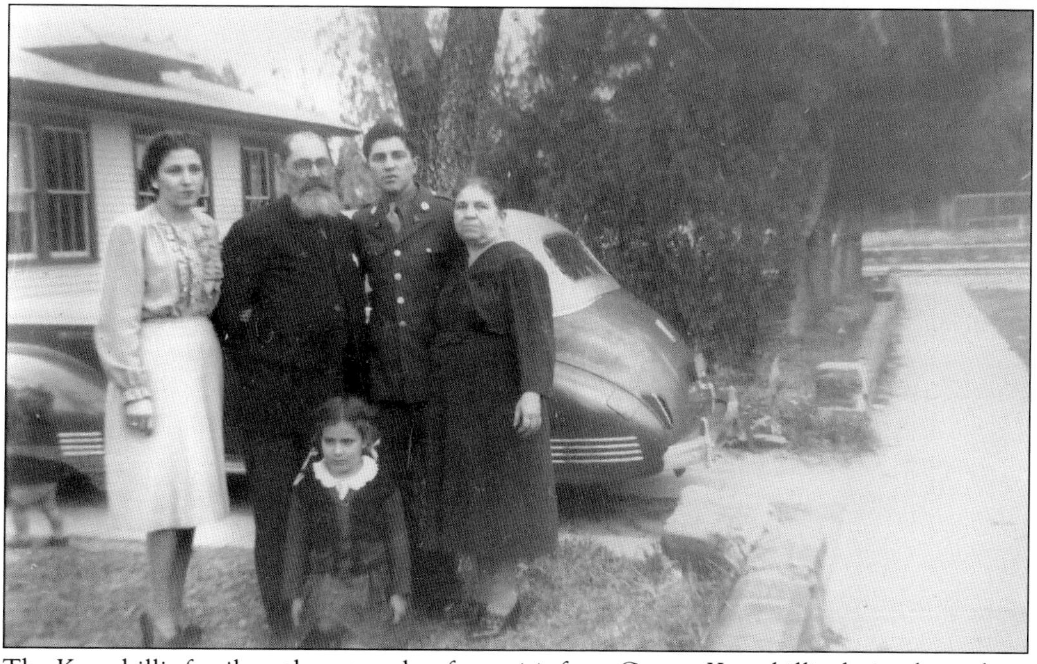

The Karaphillis family gathers together for a visit from George Karaphillis during leave from his duties during World War II. From left to right are Katina Karaphillis Nicholis, the Reverend Father Theophilos Karaphillis, Esther Jordan Raptis (kneeling), George Karaphillis (in military uniform), and Kaliope Karaphillis. They are pictured in front of the former Greek school on what is now Pinellas Avenue. (Courtesy of Esther Jordan Raptis.)

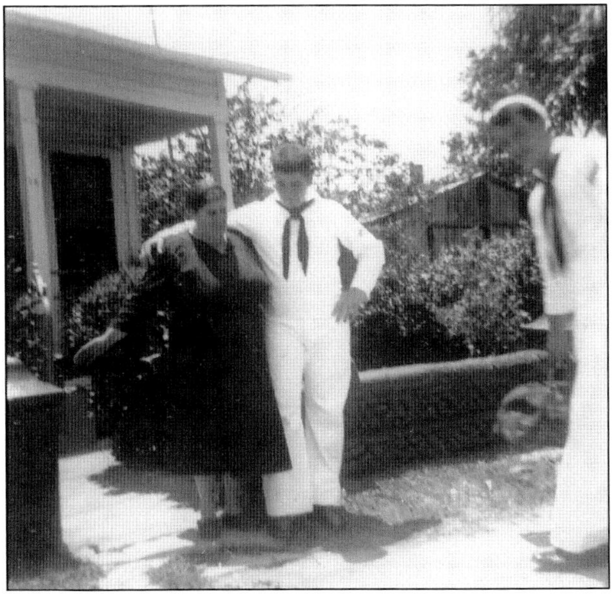

Tony Karavokiros served in the US Navy during World War II. While on leave, he and another sailor visited his mother, Maria, around 1943. Many Greek Tarponites who had observed the Axis powers invade Greece early in the war served bravely in the armed forces. Those at home collected for the Greek war relief fund. (Courtesy of Nickollet Tsourakis Henderson.)

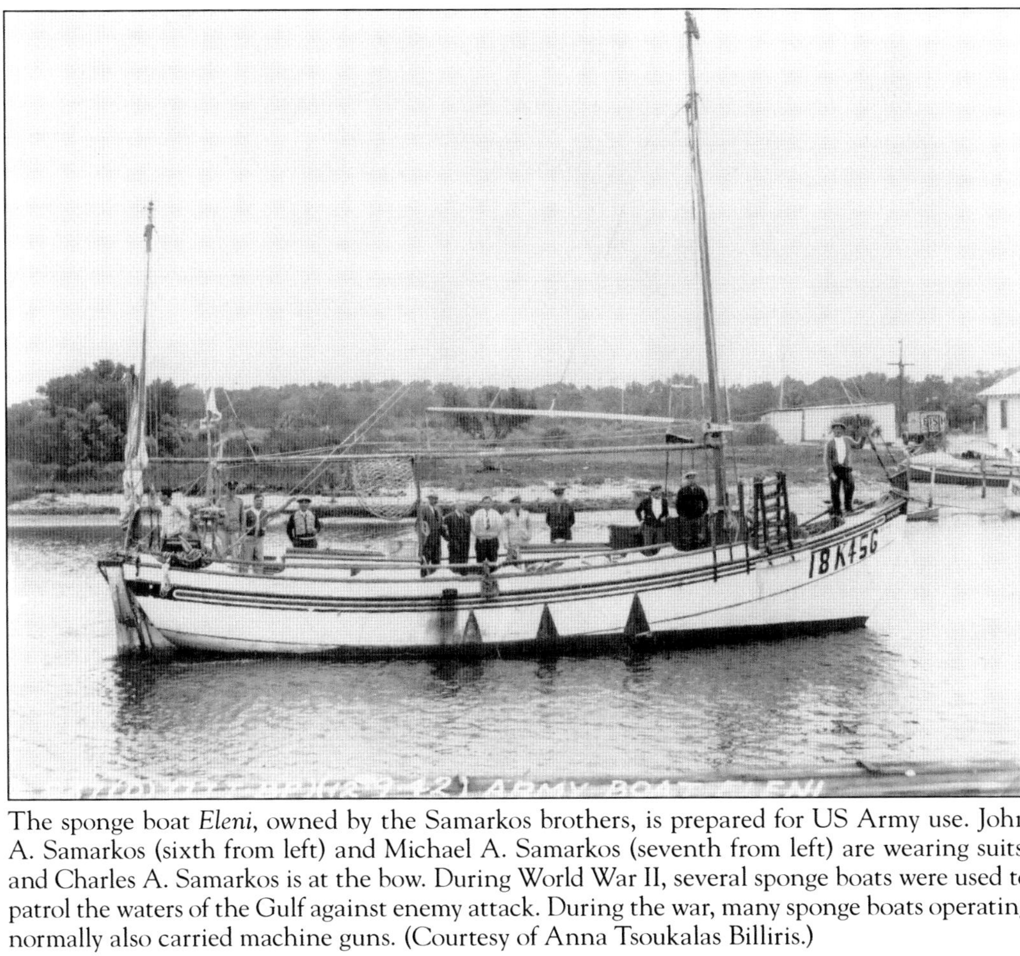

The sponge boat *Eleni*, owned by the Samarkos brothers, is prepared for US Army use. John A. Samarkos (sixth from left) and Michael A. Samarkos (seventh from left) are wearing suits, and Charles A. Samarkos is at the bow. During World War II, several sponge boats were used to patrol the waters of the Gulf against enemy attack. During the war, many sponge boats operating normally also carried machine guns. (Courtesy of Anna Tsoukalas Billiris.)

Three

Religious Traditions

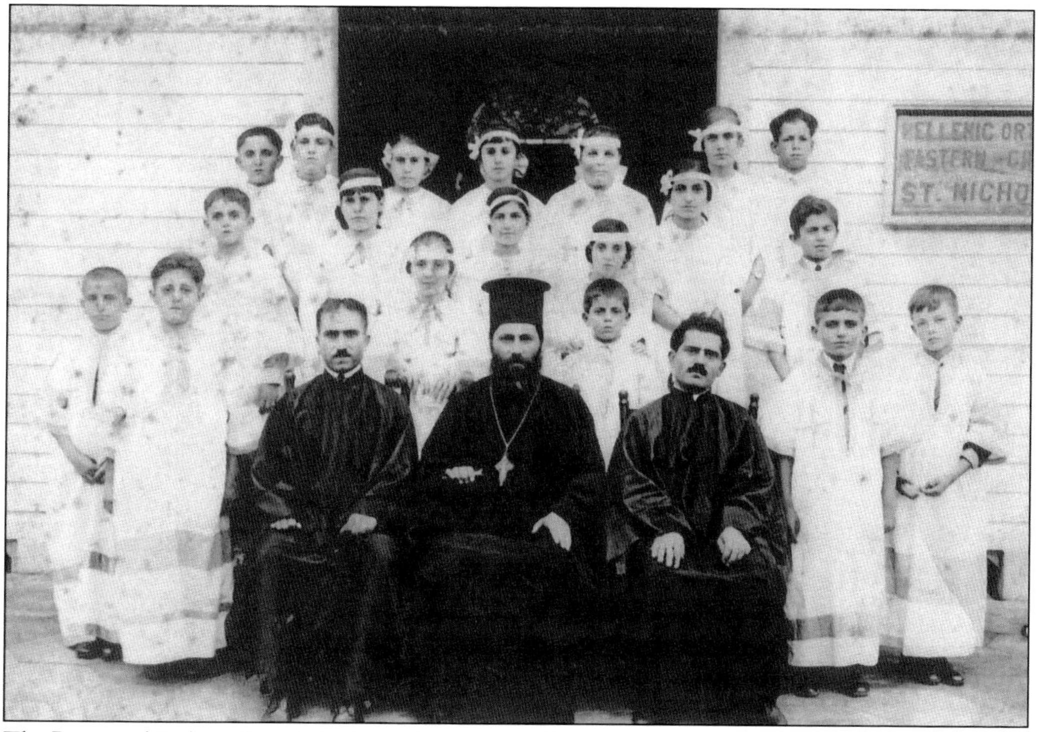

The Reverend Father Theophilos Karaphillis (1883–1963) is seen at center, with George Anastassiou at left and Vasile Faklis (then Papafaklis) at right. They are pictured with the first choir in front of the old St. Nicholas Greek Church around 1925. Karaphillis came from Kalymnos in 1922 and served at St. Nicholas and in neighboring communities until he retired in 1954. He was revered in the community for his dedication and patience and for overseeing the building of St. Nicholas Greek Orthodox Cathedral. After Karaphillis's funeral, parishioners followed his casket on foot to Cycadia Cemetery. (Courtesy of the Faklis family.)

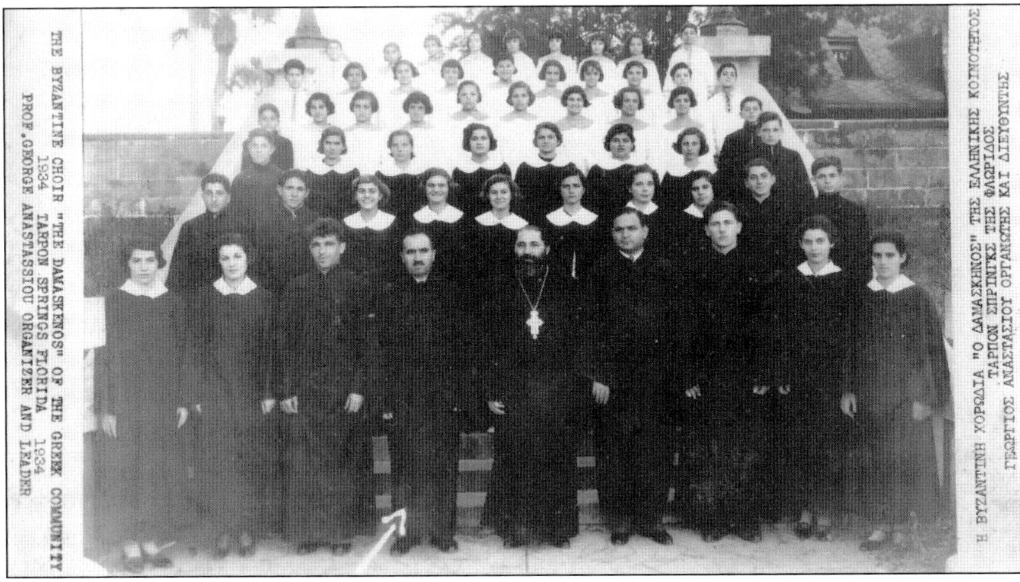

The Damaskenos, a Byzantine choir led by Fr. George Anastassiou (1900–1962), poses on the steps leading to the Spring Bayou pier in 1934. In the early 20th century, priests and others in America began to compose new Greek Orthodox liturgical music in European scales. The new music was often presented in a westernized style through choirs accompanied by organs. Associated with the progressive style, Anastassiou arrived from Cyprus in 1920. In 1924, he settled in Tarpon Springs, where he served as principal of the Greek Parochial School and head chanter at St. Nicholas from 1931 to 1941. He organized the Byzantine choir, composed liturgical music, and edited the *Liturgical Hymnal* used in most Greek Orthodox churches of his time. (Courtesy of Esther Jordan Raptis.)

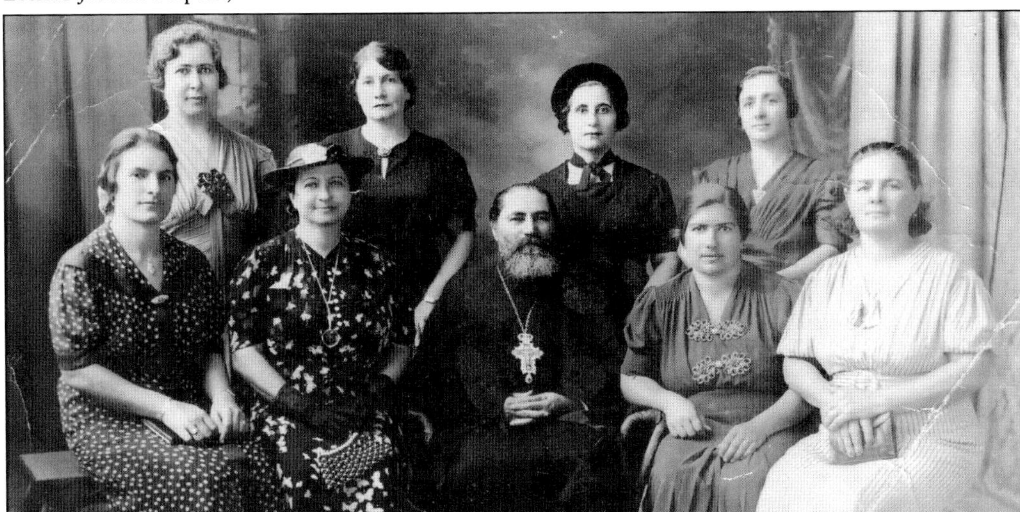

This early image of Philoptochos members is probably from the late 1930s. The Greek Orthodox Ladies Philoptochos Society is a women's philanthropic society associated with the Greek Orthodox Archdiocese of America. Its mission is to aid those in need, promote the charitable purposes of the church, and preserve Orthodox traditions and doctrine. The first formal chapter was founded in New York City in 1902, but branch societies were soon established at each Greek Orthodox church. (Courtesy of Evelyn Miaoulis Bilirakis.)

Members of Philoptochos pose with the Reverend Father Theophilos Karaphillis in 1940 at the ground breaking for the Philoptochos Building that was erected on Hope Street and completed in 1942. From left to right are (first row) Maria Miaoulis, Karaphillis, and Assimina Velousis; (second row) Paraskevi Christou, two unidentified, and Stamatia Tsalichis; (third row) Katina Krouskos, Eleni Psaras, Irene Diamantes, and Angeliki Boudoucies. The little girl in the lower right corner is Evelyn Miaoulis Bilirakis. (Courtesy of Nick and Betty Krouskos.)

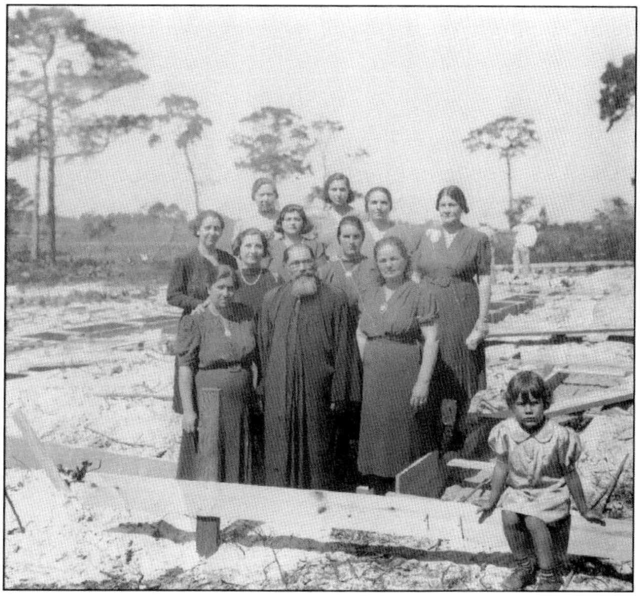

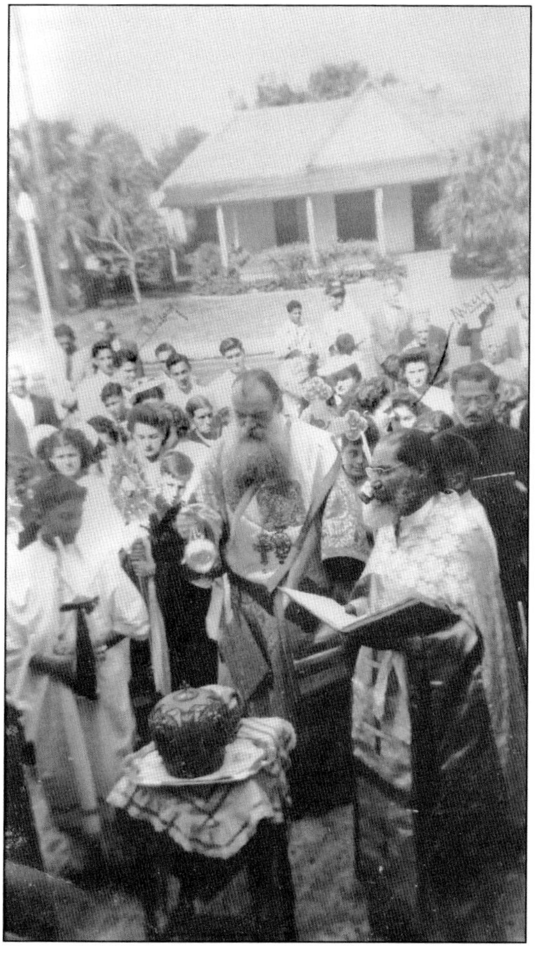

Archbishop Athenagoras (center) and the Reverend Father Theophilos Karaphillis (right) are pictured at the consecration of the new St. Nicholas Greek Orthodox Church in 1943. Chanter Vasile Faklis is at far right behind Father Karaphillis. Completed at the height of World War II, it replaced the earlier wood-frame church, which had been damaged by fire and was too small for the community. The sponge industry experienced a boom during World War II, as European sponge markets were closed to the United States and sponges were needed for the war effort. Much of the money needed to construct the church came from the spongers, who donated a percentage of their harvest to the cause, as well as through the fundraising efforts of the Greek fraternal organizations. (Courtesy of Nellie Peronis Tiliakos and Magdaline Peronis Tiliakos.)

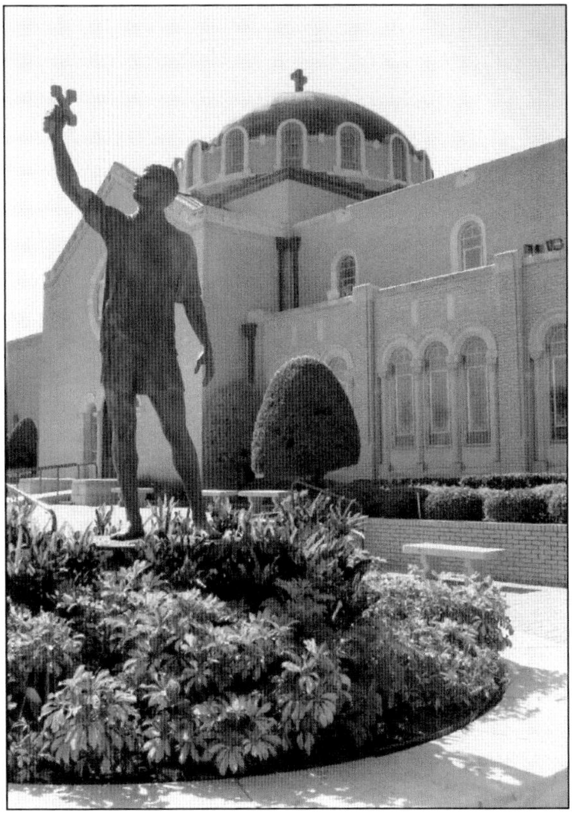

St. Nicholas Greek Orthodox Cathedral is shown behind the statue depicting a youth who has retrieved the Epiphany Cross. St. Nicholas was modeled after Agia Sofia, the famed Byzantine church in what is now Istanbul. The builders utilized 60 tons of marble from Mount Pentele, near Athens. The Greek government had sent it to the 1939 World's Fair in New York, but then donated it to the church. It was designated a cathedral in 1975. Today, it is one of the best-known Greek Orthodox churches and plays an important part in the most elaborate Epiphany observances in the United States. The statue was created by local artist Mitchell Kolbe and unveiled in January 1994. (Author's collection.)

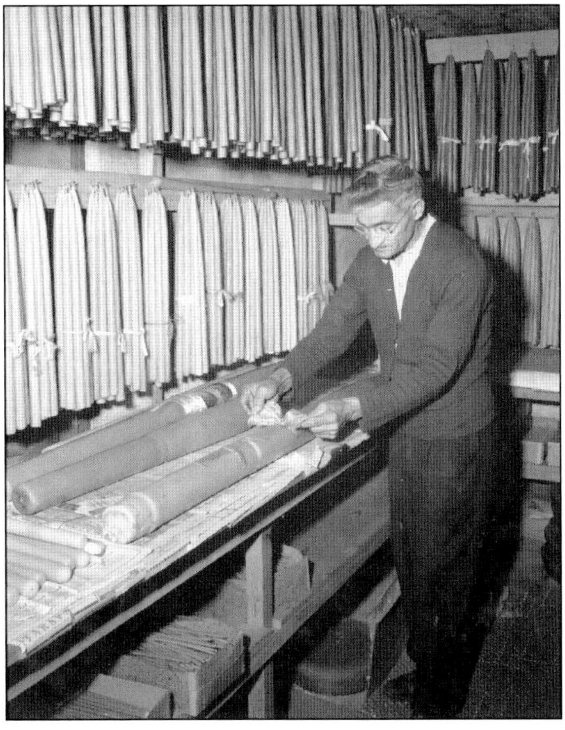

Louis Peronis (1884–1948), master candle maker, is seen at work in a miniature candle factory in the basement of St. Nicholas Greek Orthodox Cathedral on January 6, 1947. He puts the finishing touches on a four-foot candle weighing 15 pounds that later sold for $75. It was one of 9,000 assorted candles made by hand in a three-month period for the Epiphany celebration. In addition to being the master candlemaker for St. Nicholas, Peronis was also known for playing Greek music on the violin. He is heard on several recordings at the Library of Congress that were made by the WPA in Florida. (Photograph by the Department of Commerce, courtesy of State Archives of Florida, Florida Memory.)

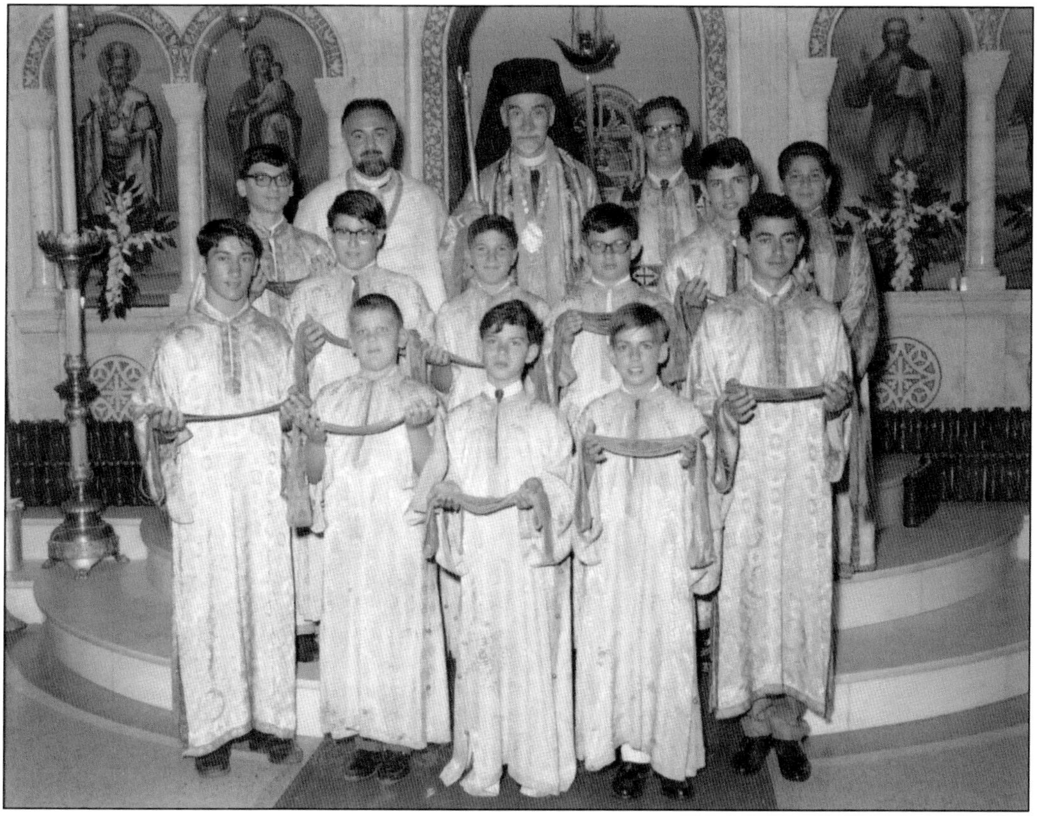

Altar boys at St. Nicholas take time out from their duties to pose with, from left to right, the Reverend Father Constantinos Raptis, Metropolitan Germanos, and Nikitas Manias on April 21, 1966. From left to right are (first row) Jim Krouskos, Skevos Koulias, Costa Tsourakis, Nikitas Lulias, and Bill Saroukos; (second row) Nick Koulianos, Nicholas Toth, John Raptis, Dean Tsourakis, Nick Houmis, and John Xipolito. Upon reaching eight years old, Greek Orthodox boys may assist the priests on Sundays and at special services as acolytes, or altar boys. Over the years, the altar boys can achieve progressive levels of responsibility. (Photograph by Flash Jarocki, courtesy of Mary Lerios Toth.)

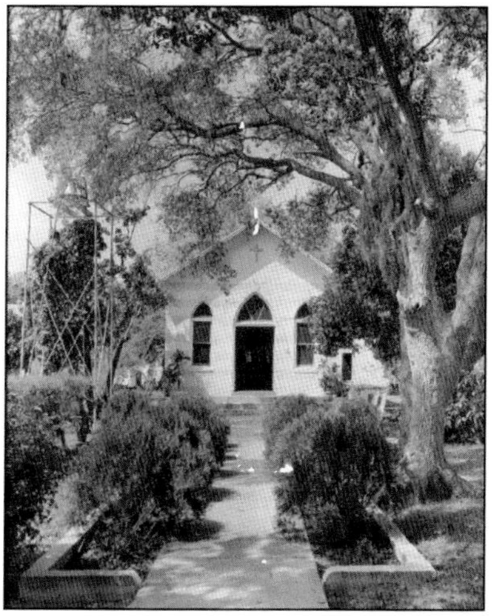

The St. Michael Shrine, a one-story chapel on Hope Street, was developed as a memorial by the Tsalichis family to honor the Archangel Michael for healing their 11-year-old son, Steve. Like St. Nicholas, it was completed in 1943, but unlike the cathedral, it was constructed without formal plans by local masons and carpenters. Greek Orthodox believers from throughout the country visit the chapel to pray for healing. St. Michael is the patron saint of the island of Symi, where the family originated. (Photograph by J.J. Steinmetz, courtesy of the *Tampa Tribune*.)

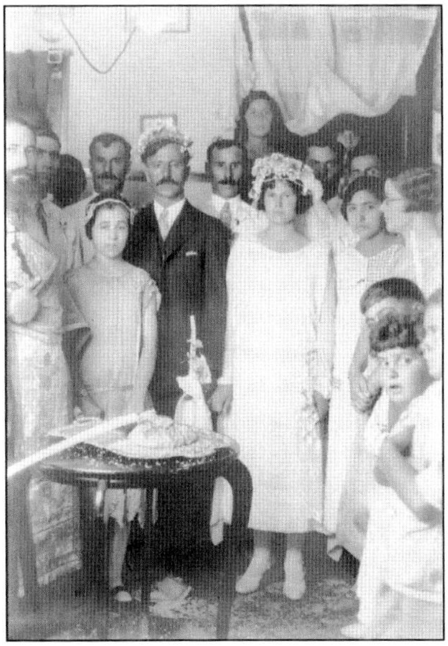

The Reverend Father Theophilos Karaphillis performed the marriage of Nickolas Lerios and Sievesta Samarkos inside a home in 1927. Greek weddings are traditionally conducted around a small table with a wedding tray containing the wedding crowns, Book of Gospels, rings, cup of wine, and two white candles needed for the ceremony. It looks like the cloth may contain the sugar-coated almonds usually distributed to wedding guests. Each guest receives an odd number of almonds; the odd number symbolizes the indivisibility of the couple, and the almonds signify the sweetness and bitterness of married life. Candles remind the couple of the light of Christ, who is with them in both the sacrament and their married life. Drinking from the common cup of wine symbolizes sharing all that life will bring, but their sorrows will be divided in half and their joy will be doubled. (Courtesy of Kaliope Lerios George.)

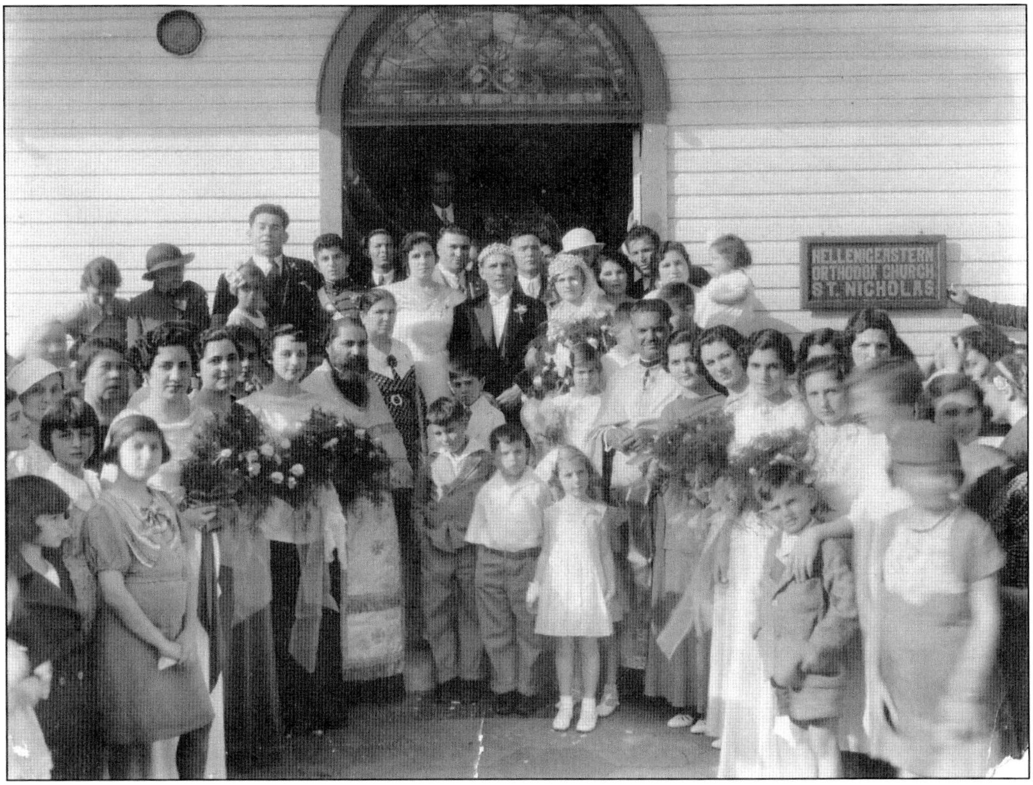

The Reverend Father Karaphillis presided at the marriage of his daughter Helen Karaphillis to George Jordan at the original St. Nicholas Church in July 1935. Greek Orthodox weddings are particularly rich in tradition. For instance, the *stefana* (crowns linked with a ribbon) worn by the bride and groom symbolize the couple's union and their status as king and queen of a new household. After the wedding, these elaborate creations are displayed in a special case and may ultimately accompany their owners to the grave. (Courtesy of Esther Jordan Raptis.)

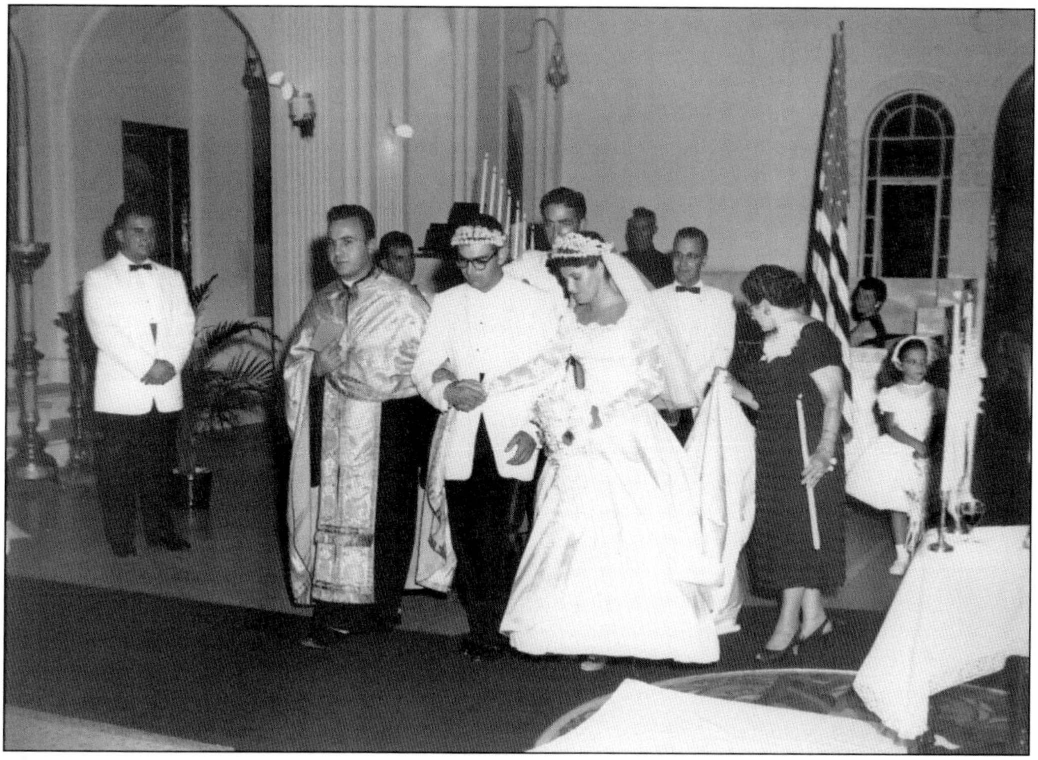

Themistocles "Tommy" and Kalotina Assimack wear *stefana* during their wedding ceremony in 1958. The Reverend Father Constantinos Raptis is on the left, and Garifalia Gillas, the *koumbara*, is on the right. Being a *koumbaros* or *koumbara* (sponsor) for a wedding is a position of great honor. *Koumbaroi* participate in the wedding by exchanging the crowns over the heads of the couple and providing necessary items. (Courtesy of the Tarpon Springs Area Historical Society.)

Uncle and godfather Theophilos Samarkos hands young Anna Tsoukalas Billiris to the Reverend Father Constantinos Raptis for her immersion into the baptismal font at St. Nicholas in 1956. Baptism marks the entry of the child into the church and usually occurs a few months after birth. In the church, the infant is immersed in a baptismal font, and the godparents assist the priest in anointing the child with oil. Being chosen as a *nounos* (godfather) or *nouna* (godmother) for a child is both an honor and a lifelong commitment. (Courtesy of Anna Tsoukalas Billiris.)

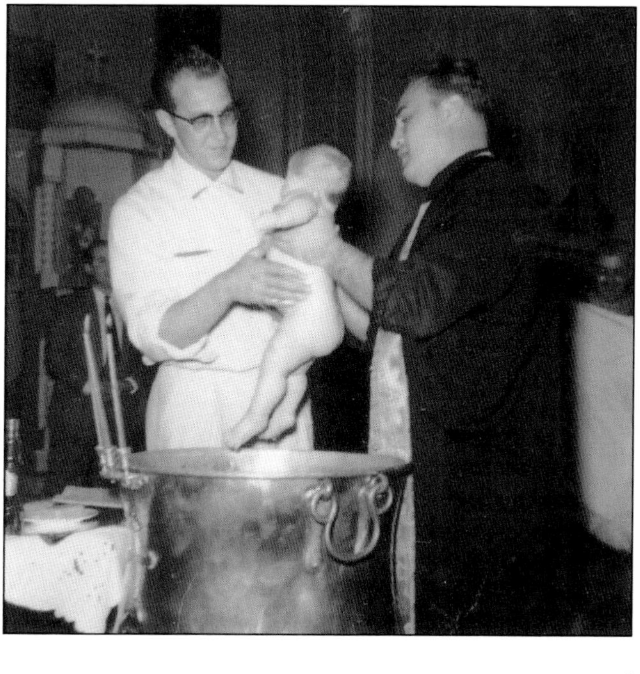

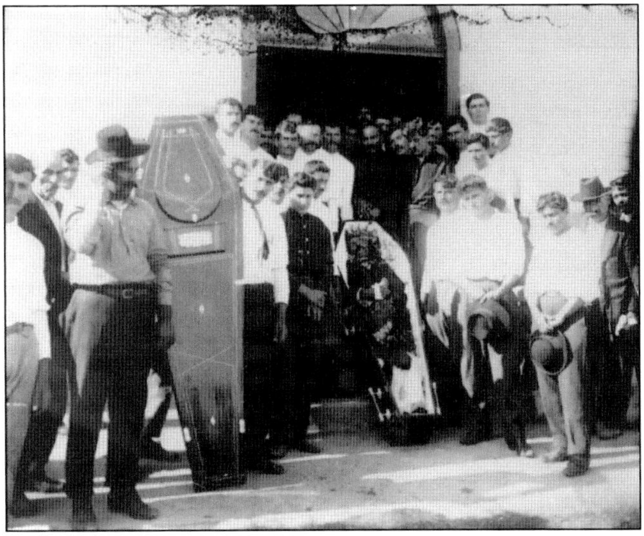

Outside St. Nicholas Church, mourners pose with the deceased before the burial in the 1920s. At the time, it was a widely accepted practice to photograph the deceased. Especially in the case of immigrants, this might have been the only glimpse of a loved one whom the families back home had not seen in years. Following the burial, mourners usually gather for the *makaria*, a meal to celebrate the life of the departed. The traditional menu includes a shot of Metaxa, fish, and *paximadia*, a dry cookie like biscotti. (Courtesy of the City of Tarpon Springs.)

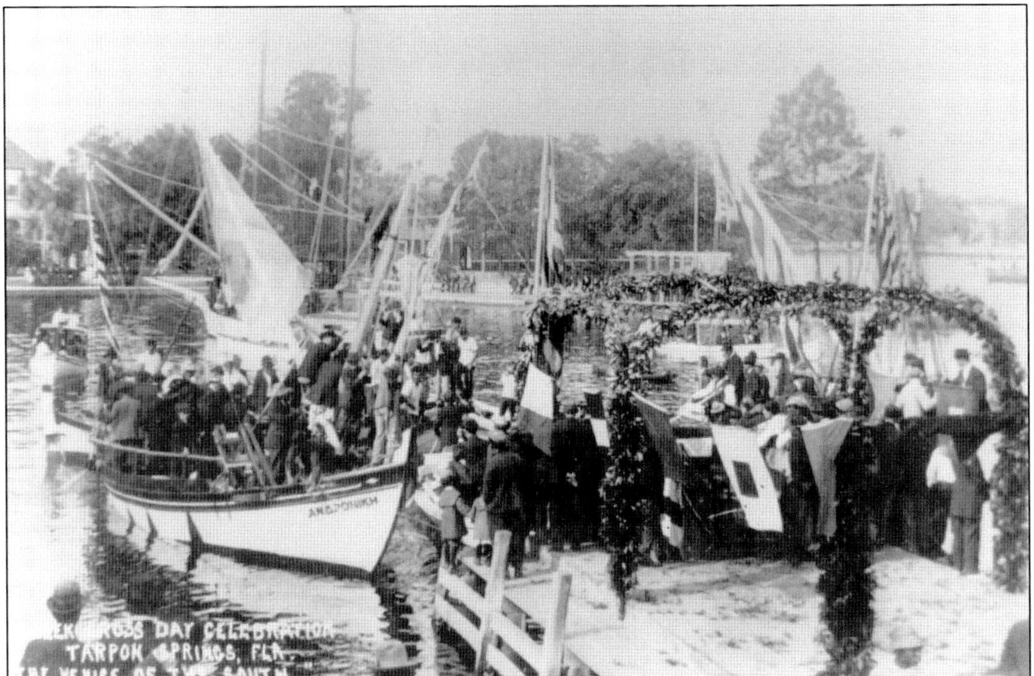

The Epiphany celebration in Tarpon Springs is the largest and most widely known in the United States. Epiphany commemorates the baptism of Jesus in the River Jordan, when the Holy Spirit descended in the form of a dove. This 1914 image is one of the earliest of an Epiphany celebration in Spring Bayou. Residents joined visitors at an array of events, commencing with an early Liturgy at St. Nicholas Cathedral and then the Agiasmo (Blessing of Water) at noon. Afterward, church officials led a procession with altar boys, the Byzantine choir, Greek clubs and societies, bands, and many more to Spring Bayou. During the earliest years of Epiphany until 1922, the ceremonies were attended by Metropolitan Germanos Shehadi of the Syrian Antiochian Church of North America. (Courtesy of the City of Tarpon Springs.)

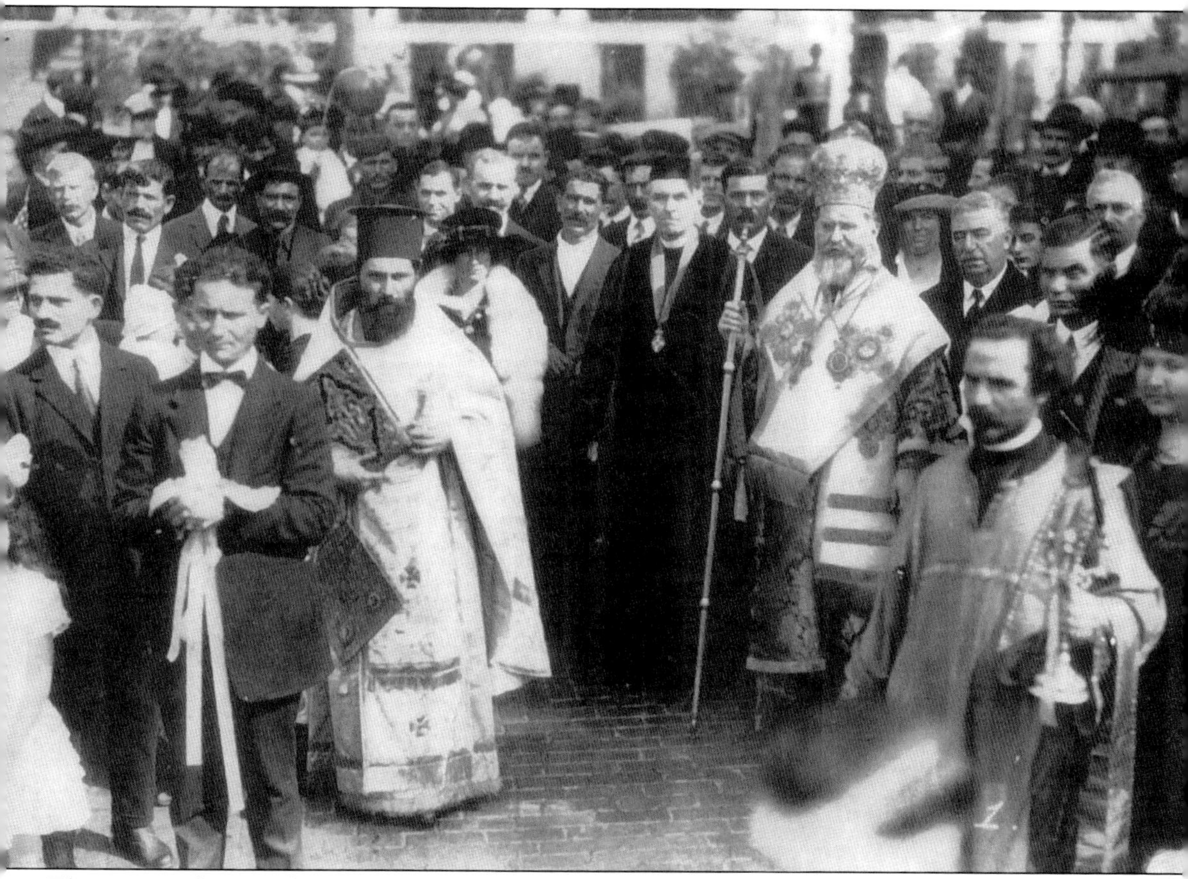

This image of an Epiphany procession from the early 1920s shows the dove bearer at left. From 1920 to 1934, the dove bearer was Kostas Tsimpikas from Halki. In 1935, the Byzantine choir started the tradition of electing a young girl as the annual dove bearer. To the right of the dove bearer is the Reverend Father Theophilos Karaphillis. The Protestant clergyman in the center is Rev. Thomas J. Lacey. Depending on the date, on the right may be Archbishop Alexander (1876–1942), the first leader of the Greek Orthodox Archdiocese of North and South America, which was formed in May 1922. (Courtesy of the Faklis family.)

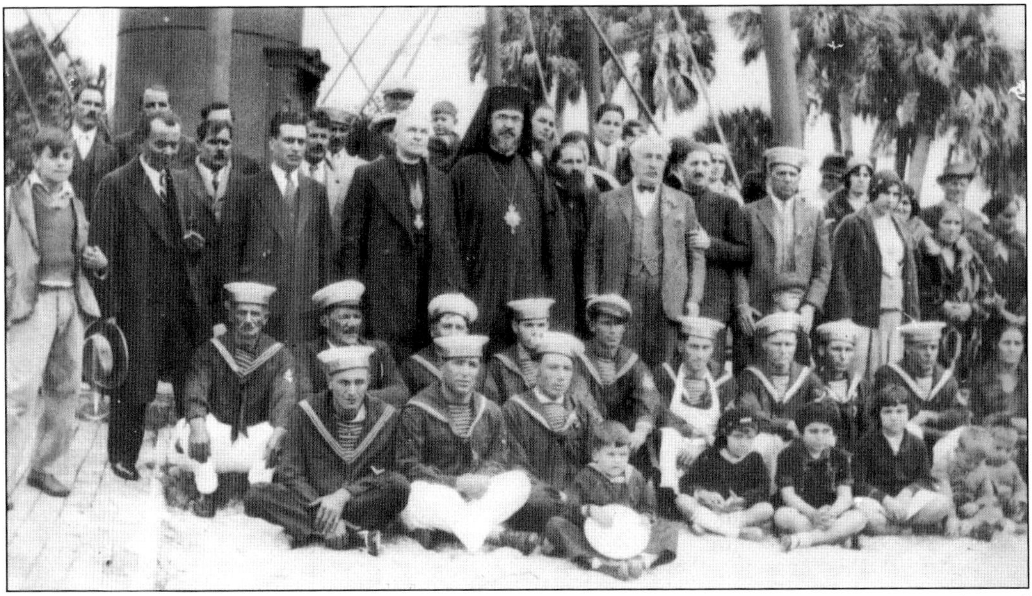

Sailors from Halki join an unidentified bishop, Rev. Thomas J. Lacey from New York, and community members for a picnic at Anclote Key on the day following Epiphany in 1930. In the early years, picnics at Anclote Key were commonly held after Epiphany and on other festive occasions. (Courtesy of Dr. Themistocles J. Diamandis.)

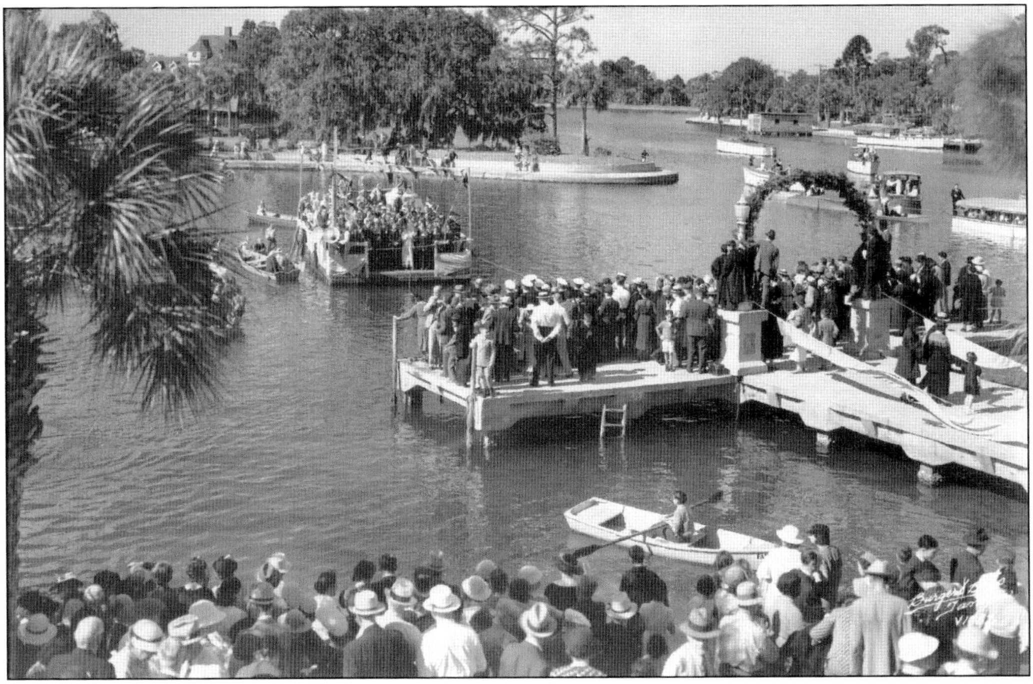

Residents and visitors at Spring Bayou wait for the annual cross dive during the Epiphany celebration of 1937. Before 1956, the archbishop, priests, and choir would board a barge that took them to the center of Spring Bayou. The archbishop would bless the waters before the young men dove for the cross. (Photograph by Burgert Brothers, courtesy of Special Collections Department, Tampa Library, University of South Florida.)

On Epiphany, January 6, 1938, the Reverend Father Theophilos Karaphillis (left), Rev. Thomas J. Lacey (center), and Bishop Callistos stand while cross retriever Anthony Houllis kneels. The dive is the highlight of Epiphany. Since 1920, young men have braved the chilly January waters in hopes of capturing the coveted cross to ensure a year of blessings. (Courtesy of the Tarpon Springs Area Historical Society.)

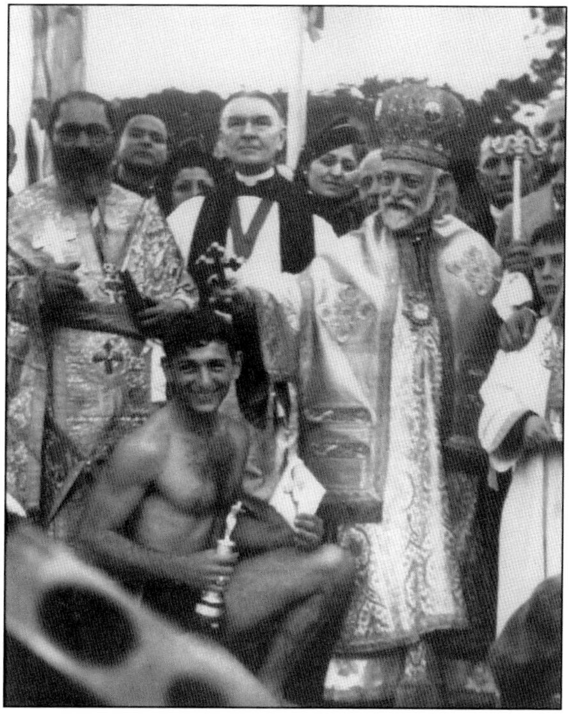

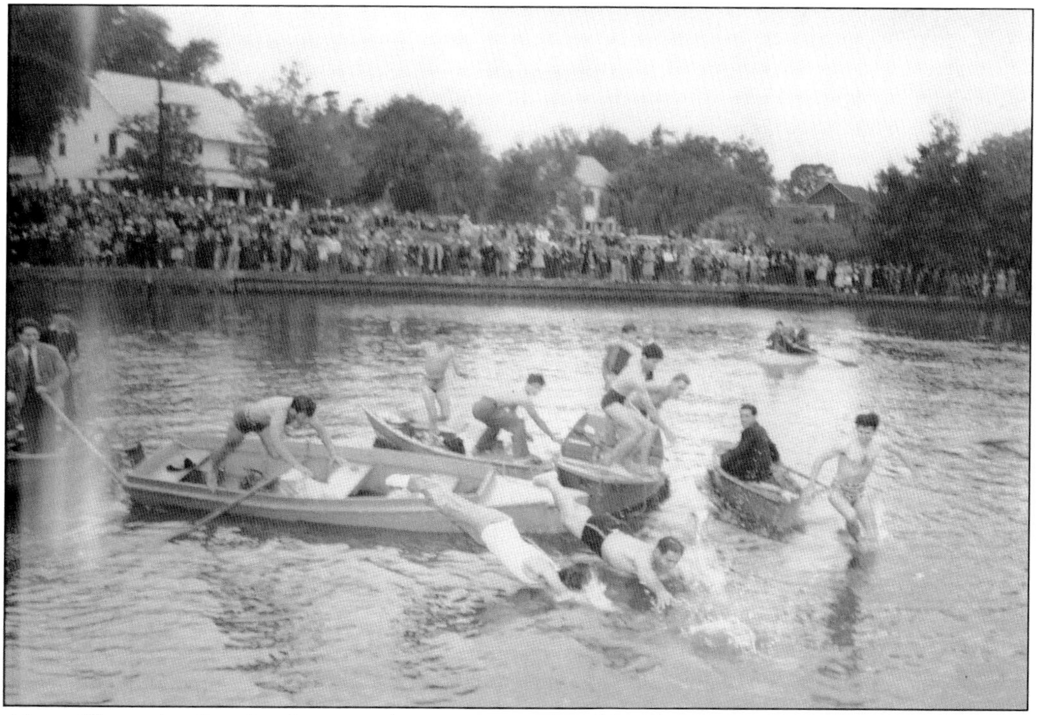

About 50 youths dive for the cross from a semicircle of dinghies in Spring Bayou on Epiphany, January 6, 1941. When a lucky diver finds the cross, he shoots up through the water, triumphantly holding it above his head. (Photograph by Burgert Brothers, courtesy of the Tampa-Hillsborough County Public Library System.)

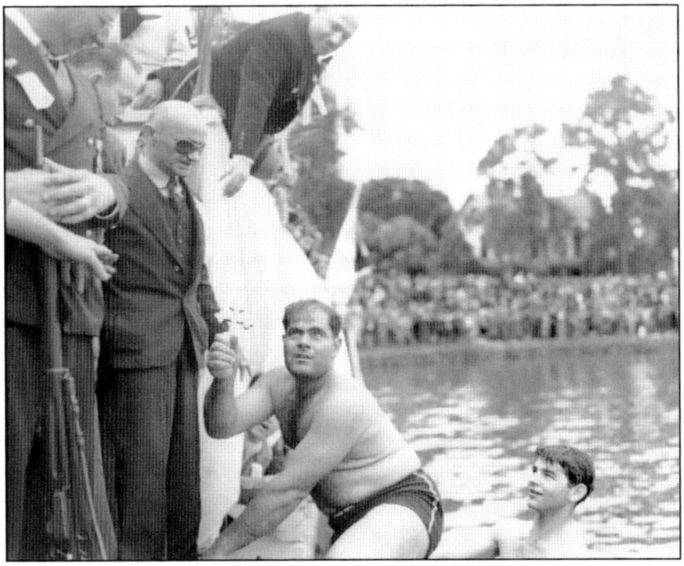

Theophilos Katras displays the cross that he retrieved from Spring Bayou on January 6, 1941. The young man who finds the cross is greeted with cheers of delight, then carried on his friends' shoulders back to St. Nicholas Cathedral to be blessed. The youths parade throughout town singing hymns before proceeding to the *glendi*, a celebration with food, dancing, and music. (Photograph by Burgert Brothers, courtesy of the Tampa-Hillsborough County Public Library System.)

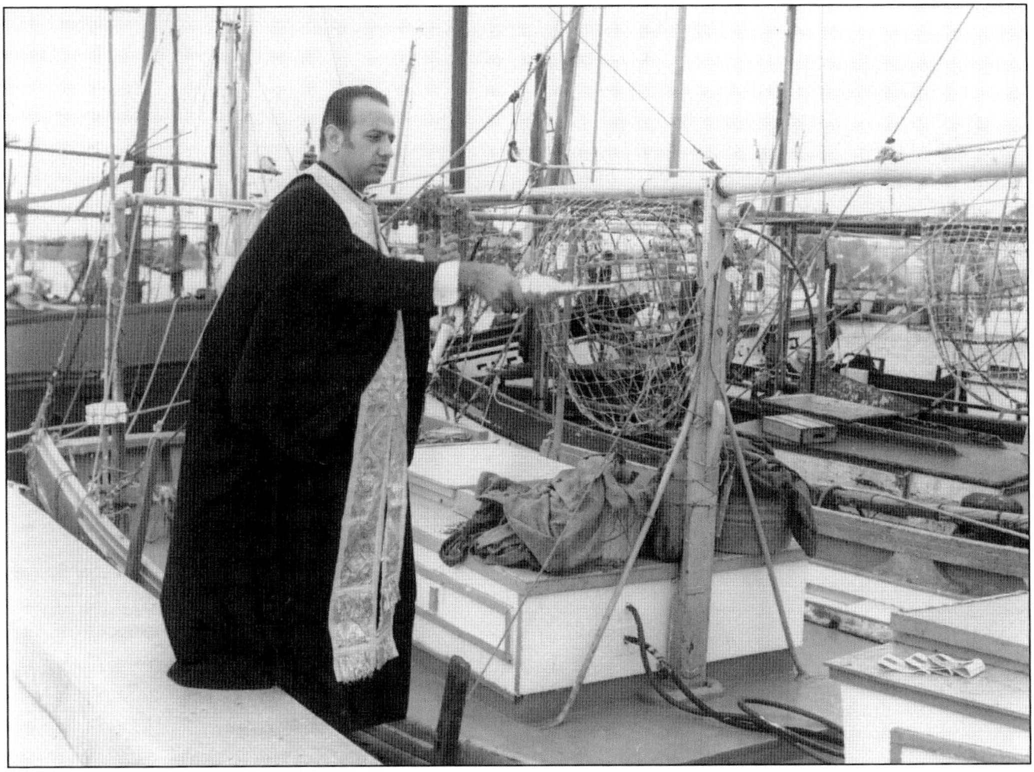

The Reverend Father Elias Kalariotes of St. Nicholas performs the annual blessing of the fleet ceremony at the Sponge Docks on January 5, 1970, the day before Epiphany. He boarded each boat and sprinkled holy water as he chanted the blessing. He also blessed those who watched the ceremony as well as nearby businesses. For centuries, Greek priests have blessed boats and the sea as part of Epiphany ceremonies—an essential event for seafaring communities since boats traditionally would not sail in the unhallowed sea between Christmas and Epiphany. (Courtesy of the *Tampa Tribune*.)

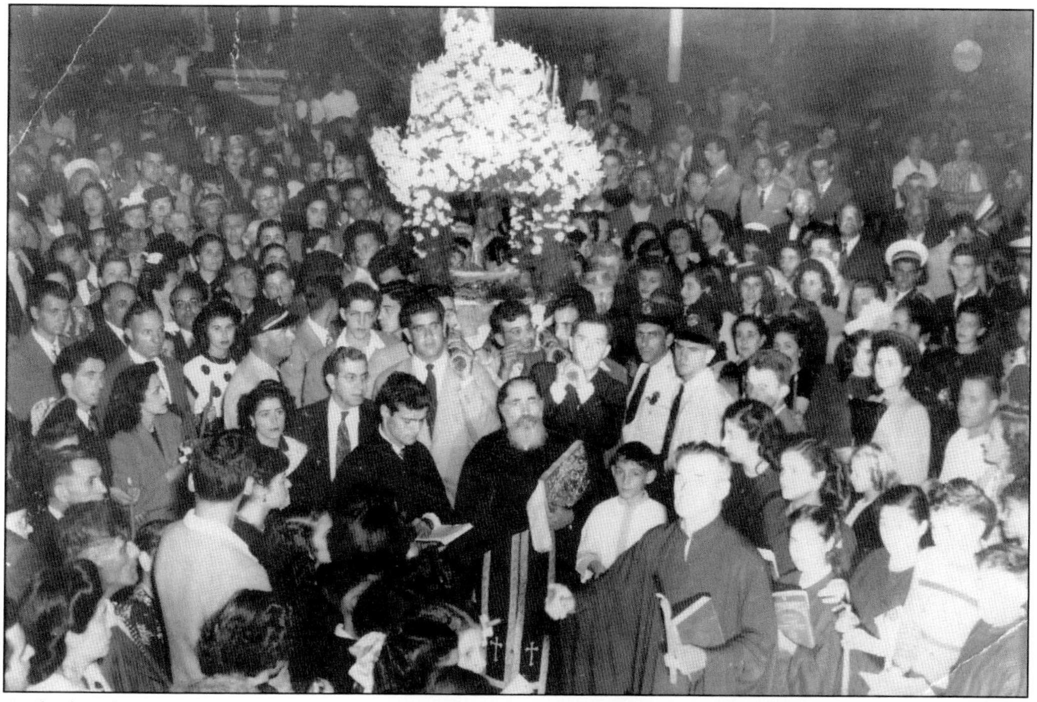

As befits the most important day in the Greek Orthodox calendar, Easter traditions are extensive. On Holy Friday, the *kouvouklion*, representing the tomb of Christ, is decorated by young parishioners. That night, it is carried from the church through the surrounding area in a procession followed by hundreds of mourners. In this photograph, the Reverend Father Theophilos Karaphillis leads a procession during the 1940s. (Courtesy of Eleni Christopoulos-Lekkas.)

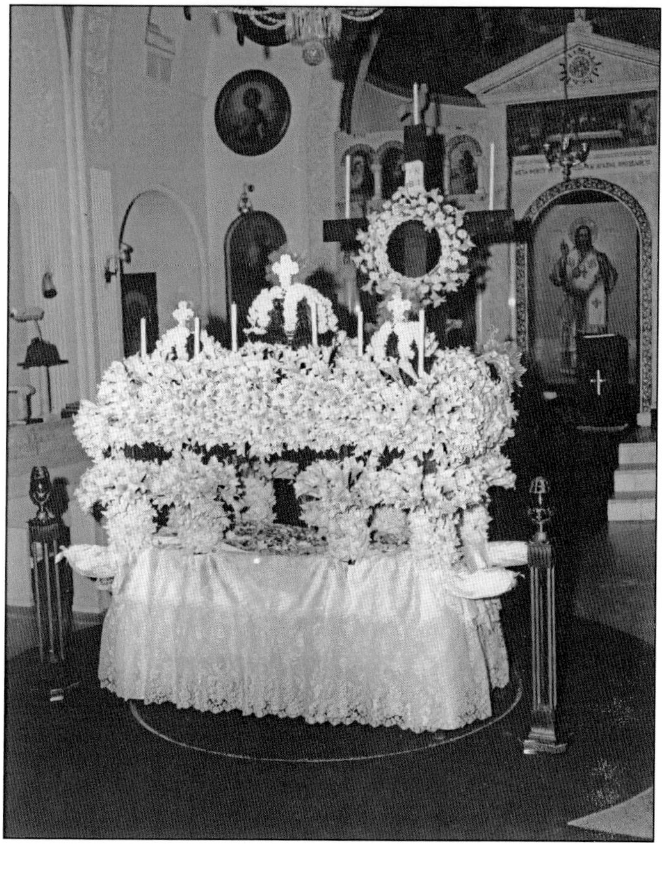

Decorated with hundreds of lilies, the kouvouklion is displayed in front of the altar inside St. Nicholas on Holy Friday in this image dating from the late 1940s. Young women from the parish had decorated the kouvouklion that morning. (Courtesy of Kaliope Lenos George.)

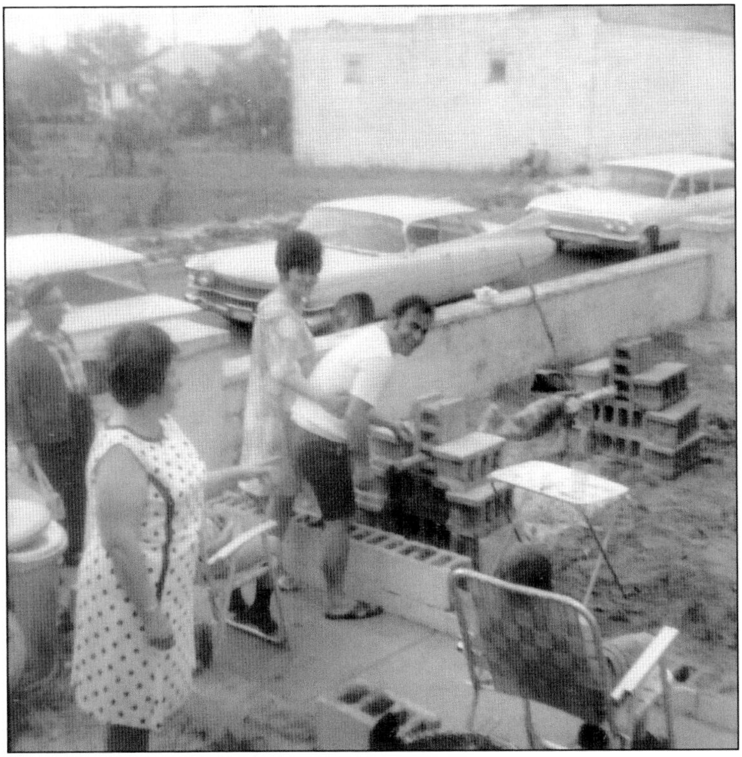

Easter Day is celebrated with a feast of roast lamb and other dishes avoided during the 40 days of Lenten fasting. Like many others, Panagiotis and Mary Christopoulos are roasting a lamb on their homemade rotisserie on an Easter morning in the 1960s. (Courtesy of Eleni Christopoulos-Lekkas.)

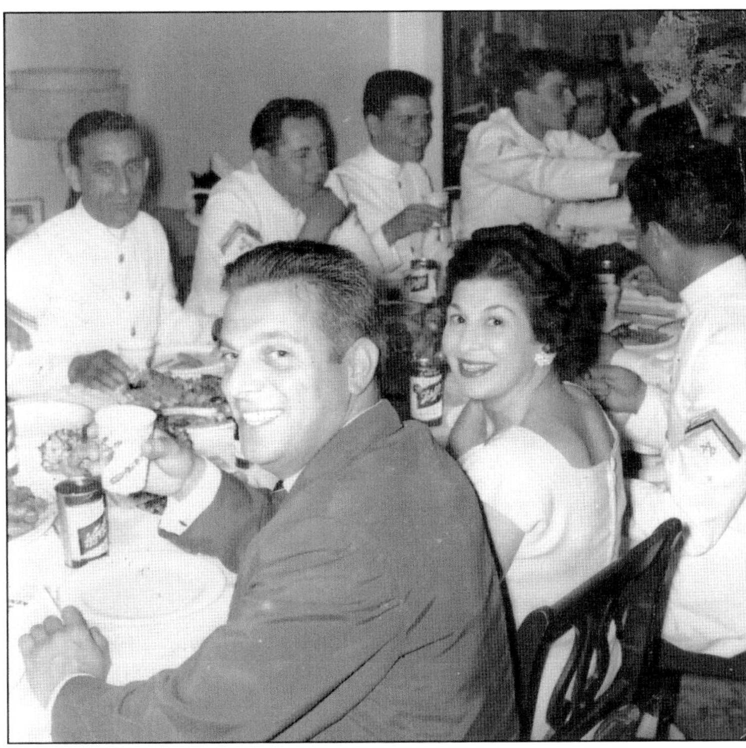

Gus and Lula Dalacos share a festive Easter dinner with about 30 Greek naval officers at the home of Michael and Eleni Billiris in 1962. The US Navy gave three ships to the Greek Royal Navy, and the men in uniforms were Greek Royal Naval officers who were in Jacksonville for training to take the ships to Greece. (Courtesy of Eleni Christopoulos-Lekkas.)

Four

Sponge Fishing and Related Occupations

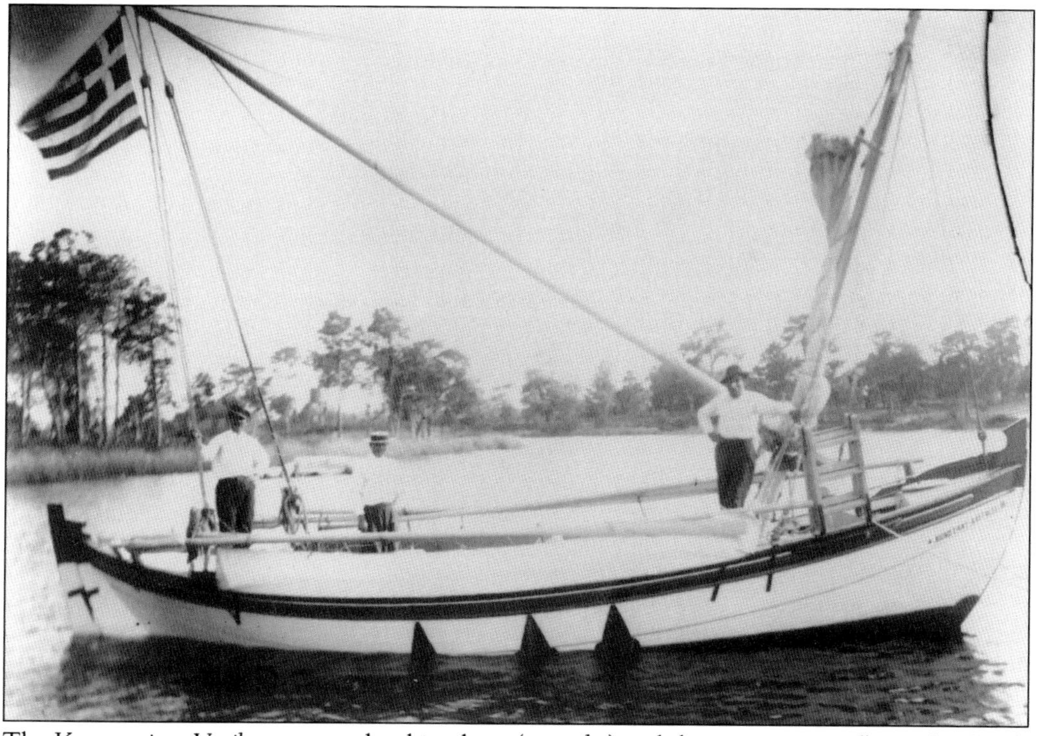

The *Konstantinos Vasileus* sponge-hooking boat (*gazeriko*) with lateen rigging is flying the Greek flag while anchored in the Anclote River in 1909. The first boats used by the Greeks for sponge fishing were modified American boats, but soon, two sponge boats were shipped from Greece. In addition, Greek boatbuilders turned out more than 200 Greek-style sponge boats over the next six decades. (Courtesy of the Tarpon Springs Area Historical Society.)

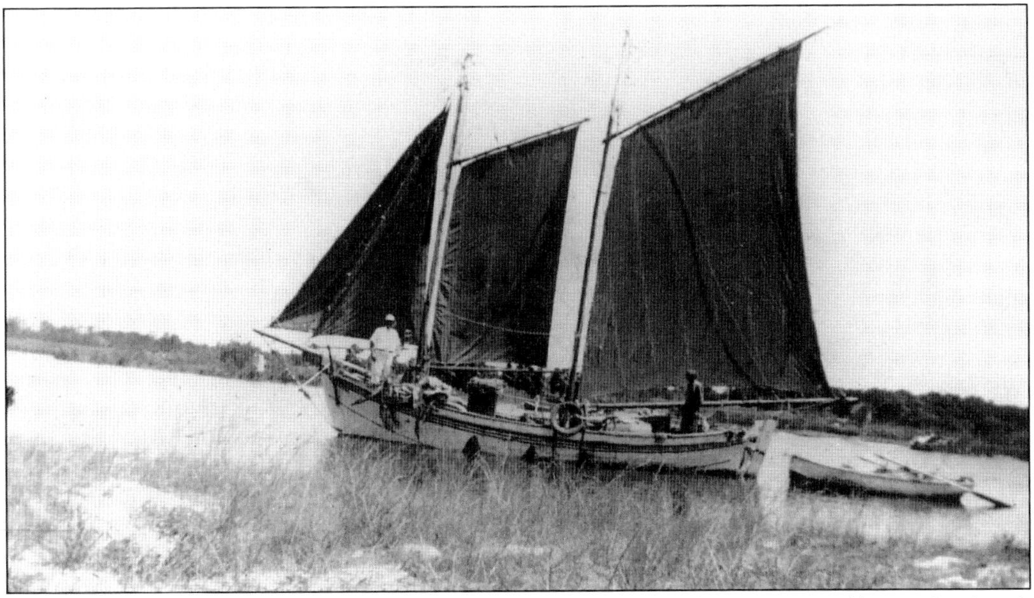

The sponge schooner *Elias*, built in 1918 and later named *Treandria*, is seen pulling a dinghy. A schooner is a sailing vessel with fore-and-aft sails on two or more masts. The *Elias* is painted white like most working Greek sponge boats, with a black base and colored trim. Triangular markings mask runoff stains. Sponges were hooked from dinghies using a long pole with a grapple at the end. The collected sponges were then stored in the larger boat until their return. (Courtesy of the Tarpon Springs Area Historical Society.)

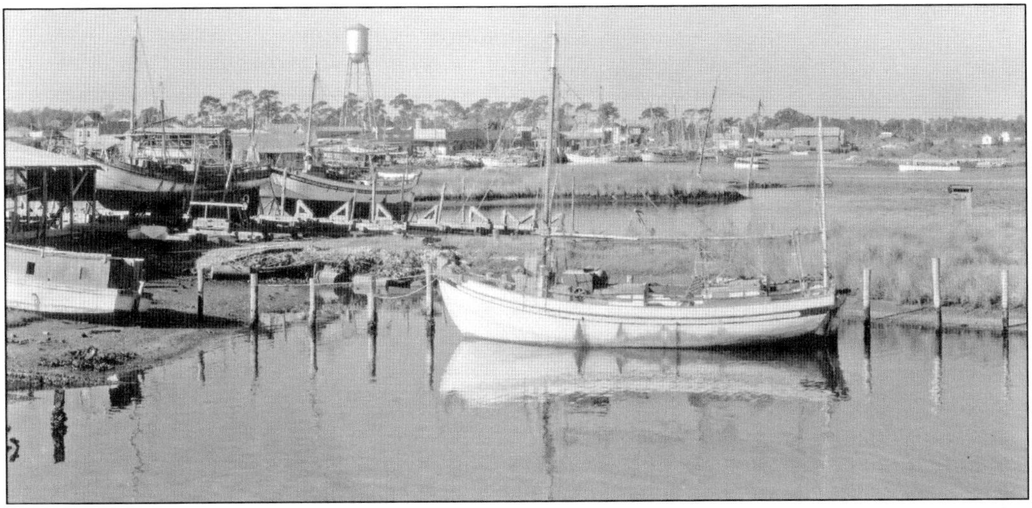

In this March 1932 image, a boatyard is in the foreground and the sponge fleet appears in the distance. The 1910 census reveals that six Greek ship carpenters resided in Tarpon Springs. The Greeks learned their skills as apprentices to master shipbuilders, and many worked full-time in the construction and repair of diving and hooking boats. During the first half of the 20th century, hundreds of boats based on the *achtarmas*-style sponge boat (a subtype of the *trechantiri*) common in the Dodecanese islands were built by Greeks from Tarpon Springs to Apalachicola. Among Tarpon Springs boatyards were those of the Kaminis, Sarris, Arfaras, and Macrenaris families. (Photograph by Burgert Brothers, courtesy of the Tampa-Hillsborough County Public Library System.)

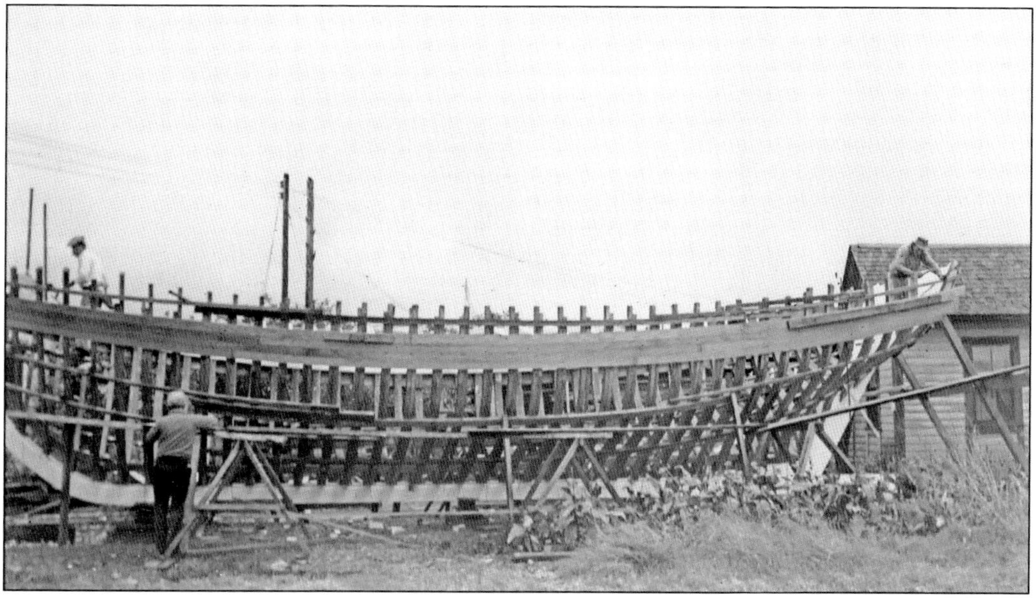

In 1937, George Coutroulis and his son Christ Coutroulis built the *Fannie C. Angeli* with pine and cypress. They fitted it with the latest devices, including diesel power and an air compressor. Around 1920, Greek sponge boats were adapted to new technologies with diesel engines replacing or supplementing sail power. When it was launched to join the sponge fleet on July 21, 1937, the *Fannie C. Angeli* was 46 feet long and 15.8 feet wide, with 6 feet draft aft and 3.5 feet forward and a gross tonnage of 35. (Courtesy of State Archives of Florida, Florida Memory.)

Sponge boats often do not work during winter months because of the wind from cold fronts. In the winter, the fishermen complete tasks for which they did not have time during the busy working season, such as cleaning and repairing boats or equipment. In this image, a crew member is painting a boat at the Sponge Docks in 1946. (Courtesy of State Archives of Florida, Florida Memory.)

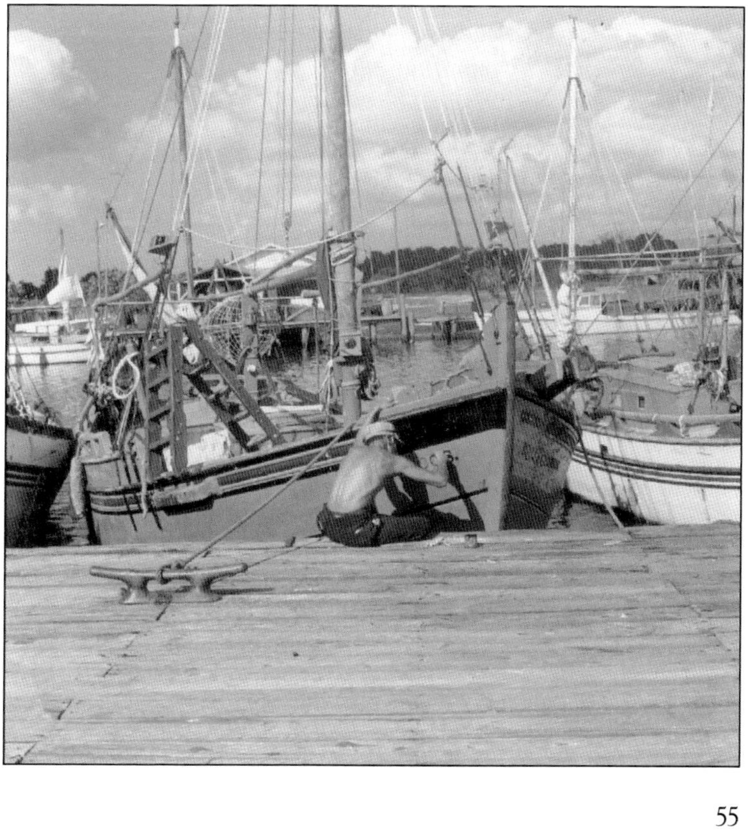

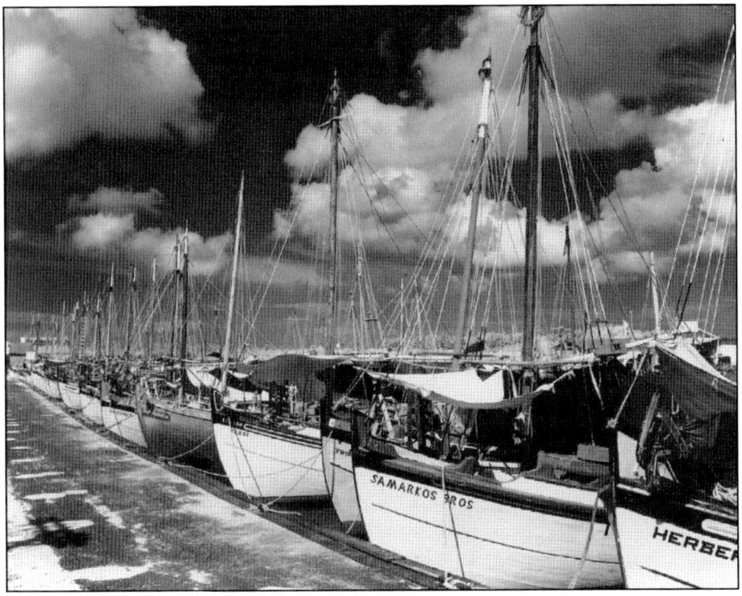

Sponge boats *Samarkos Bros*, *Eleni*, *Posidon*, *Anna*, *Democratia*, and *Anastases* are moored at the Sponge Docks in 1949. Despite the many boats seen here, by the late 1940s, the sponge beds had been devastated by a red tide that killed the sponges. Many businesses closed, and most men found other occupations or went to work for the steel mills in the North. (Photograph by the Florida State News Bureau, courtesy of the *Tampa Tribune*.)

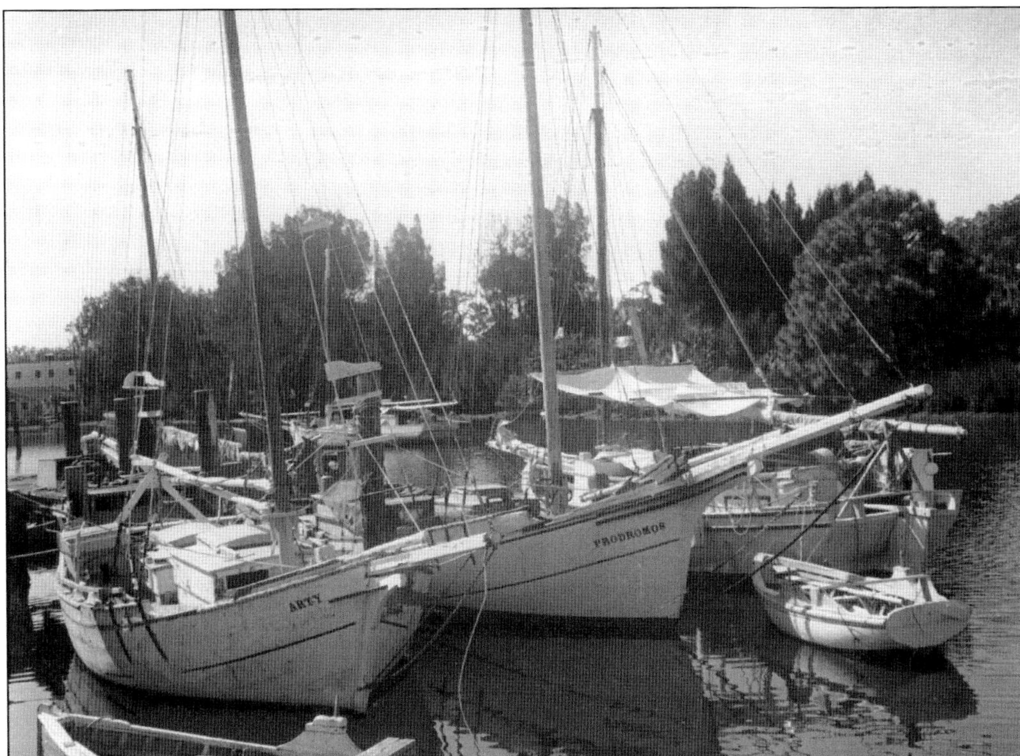

Sponge-hooking schooners, such as these docked in an inlet off the Anclote River on October 18, 1973, originally composed a large part of the sponge fleet. The *Arty* was converted to a sponge boat by George Tsourakis. Although equipment for hooking sponges remained fairly stable, the divers had by this time abandoned the heavy hard hat diving suits for modified scuba gear with air supplied into the diving mask from a compressor on the boat. (Photograph by Connie Standish, courtesy of the *Tampa Tribune*.)

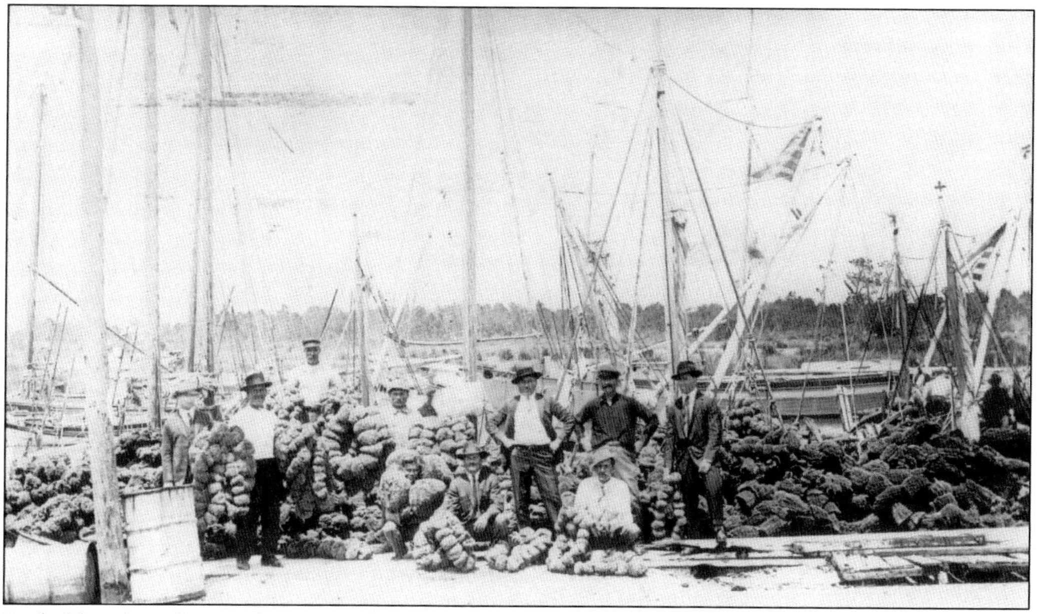

Probably taken during the 1910s, this is one of the oldest images of the Sponge Docks. Not only their caps and mustaches but also the Greek-style boats in the background provide evidence that these are Greek sponge fishermen. The focus of the sponge business shifted from the Bailey's Bluff area on the north side of the Anclote River in the 20th century. Originally wooden, the Sponge Docks was rebuilt in concrete by the 1960s. (Courtesy of the Tarpon Springs Area Historical Society.)

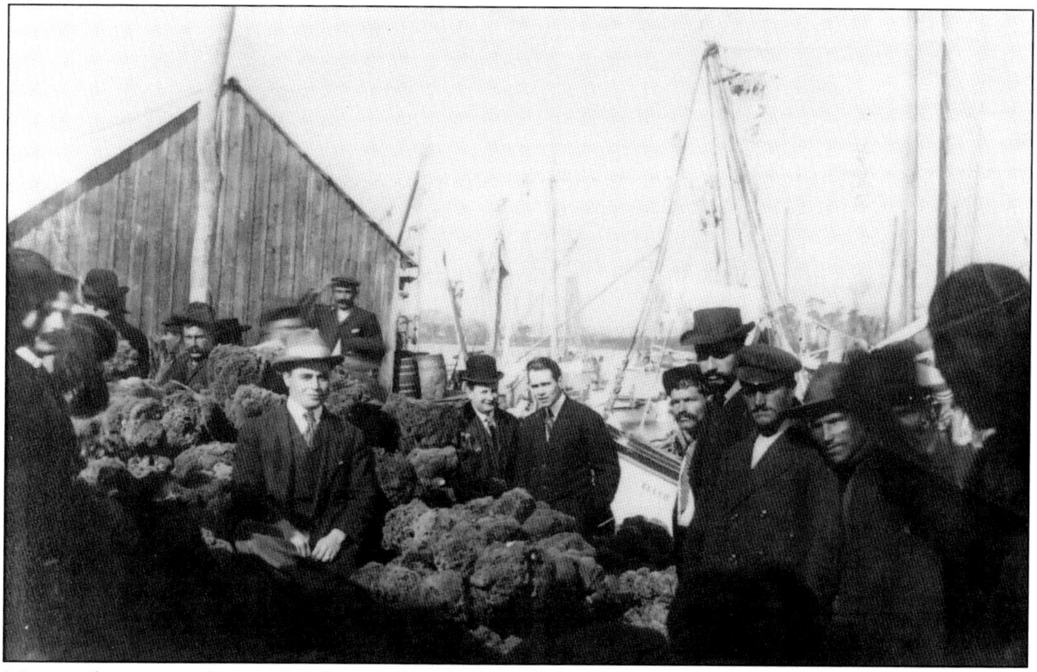

Men gather around a six-foot-high pile of sponges near the Anclote River, probably during the 1920s. Among the Greek boats in the background is the *Ellpis* [*sic*], or the *Hope*. (Courtesy of Dr. Themistocles J. Diamandis.)

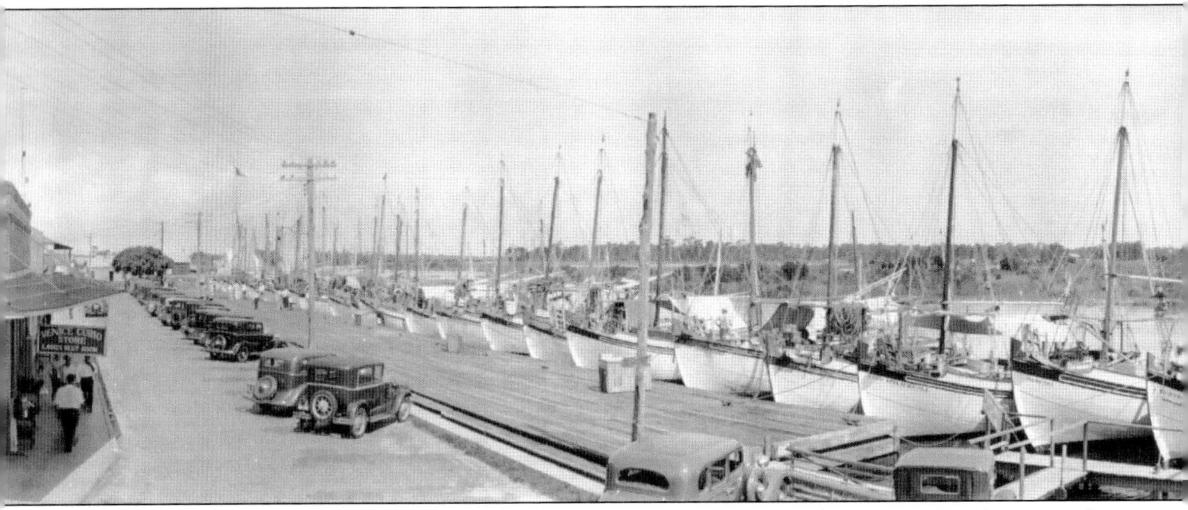

This remarkable panoramic view shows a line of sponge boats at the Sponge Docks across from the shops along Dodecanese Boulevard, as well as some boats moored east of the docks along the banks of the Anclote River in 1932. The new bridge that replaced the wooden one can be seen at

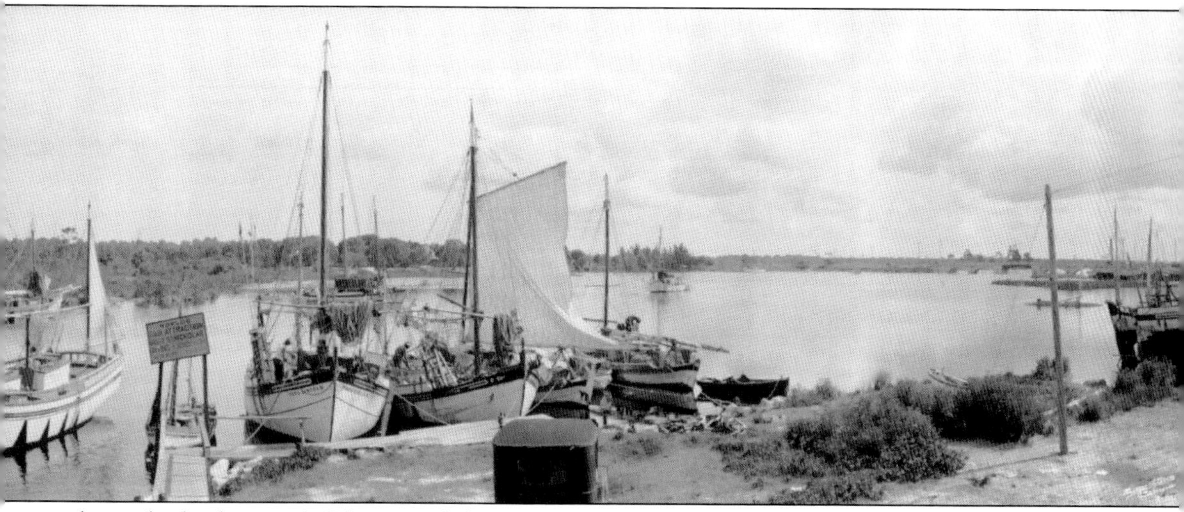

right in the background. (Photograph by Burgert Brothers, courtesy of the Tampa-Hillsborough County Public Library System.)

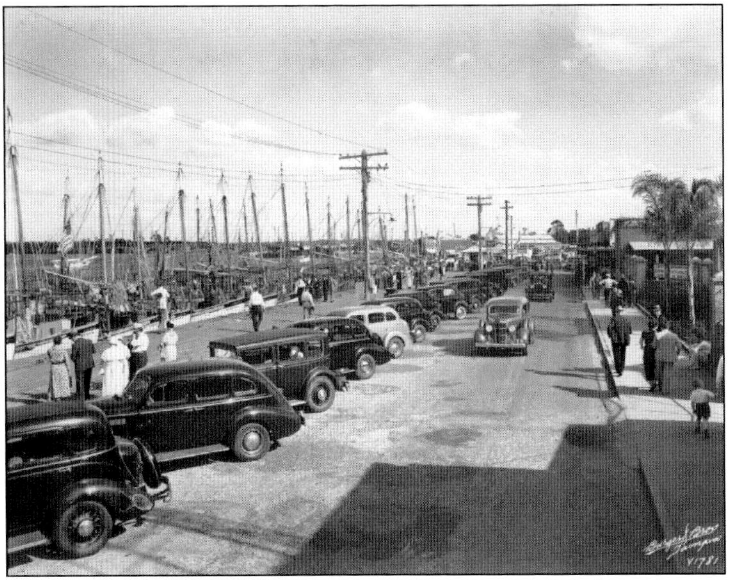

By 1937, the Sponge Docks are bustling with visitors. Note the many cars parked in front of the sponge fleet, the tourist boat ride at the end of the Sponge Docks, and the large sign announcing the function of the Sponge Exchange to visitors. (Photograph by Burgert Brothers, courtesy of Special Collections Department, Tampa Library, University of South Florida.)

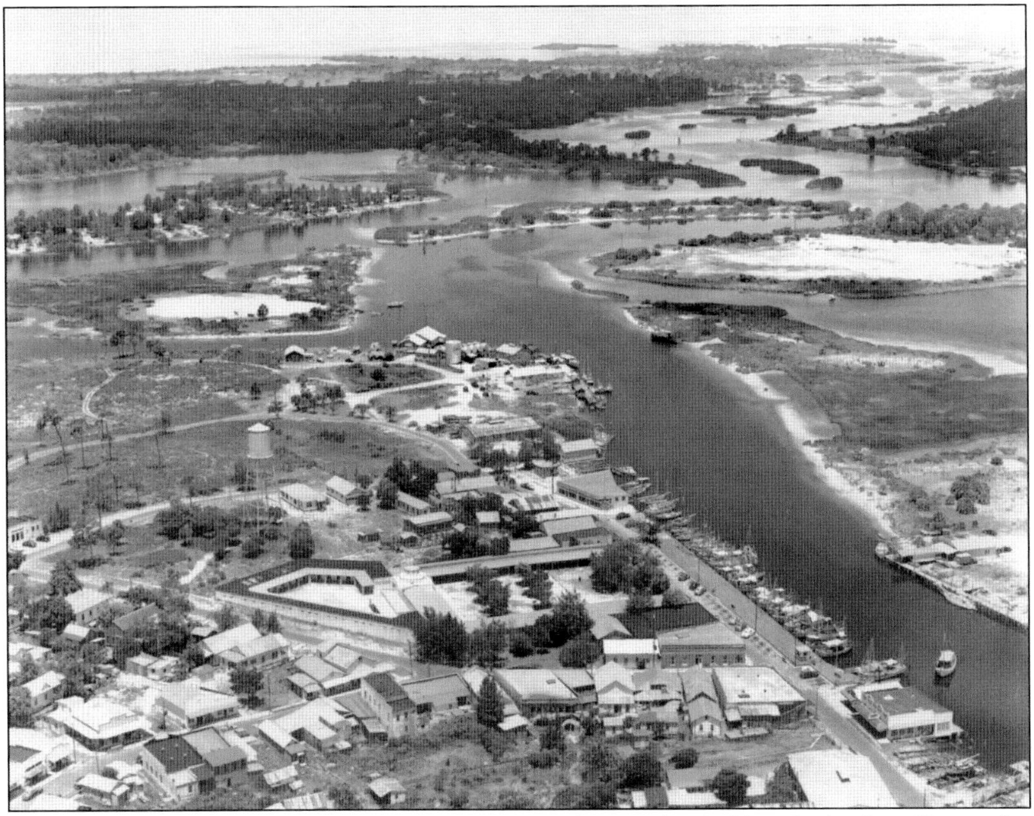

This 1947 aerial view shows the Anclote River winding to the Gulf, with Anclote Key in the background. It also reveals more limited activity on the Sponge Docks, where there are fewer boats and cars. The beginnings of the Greektown residential area and the section known as the Fish House are seen on Athens Street in the lower left. (Photograph by Burgert Brothers, courtesy of Special Collections Department, Tampa Library, University of South Florida.)

Here, crowds walk along the Sponge Docks where the sponge boats have been moored in 1947. Signs in the background announce a café and an explanation of ceremonies, so perhaps this image was taken during Epiphany. (Photograph by Burgert Brothers, courtesy of Special Collections Department, Tampa Library, University of South Florida.)

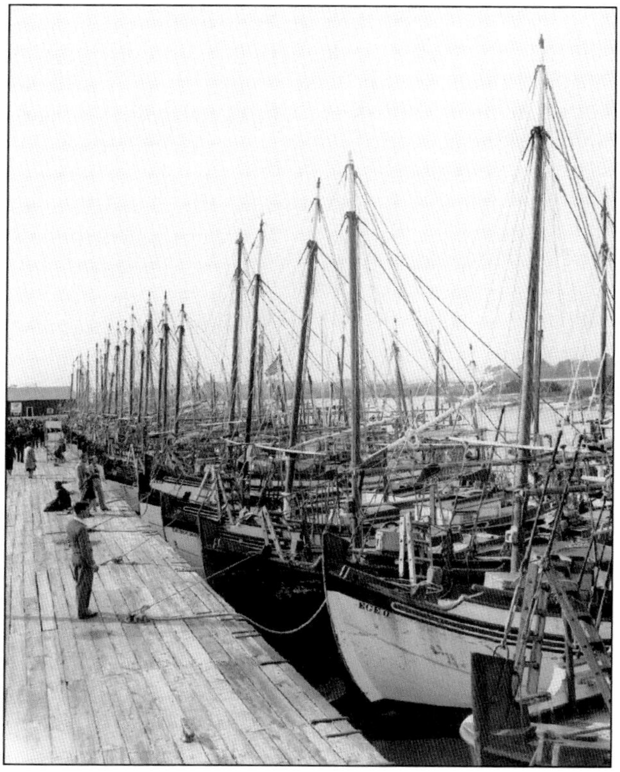

On October 2, 1970, the crew of the sponge boat *Eleni* hauls strings of sponges off the boat to store in the Sponge Exchange until they are auctioned later in the day. (Photograph by Connie Standish, courtesy of the *Tampa Tribune*.)

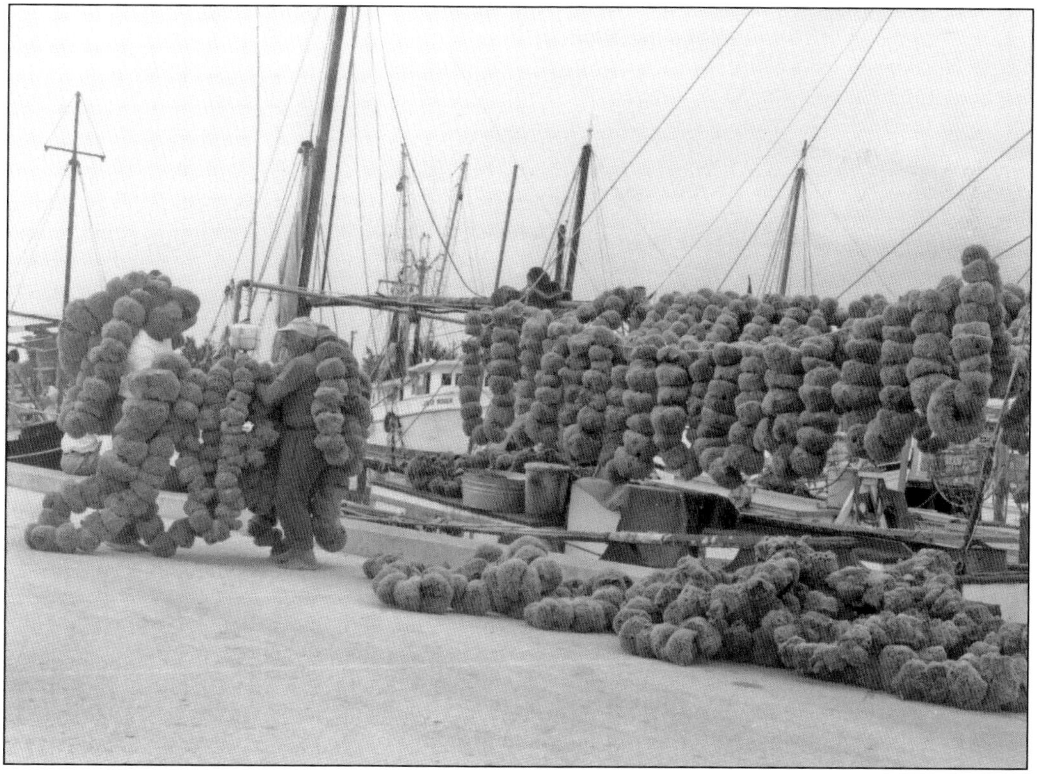

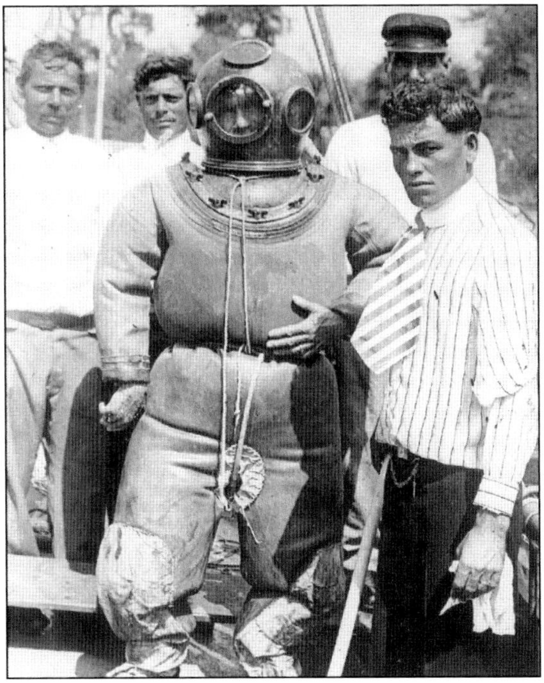

A sponge fisherman wears a diving suit in the early 20th century. Sponges had long been harvested in Greece with breath-hold diving and hooking, but in 1863, deep-sea diving with a rubberized canvas suit attached to a metal helmet and hand-cranked air compressor was introduced on the Dodecanese island of Symi. This innovation was a mixed blessing. While production increased dramatically, it was extremely dangerous because little was understood about the crippling bends (decompression sickness) until diving timetables were created in 1908. (Courtesy of State Archives of Florida, Florida Memory.)

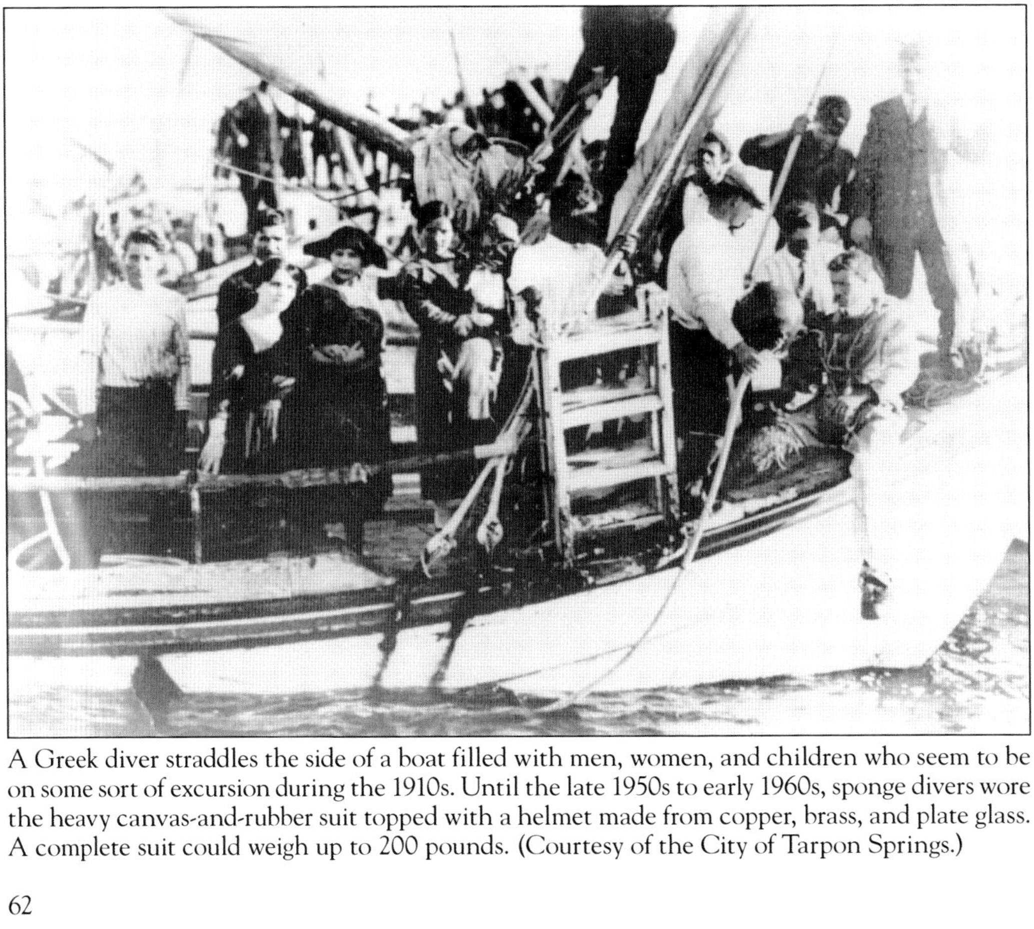

A Greek diver straddles the side of a boat filled with men, women, and children who seem to be on some sort of excursion during the 1910s. Until the late 1950s to early 1960s, sponge divers wore the heavy canvas-and-rubber suit topped with a helmet made from copper, brass, and plate glass. A complete suit could weigh up to 200 pounds. (Courtesy of the City of Tarpon Springs.)

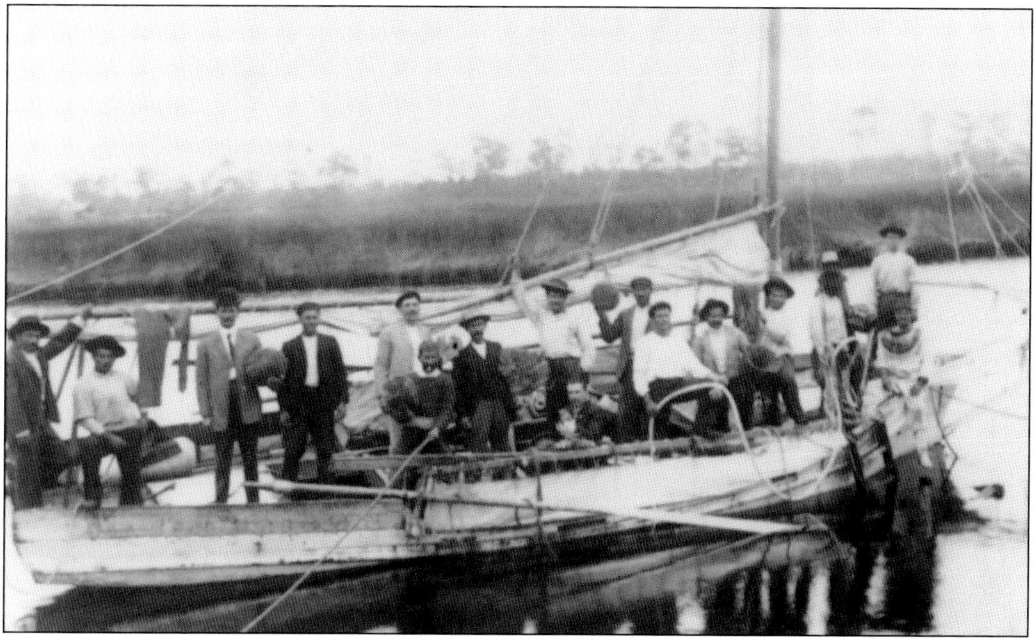

Greek sponge fishermen pose on a schooner that has been adapted as a diving boat. Since the image includes a man in formal dress with a bowler hat and tie, it could have been taken to send to families back home whom the men might not see for many years. (Courtesy of Dr. Themistocles J. Diamandis.)

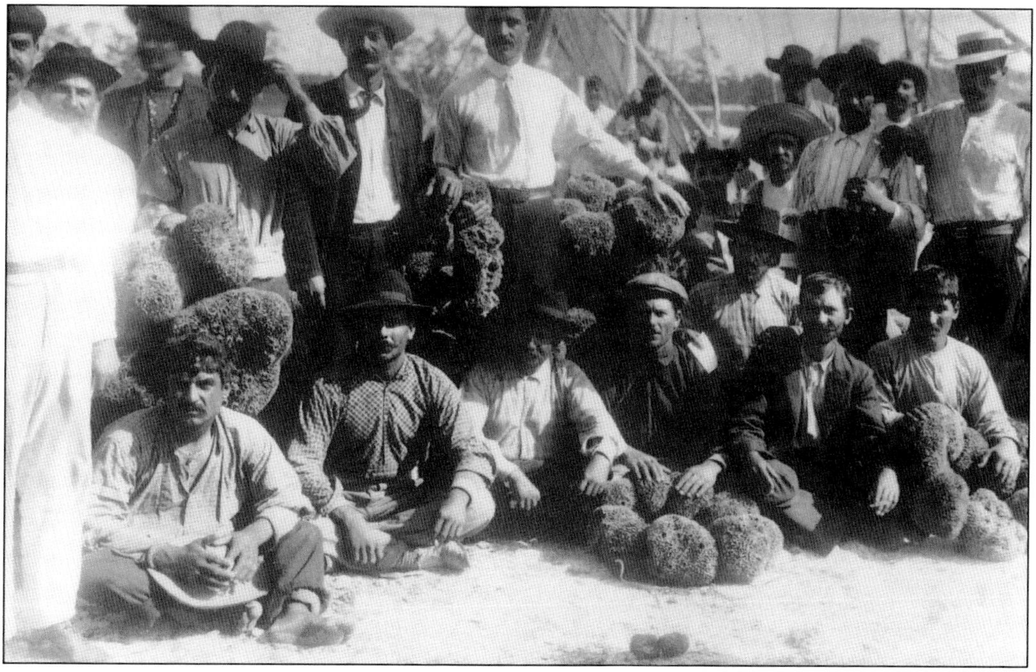

The men gathered in front of the Sponge Docks with strings of large harvested sponges reflect a variety of levels within the sponge industry. No doubt those wearing everyday work apparel are sponge boat crews, while those with white shirts and ties are probably merchants. (Courtesy of Dr. Themistocles J. Diamandis.)

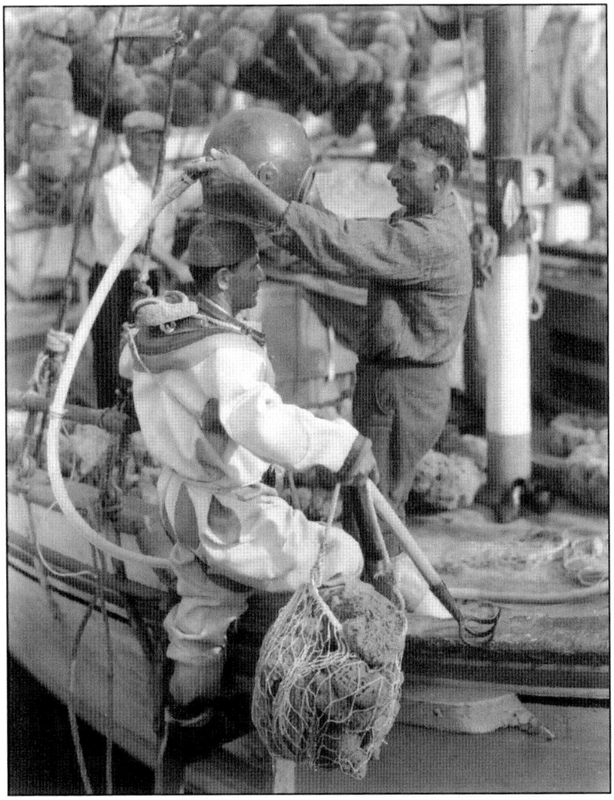

Pictured in 1936, a Greek diver returns to the surface holding a net bag of sponges and the sponge hook that he used to harvest them. There are dozens of types of sponges in the Gulf, but only a few are commercially viable. Divers must be able to identify and harvest those that will sell. The most desirable are Rock Island wool, Hudson grass, and yellow sponges. Finger and vase sponges are also sought as decorative items. (Photograph by Burgert Brothers, courtesy of the Tampa-Hillsborough County Public Library System.)

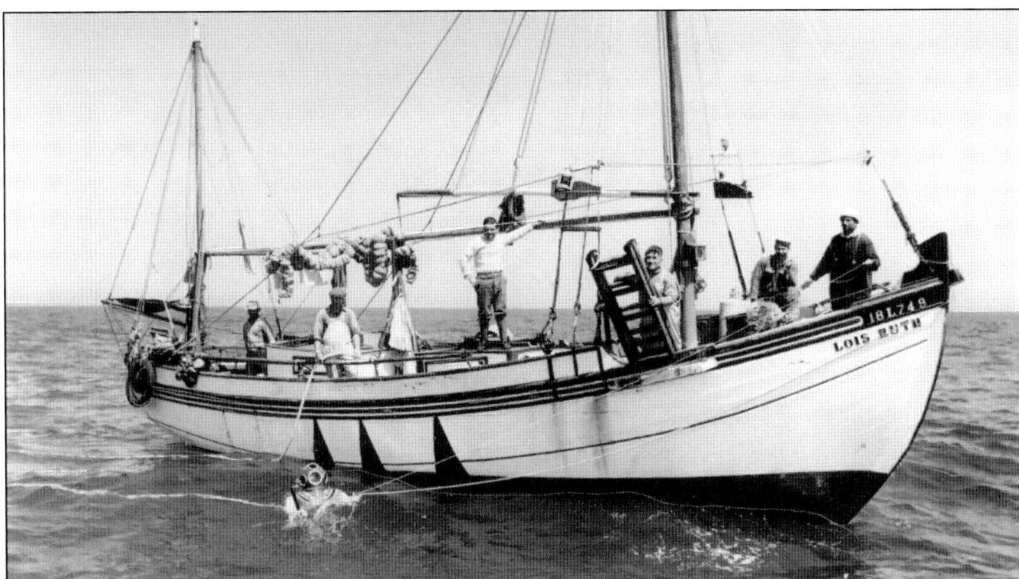

On a trip during the 1940s, crewmen on the *Lois Ruth* hold the diver's air hose and a line attached to his catch net. Sponge boats often stayed out in the Gulf of Mexico for months at a time. To break up the monotony of eating fish and *kavourmas*, men also made *spinialo*—conch, mussels, or other shellfish that they cleaned, then pickled in seawater and stored in bottles—another dish that did not require refrigeration. (Courtesy of the Tarpon Springs Area Historical Society.)

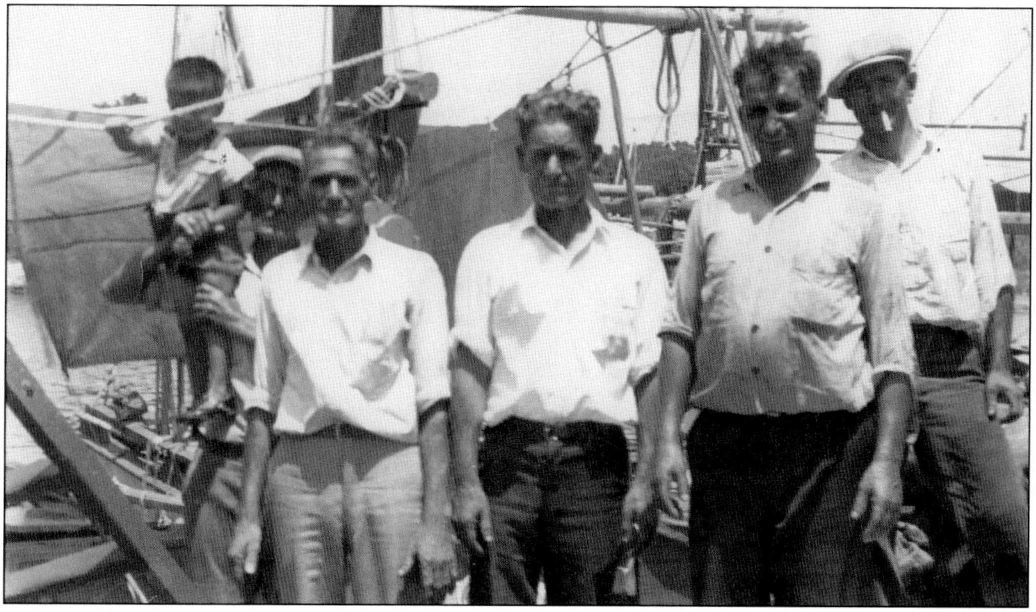

A sponge boat crew poses for the camera around 1940. From left to right are young George Tsalichis held by an unidentified man, James Tsalichis, Chris Hatzie, Anargiros Filaretou, and Nick Zouroudis. Usually included among the crew were a captain, diver(s), engineer, cook, and deckhands. A lifeline tender watched the diver at all times to ensure that he was not pulled by the boat, his line was clear, and the boat was steered in the direction needed by the diver. (Courtesy of Goldie Tsalichis Parr.)

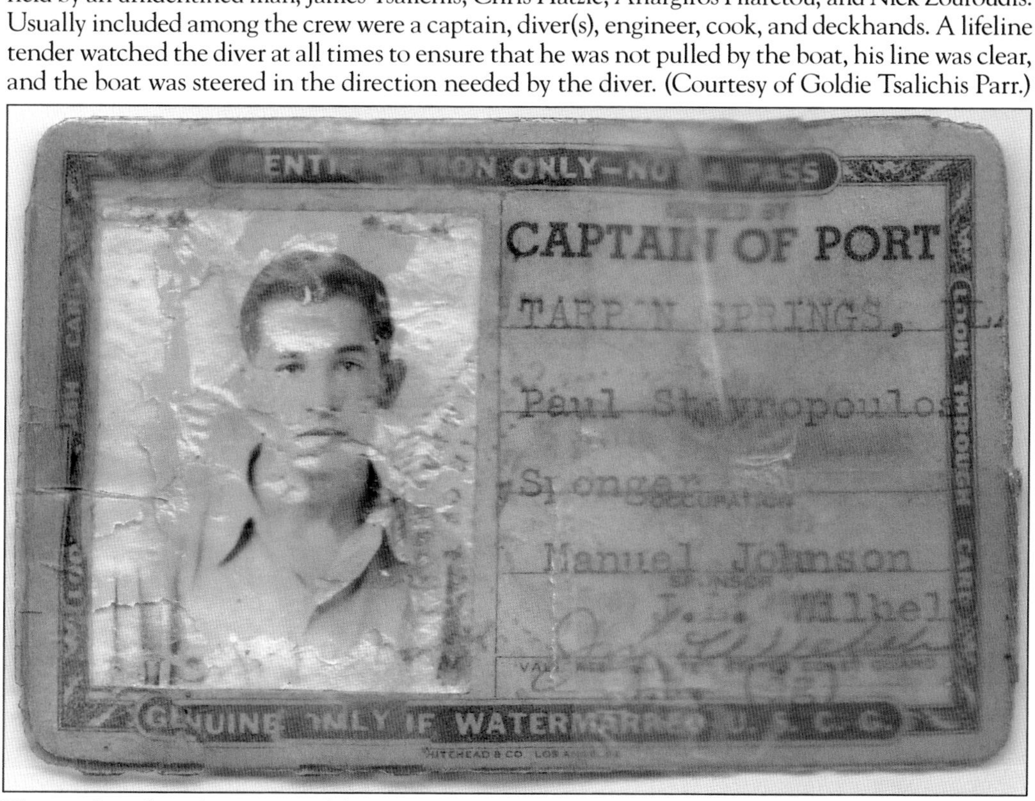

This is the identification card for sponge fisherman Paul Stavropoulos. During World War II, sponge fishermen needed identification cards issued by the captain of the port in order to journey out to the sponge beds. (Courtesy of Paul Stavropoulos.)

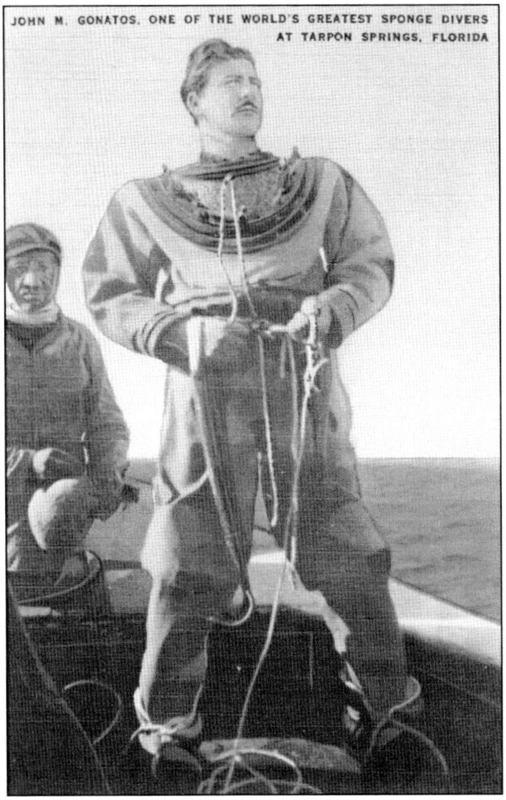

This postcard was derived from the iconic image of John Gonatos putting on his diving suit taken by famous photographer Joseph Janney Steinmetz around 1942. The son of a sponge boat captain, Gonatos became interested in films and made a documentary about the sponge industry in 1939. (Author's collection.)

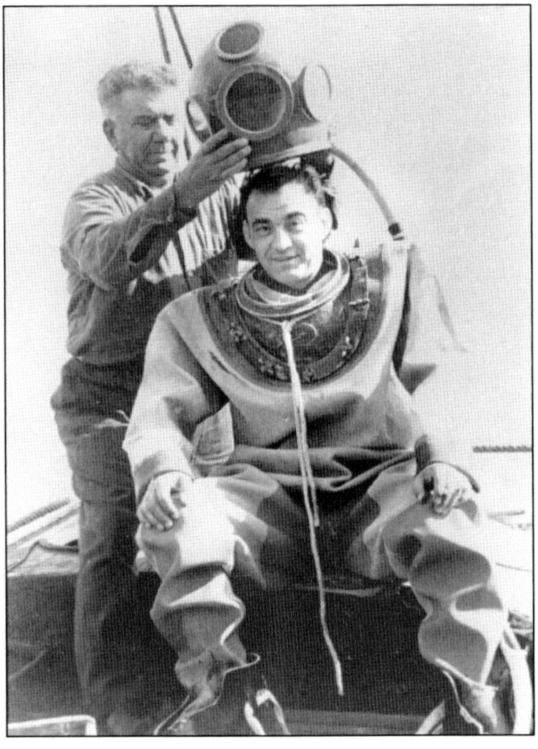

John Mehas removes the helmet from diver Leon "Roxy" Velousis. Note that the diver is holding a cigarette. Immediately after ascent, divers were often asked to smoke in order to discover whether they were developing decompression sickness. It was commonly believed that if the diver smoked without coughing or shortness of breath, his lungs were not seriously affected by gas bubbles. If they were affected, the diver might return to the water for recompression. (Courtesy of the City of Tarpon Springs.)

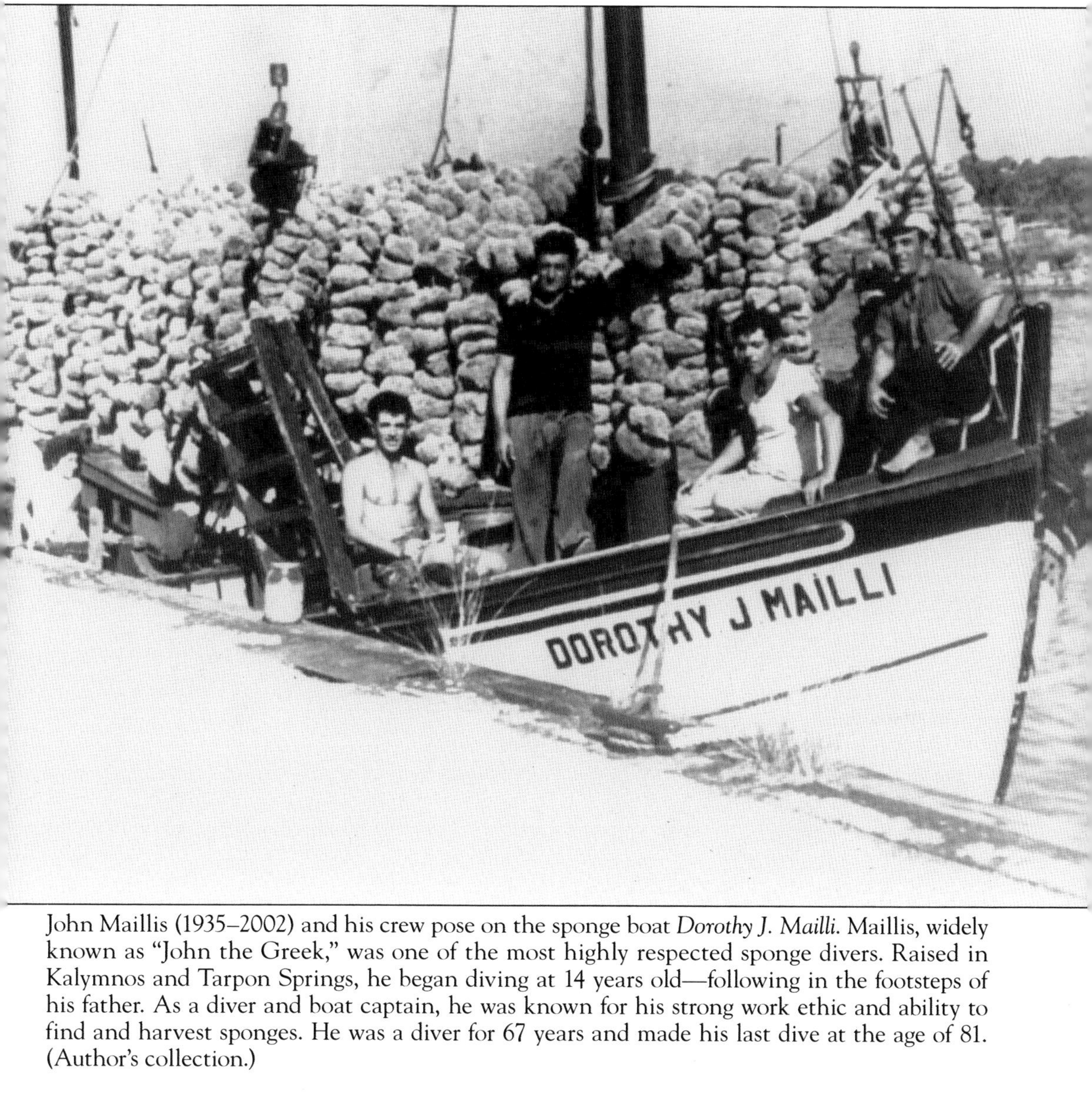

John Maillis (1935–2002) and his crew pose on the sponge boat *Dorothy J. Mailli.* Maillis, widely known as "John the Greek," was one of the most highly respected sponge divers. Raised in Kalymnos and Tarpon Springs, he began diving at 14 years old—following in the footsteps of his father. As a diver and boat captain, he was known for his strong work ethic and ability to find and harvest sponges. He was a diver for 67 years and made his last dive at the age of 81. (Author's collection.)

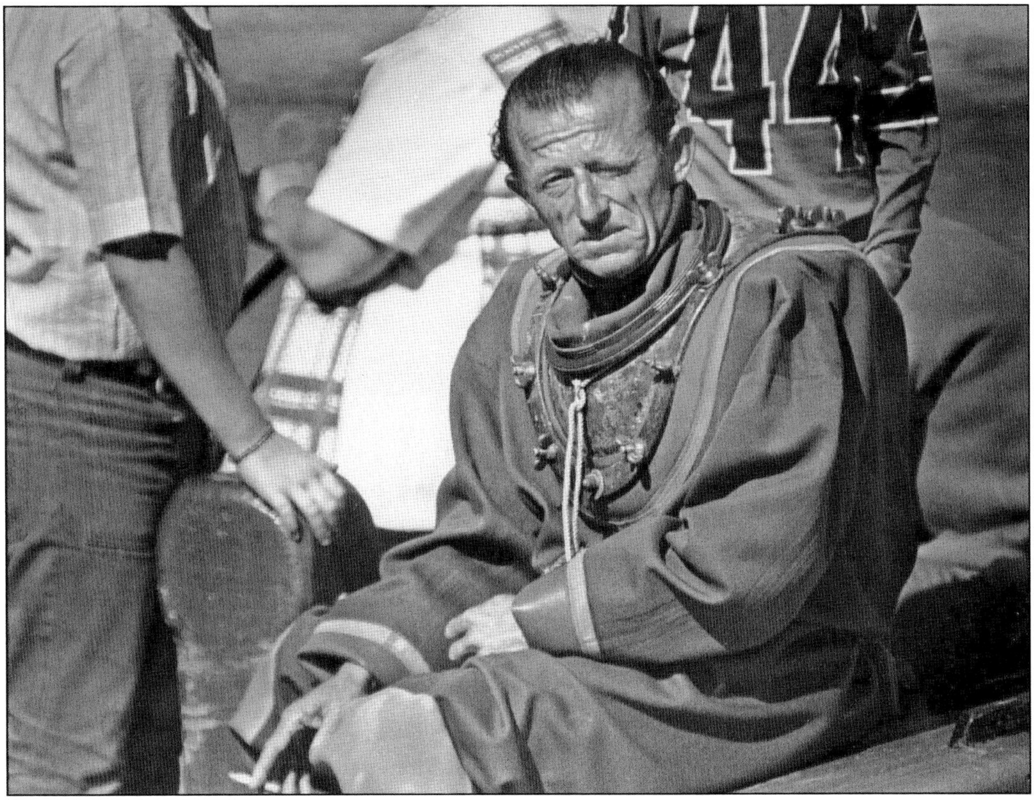

Nikolaos G. Skyllas (1926–2011) takes a break from demonstrating diving in hard hat sponge gear for tourists in February 1975. Like many, this veteran professional sponge diver turned to exhibition diving on the tourist boats in his later years. (Photograph by Jim Tuten, courtesy of the *Tampa Tribune*.)

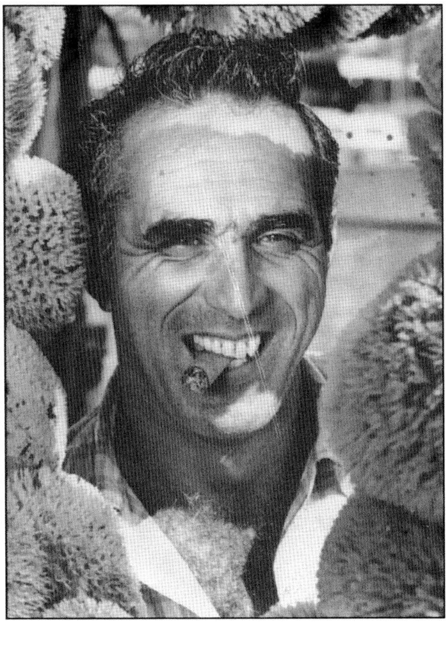

One of the last divers to have worked in the old diving helmets, Theophilos "Philip" Fatolitis (1923–2012) learned to dive from his uncle Petros Fatolitis and started working on boats with him when he was 12. His father had died when he was a child, so Philip was eager to make money to contribute to the family. He started diving professionally at 16 and soon captained his own boat. Philip dove for the Navy's Underwater Demolition Teams during World War II, then returned to Tarpon Springs with knowledge of modern diving techniques. He worked in the sponge industry for a total of 40 years, while also establishing a construction business. This 1963 photograph captures his ebullient personality. (Author's collection.)

Usually out with the sponge fleet, this boat remained at the Sponge Docks and was put up for sale in the early 1970s because of a death in the family. A memorial wreath for the deceased graces the sponge boat. (Photography by Jim Tuten, courtesy of the *Tampa Tribune*.)

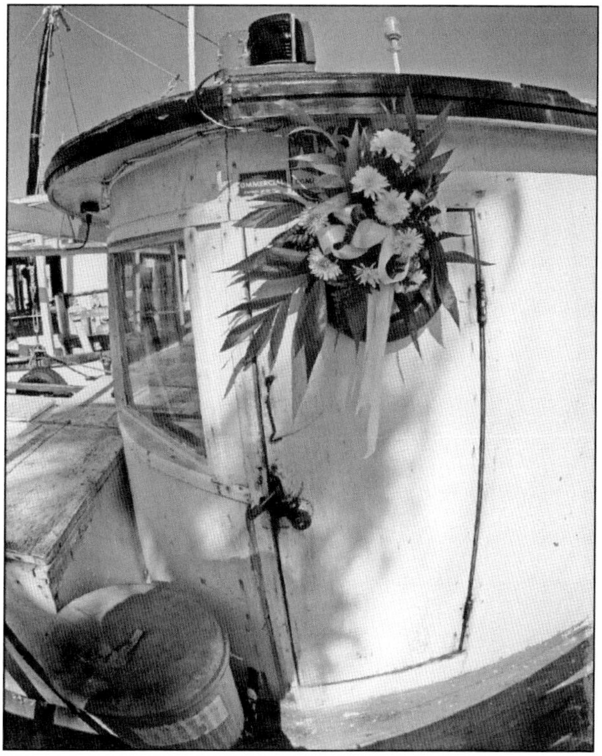

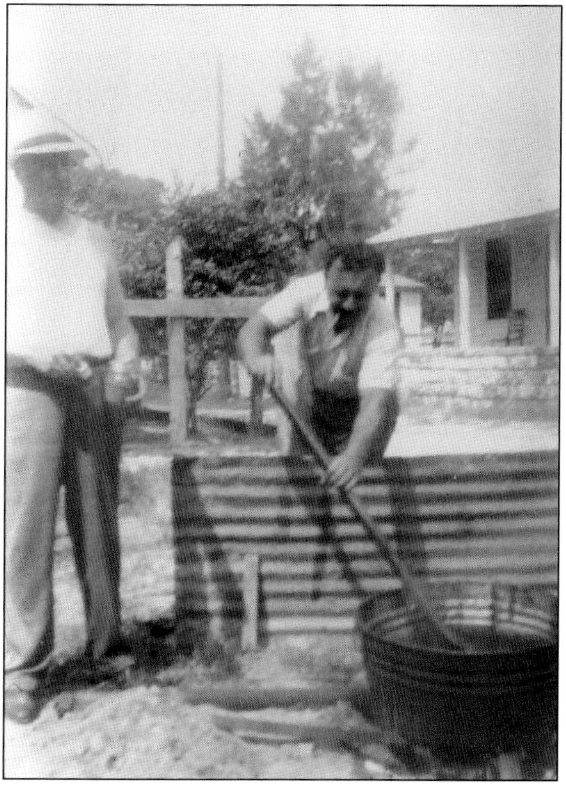

Tom Mahinis (left) and an unidentified man make *kavourmas* for the sponge fishermen in the 1940s. During the early 20th century, spongers went to sea for several months. Although the men often ate fresh fish, they broke up the monotony of their diet with a preserved meat called kavourmas. Before sailing, the crew prepared enough to last an entire trip. Outside over a wood fire, they filled a washtub with fat and heated it until it liquefied. Next, they added beef or lamb and stirred it with a small paddle as it cooked for hours, then sealed it into cans. The preparation of kavourmas became a social occasion as well as a necessity. (Courtesy of Nickollet Tsourakis Henderson.)

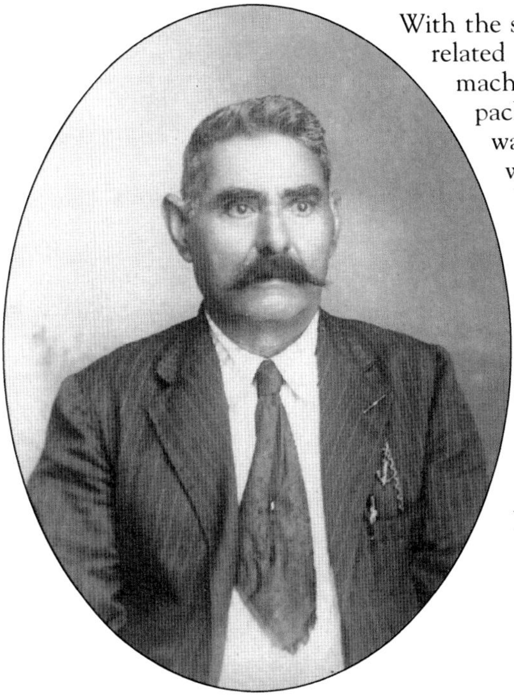

With the spongers came many other Greeks working in related maritime businesses, including ship chandlers, machine shops, boatbuilders, sail lofts, and sponge packinghouses. Antonios Avgerinos (1860–1930) was a successful diving helmet maker from Symi who established a machine shop on Aegina. Having studied helmet making in France, he was responsible for significant innovations in helmet design, such as more windows and a better airflow system. He was invited to Tarpon Springs to work as a consultant in training helmet makers and others for several months. He arrived with his 11-year-old daughter in the fall of 1911, but as they were preparing to return home in 1912, the Balkan Wars and then World War I erupted. Avgerinos stayed in Tarpon Springs, practicing his craft until the end of his life. (Courtesy of Irene Giannaras Garner.)

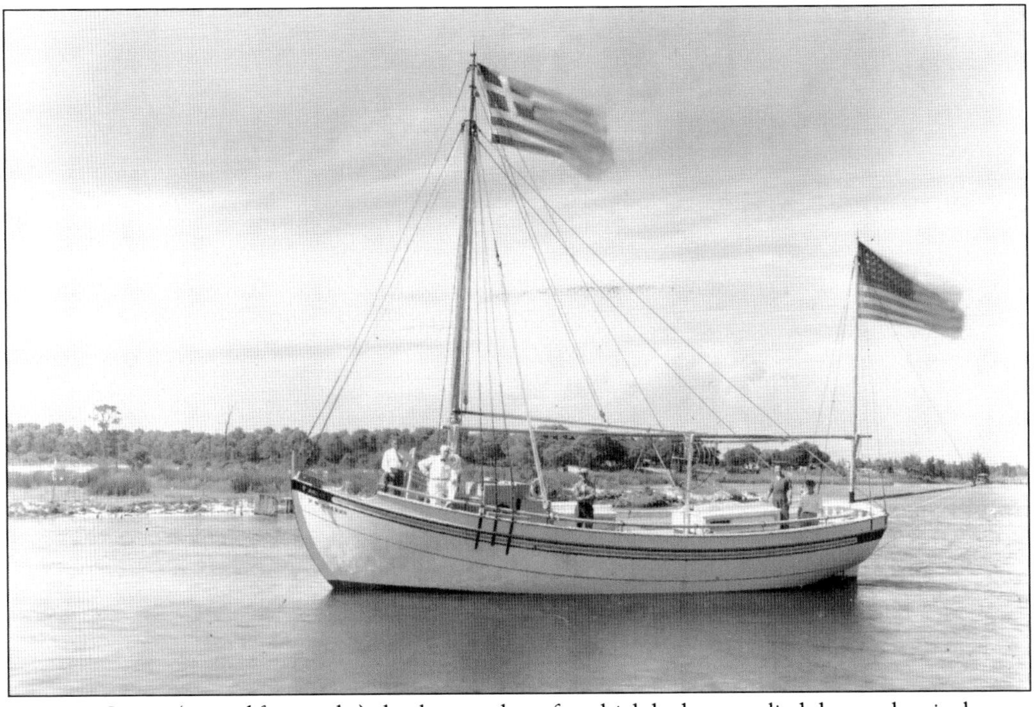

Antonios Lerios (second from right) checks out a boat for which he has supplied the mechanical parts. Born in Kalymnos, Lerios grew up in Istanbul, where he learned helmet making, ship mechanics, and other maritime crafts in the enormous shipyards. In 1913, he joined his father and brother in Tarpon Springs, where he was in great demand for making diving helmets, as well as for maintaining and producing the hardware necessary for the sponge boats. (Courtesy of Mary Lerios Toth.)

This 1986 image shows Antonios Lerios (left) and Nicholas Toth alongside a diving helmet in the shop that Lerios built in the early 20th century. Growing up in Tarpon Springs, Toth visited his grandfather's machine shop and gradually absorbed his knowledge. After college, he decided to work with his grandfather and carry on the family tradition. Toth received a prestigious National Heritage Fellowship in 2003. (Photograph by Peter Roller for the Florida Folklife Program, courtesy of State Archives of Florida, Florida Memory.)

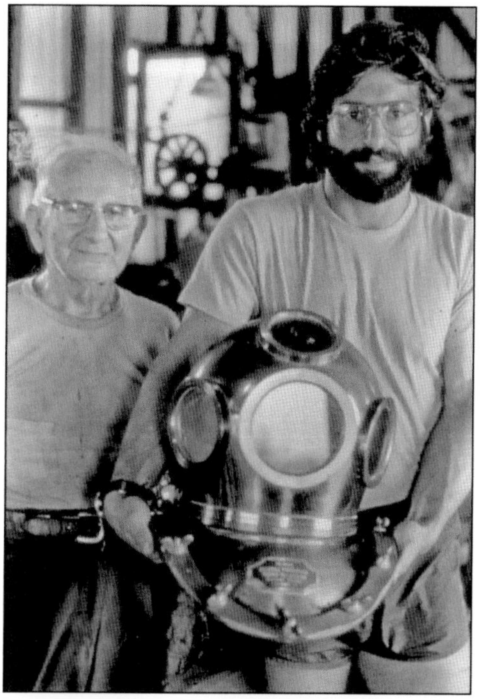

Little has changed in the basic sponge-cleaning process. Here, the man at left uses a wooden mallet to clean debris, such as small stones or shells, from a sponge in George Emmanuel's warehouse. Others trim sponges with the same type of shears used for shearing sheep. This type of heavy rustic scissors has been around for more than 2,000 years. (Courtesy of Martha Emmanuel.)

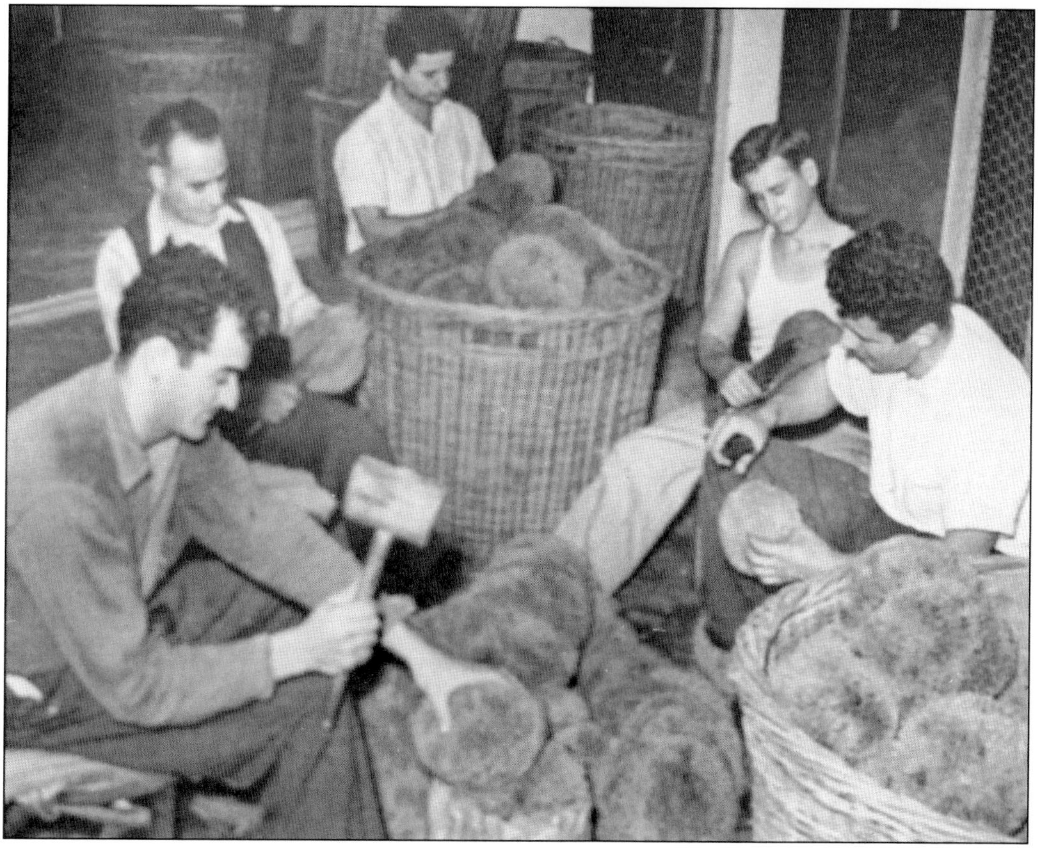

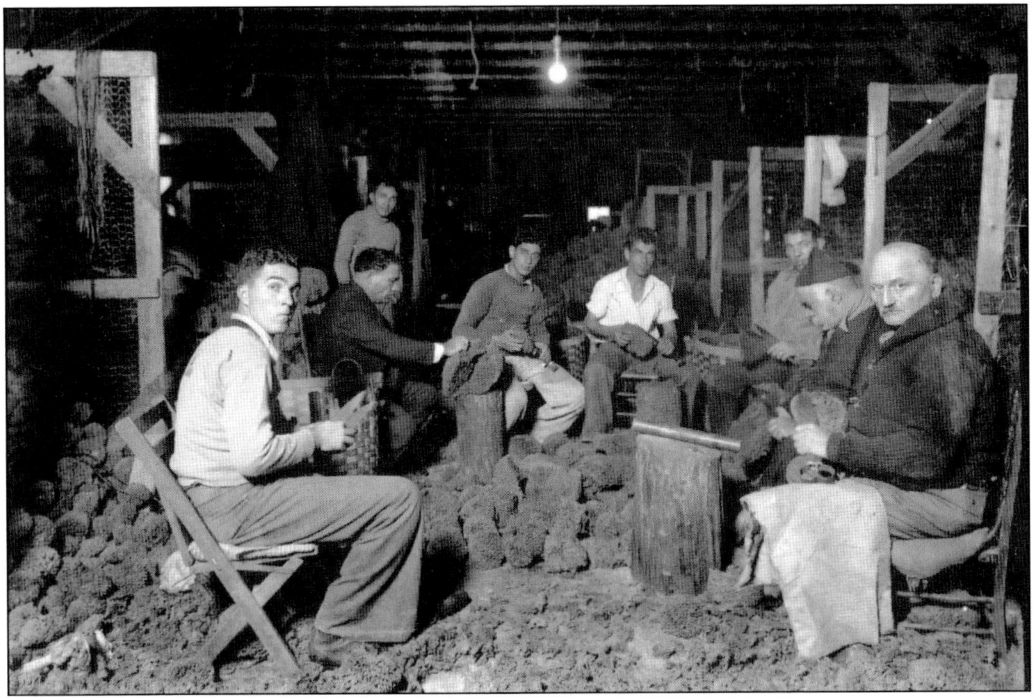

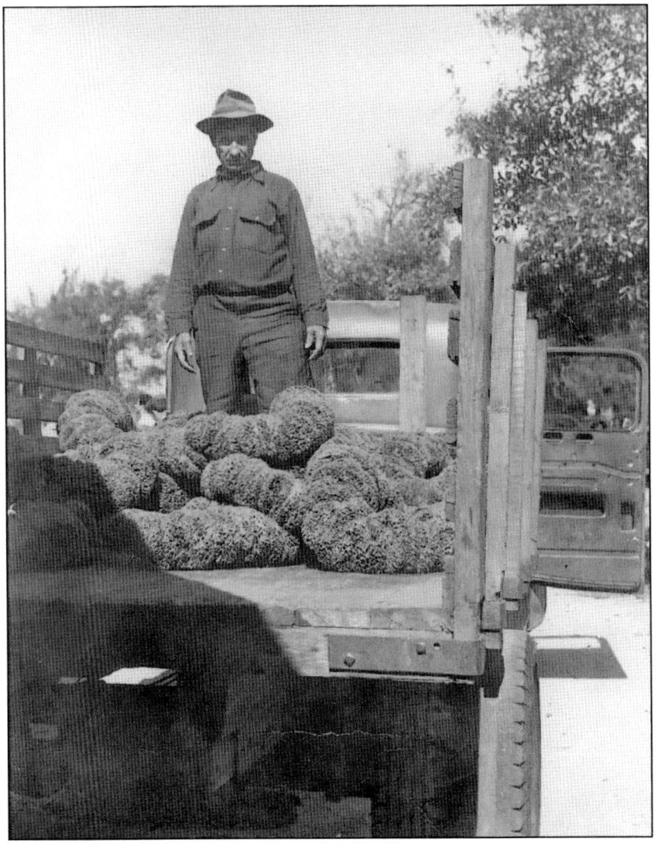

Trimming sponges in a sponge packinghouse are, from left to right, Mike Amorginos, Cosmos Giallourakis, Michael Lelekis (behind), Nick Mack, James Peterson, Costas Arvanitis, unidentified, and John Cladakis. (Courtesy of Nicholas Toth.)

Costas Tsourakis loads strings of sponges into the back of a truck during the 1940s. Tsourakis arrived from Greece in 1905. In addition to working with sponges, he made charcoal for the sponge boats at a lot on the corner of Athens and Cedar Streets. (Courtesy of Nickollet Tsourakis Henderson.)

Back in port, the crew finishes cleaning and sorting sponges for auction on October 10, 1969. Cleaning the animals entails allowing their skins to decompose, rinsing them with water, and squeezing them to eliminate internal matter and bits of skin, then scraping away small rocks or shells. Although the crew begins the process at sea, it often takes days to finish after their return. (Photograph by Connie Standish, courtesy of the *Tampa Tribune*.)

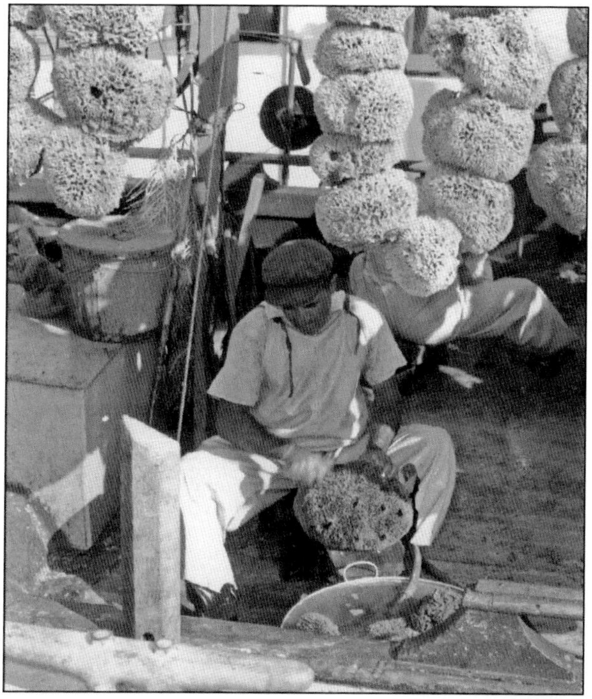

Niki Samarkos hangs finger sponges to dry on October 28, 1966. Most sponges harvested by the fishermen have some kind of personal or industrial use, but finger sponges are purely decorative. (Photograph Connie Standish, courtesy of the *Tampa Tribune*.)

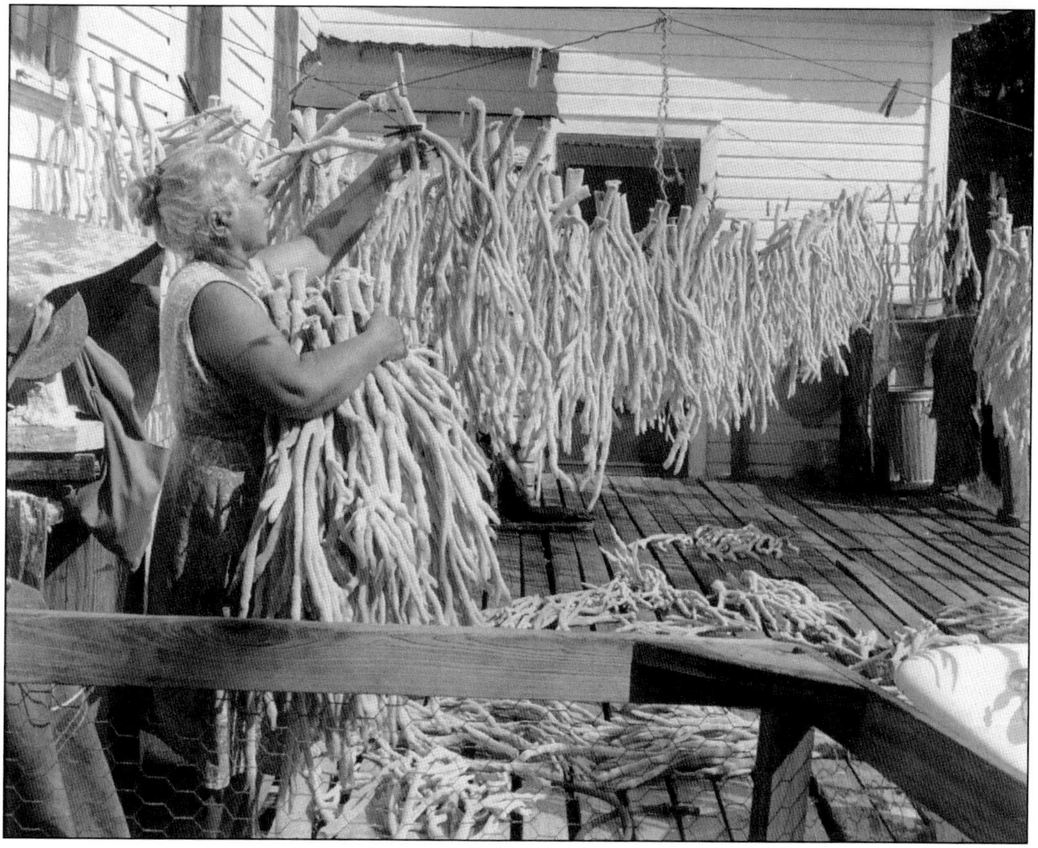

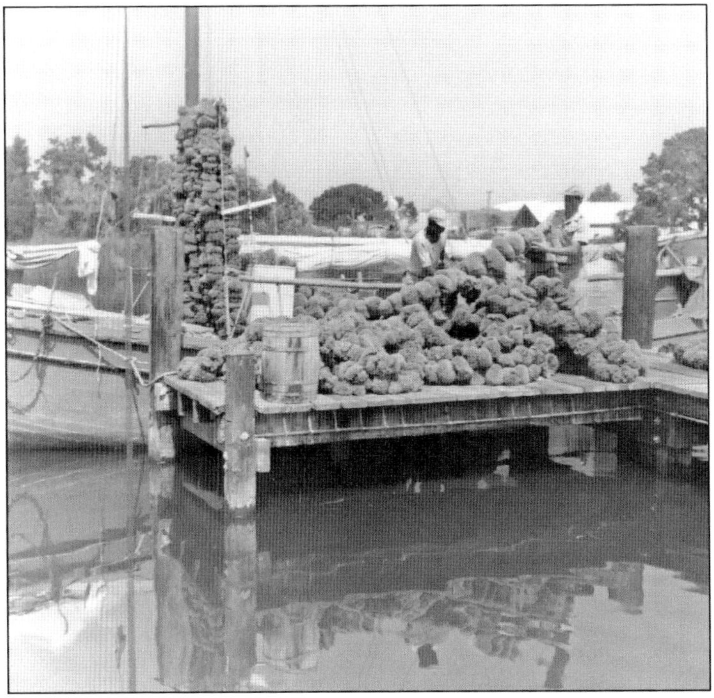

Gus Tsourakis (right) and a crew member unload strings of cleaned sponges on June 27, 1969. Tsourakis owned a hooking boat, which was smaller than the larger diving boats. On this trip, they had harvested more than 5,000 sponges, primarily wool. (Courtesy of the *Tampa Tribune*.)

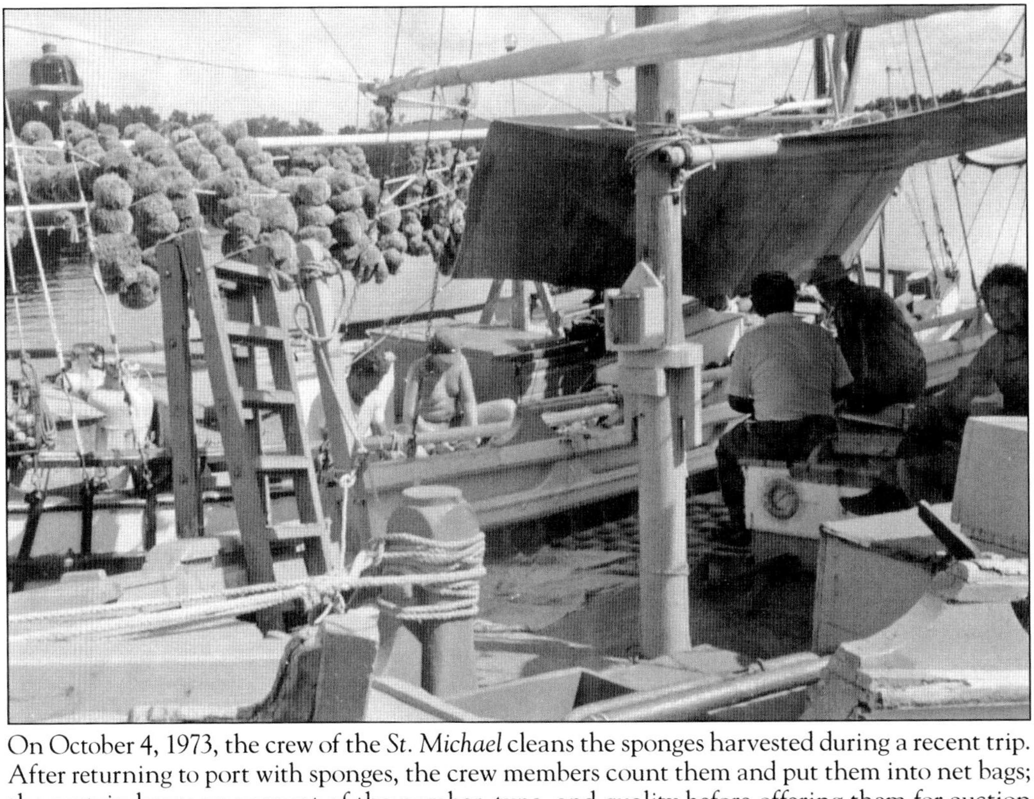

On October 4, 1973, the crew of the *St. Michael* cleans the sponges harvested during a recent trip. After returning to port with sponges, the crew members count them and put them into net bags; the captain keeps an account of the number, type, and quality before offering them for auction or sale. (Courtesy of the *Tampa Tribune*.)

A crew member finishes the grueling job of cleaning sponges on February 11, 1975. Sponges, which are simple animal organisms, must be cleaned of their skin, internal matter, and any stones or sand that have adhered to them. Crew members repeatedly squeeze and rinse them with water until they are ready to dry and sort. (Photograph by Jim Tuten, courtesy of the *Tampa Tribune*.)

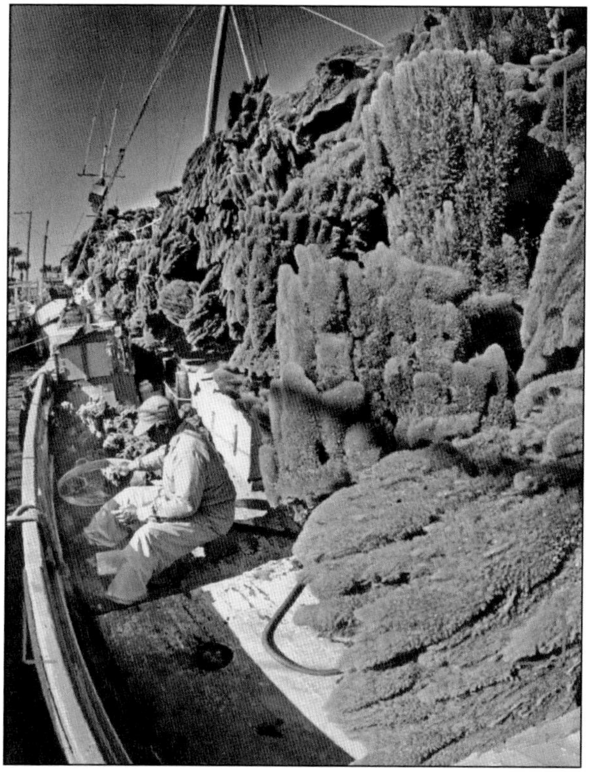

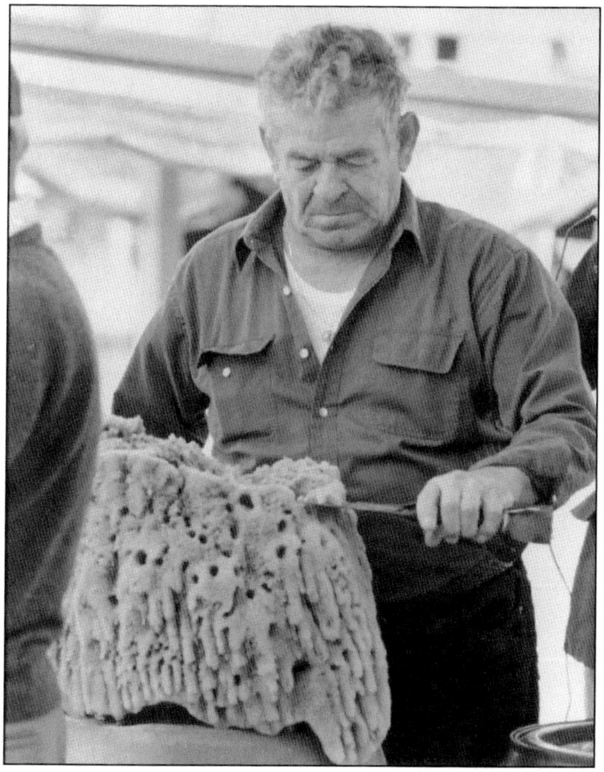

George Danapas demonstrates trimming a sponge during a festival at the Sponge Docks on March 6, 1987. Danapas was long involved in the sponge industry and had his own hook boat. (Courtesy of the *Tampa Tribune*.)

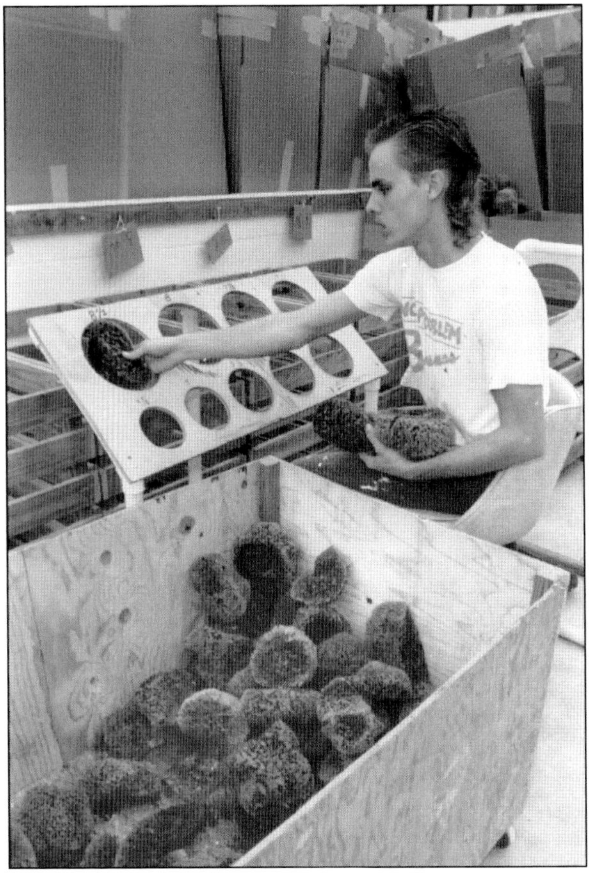

James Piccolo sizes sponges at Acme Sponge & Chamois Company, one of the largest sponge distribution businesses in Tarpon Springs. The company was established in 1938 by Michael Cantonis, who came from a family of Symian sponge merchants. Acme expanded its product line to include other cleaning items, such as chamois, loofahs, synthetic sponges, and bath brushes. (Courtesy of the *Tampa Tribune*.)

Men gather to survey heaps of large sponges in the yard of the Sponge Exchange. The early wooden buildings indicate that this photograph might have been taken in the 1910s, before the sturdier brick buildings were constructed. (Courtesy of Dr. Themistocles J. Diamandis.)

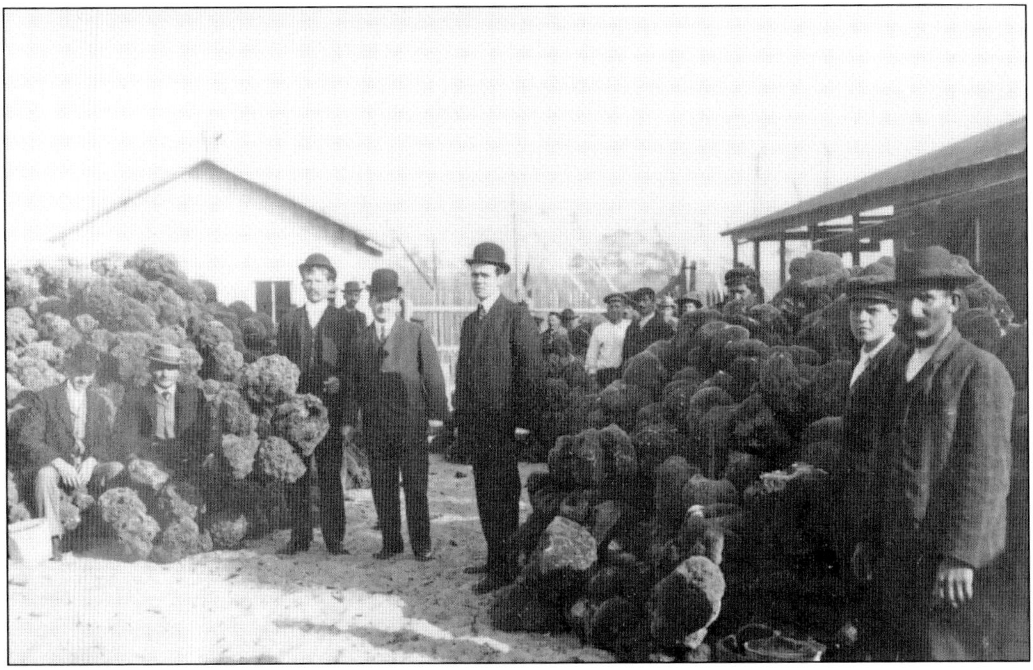

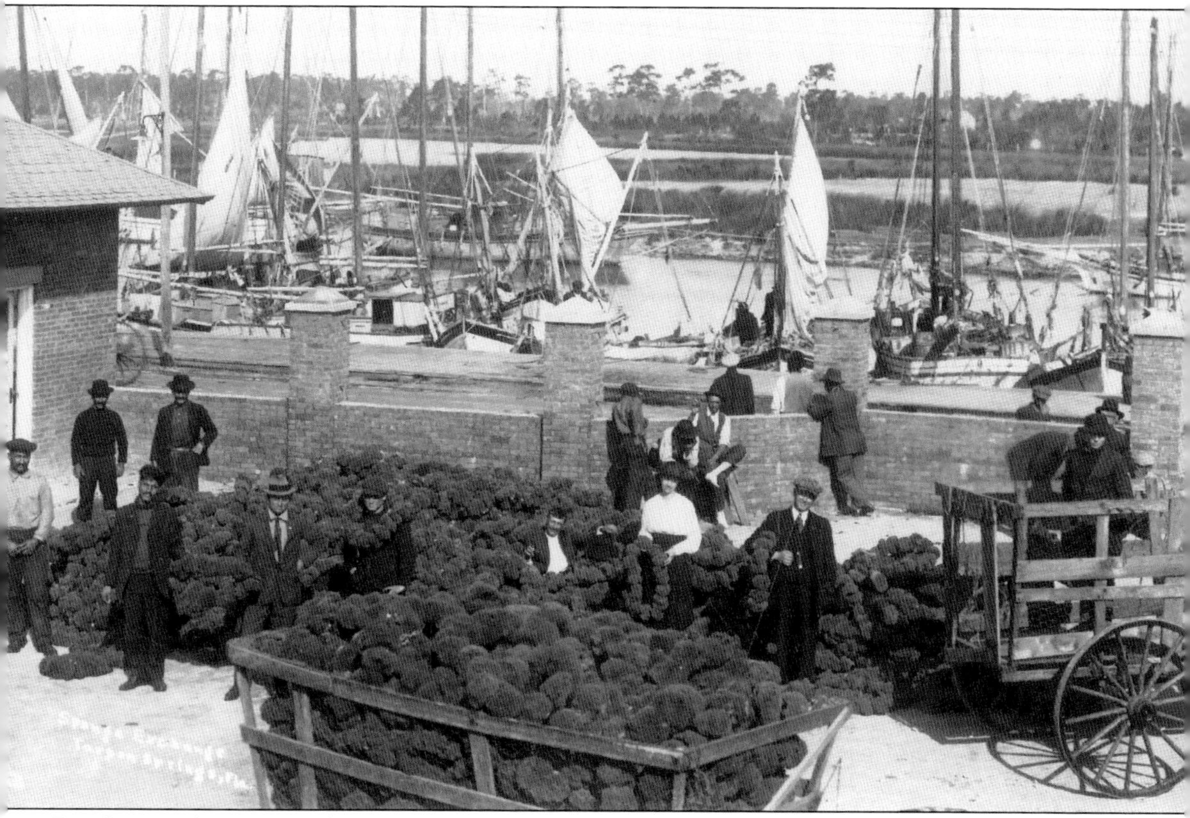

Bustling with activity, the Sponge Exchange was an organized cooperative warehouse and distribution system established around 1908. At the time of this image, iron-grilled *klouves* (storage cells) separated the catches around the perimeter. Auctions were held in the courtyard each Tuesday and Friday. (Courtesy of the Heritage Village Archives.)

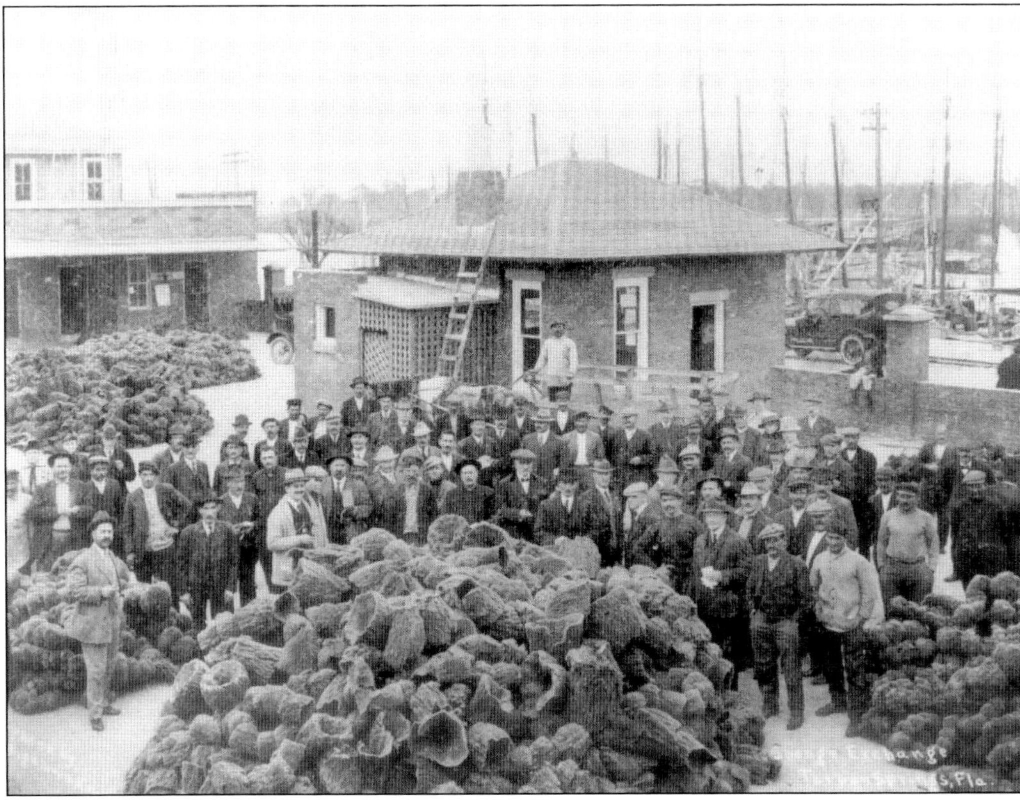

The Sponge Exchange on Dodecanese Boulevard across from the Sponge Docks was one of the most important places in Greektown. It consisted of a large courtyard for cleaning, processing, sorting, and selling sponges, surrounded by *klouves*, cells in which individual sponge catches were stored until sold. In this 1920 photograph, Emmanuel Alexiou (in a dark hat) appears front and center behind the large pile of sponges. He returned to Kalymnos in 1923. (Courtesy of Michael Alexiou.)

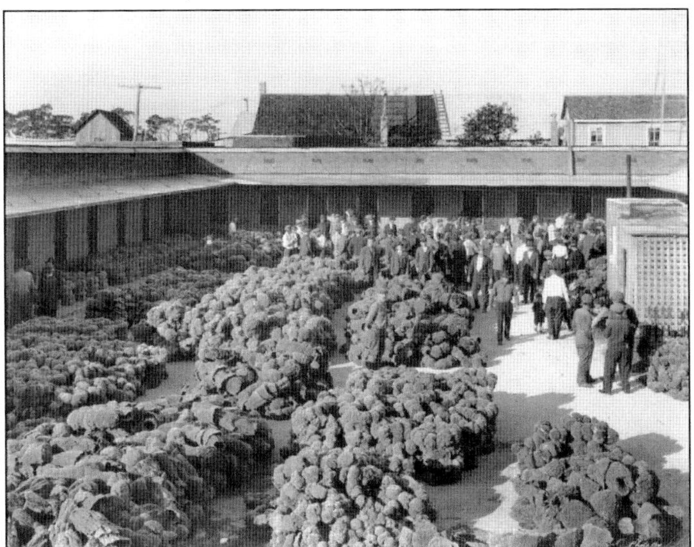

Piles of all types of sponges fill the courtyard of the Sponge Exchange on an auction day in 1921. Most of the men in the courtyard appear to be Greek, except for the African American man walking toward the camera. He is one of many who worked in the sponge industry with the Greeks, creating a close relationship between the two communities. (Photograph by Burgert Brothers, courtesy of Special Collections Department, Tampa Library, University of South Florida.)

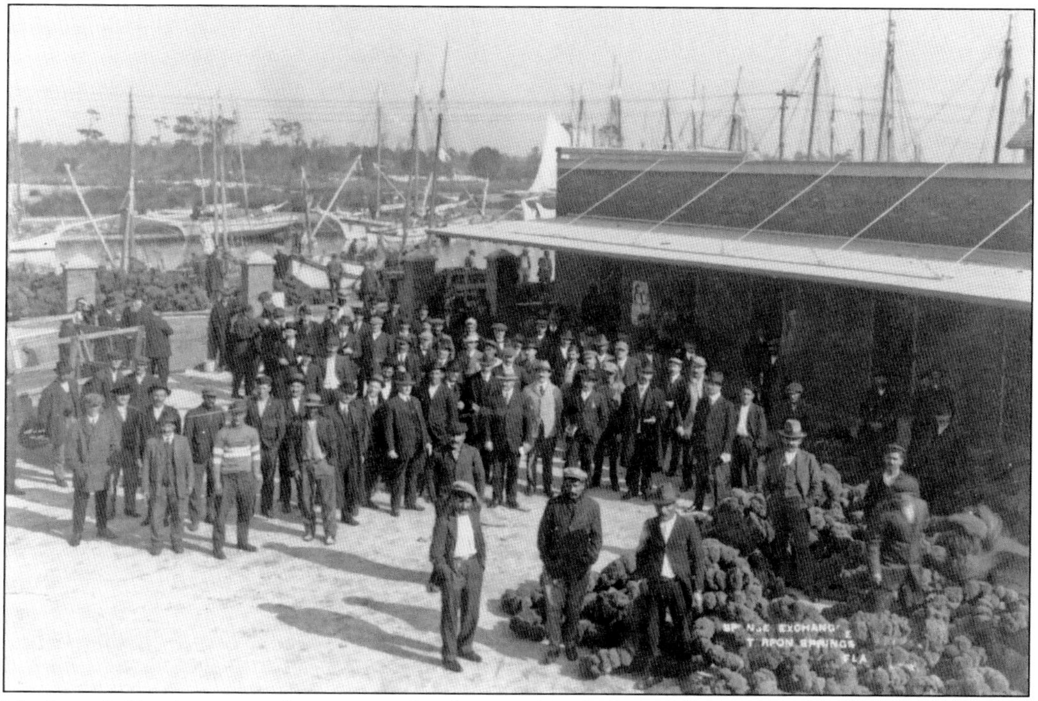

Hook and dive boats can be seen at the Sponge Docks beyond the Sponge Exchange in 1930. In addition to being the primary locus of buying and selling sponges, the Sponge Exchange functioned as a community gathering place for special occasions. For many years, the Epiphany *glendi* (celebration) was held in the courtyard, where men prepared *kavourmas* for the revelers. (Courtesy of the City of Tarpon Springs.)

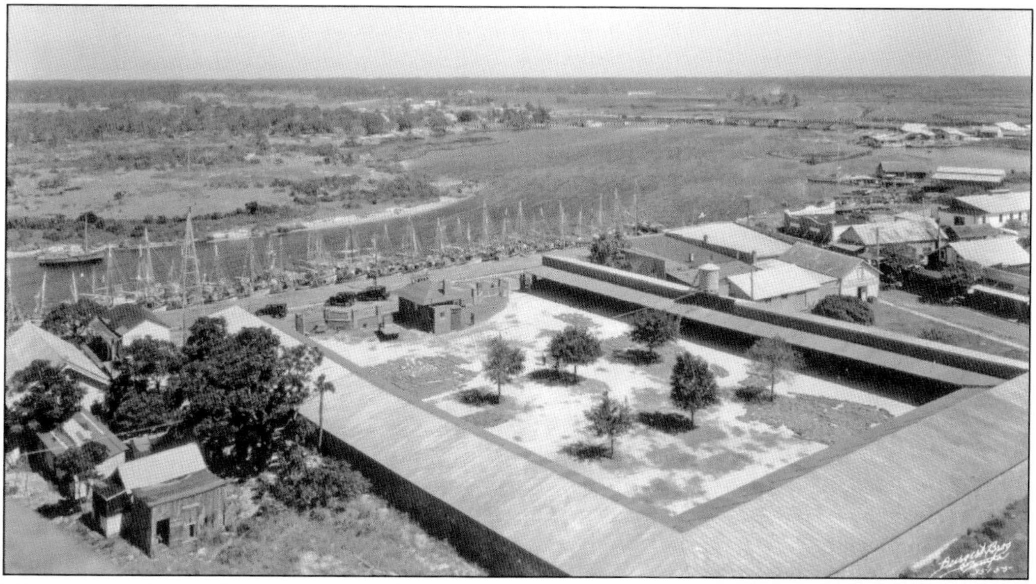

This elevated shot from 1932 reveals the sponge fleet at the Sponge Docks and the Sponge Exchange, along with a view of the bridge and surrounding area. Note the boatyard to the right of the docks, where boats were built, repaired, and cleaned. (Photograph by Burgert Brothers, courtesy of the Tampa-Hillsborough County Public Library System.)

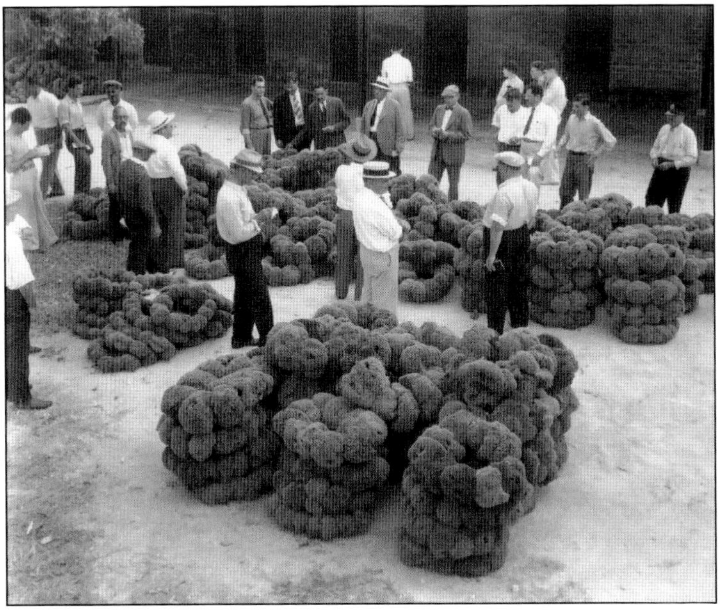

Sponge brokers examine the piles of sponges for sale in the Sponge Exchange courtyard on November 6, 1936. Many of the men are taking notes in preparation for the silent auction. (Photograph by Burgert Brothers, courtesy of the Tampa-Hillsborough County Public Library System.)

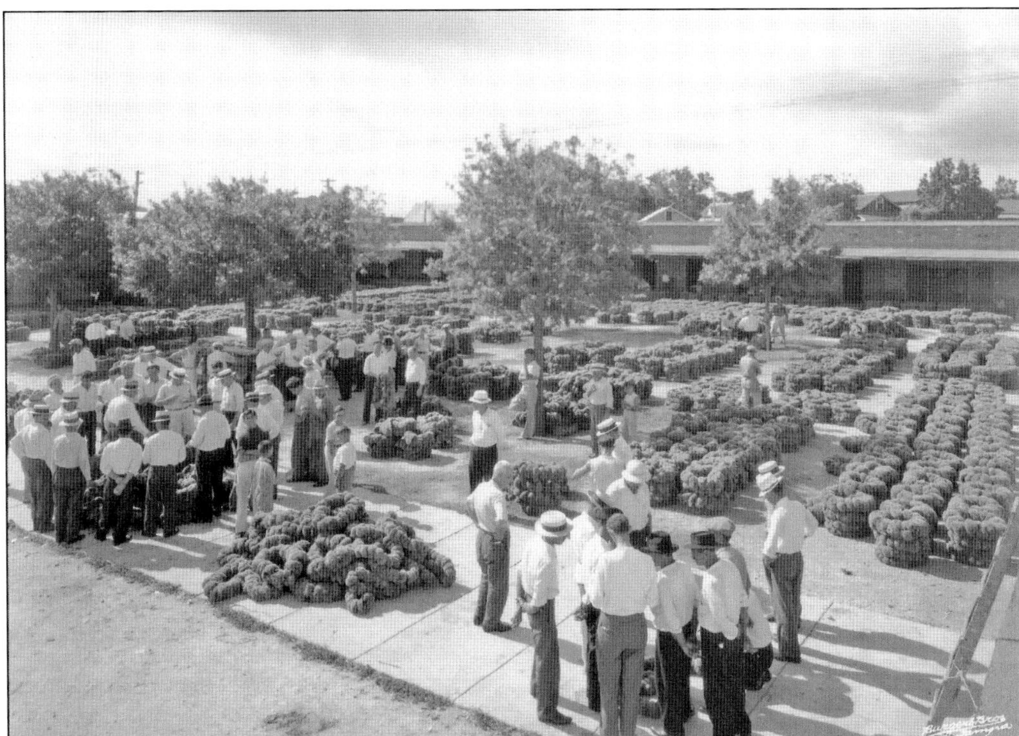

Men view sponges to be auctioned at the Sponge Exchange on July 24, 1937. By 1940, over 1,000 men were actively engaged in the sponge industry. These men and their families constituted roughly 2,500 Greeks in a town of 3,402. With the onset of World War II and closure of the European market, the supply of sponges decreased, while the demand increased dramatically, and Tarpon Springs was the world's leading sponge-producing center. (Photograph by Burgert Brothers, courtesy of the Tampa-Hillsborough County Public Library System.)

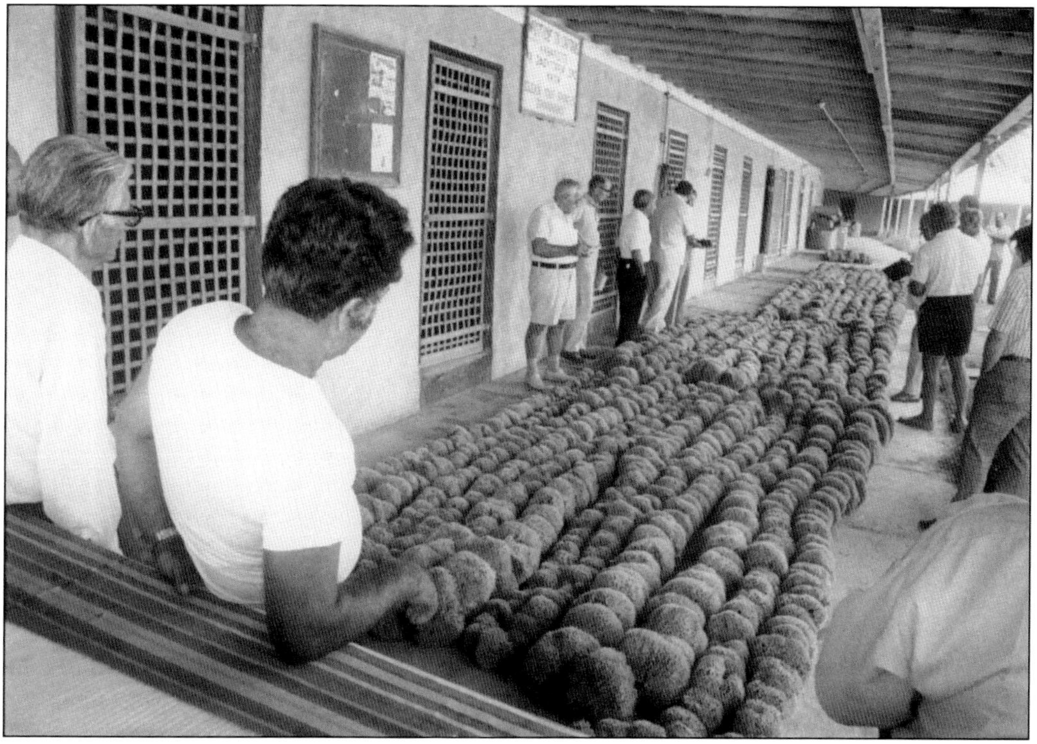

Buyers examine sponge lots during a large sale at the Sponge Exchange on June 19, 1978. Unlike sponge sales in Greece, sales at the Sponge Exchange were generally conducted through silent auctions. Each potential buyer submitted his bid on a piece of paper that he gave to the auctioneer. The highest bidder won, but the seller had the option of refusing the bid if he felt that it was not high enough. (Photograph by Dan Fager, courtesy of the *Tampa Tribune*.)

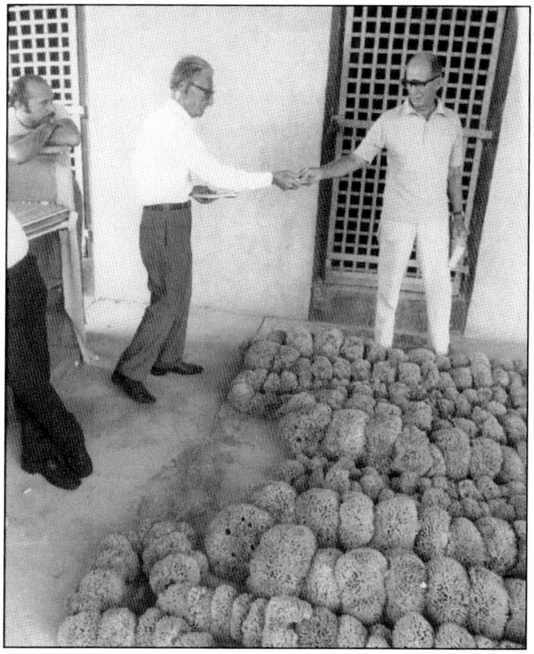

Auctioneer and former diver Costas Klimantos accepts a bid from potential buyer George Smitzes at the Sponge Exchange on June 19, 1978. After a sale, the captain or owner is reimbursed for food and boat expenses; then each member of the team receives a share proportional to their work. Most boats spend a week or two in port before commencing another trip. (Photograph by Dan Fager, courtesy of the *Tampa Tribune*.)

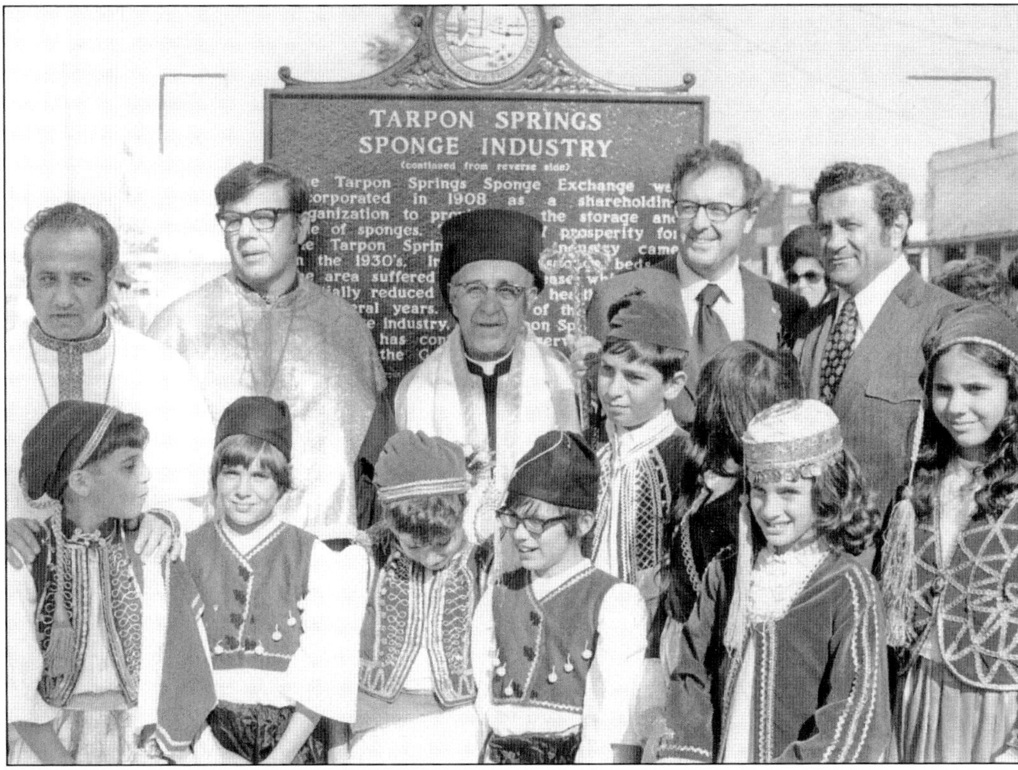

Children dressed in Greek dance costumes pose with, from left to right, the Reverend Father Elias Kalariotes, the Reverend Father John Athas, Bishop Aimilianos Laloussis, Florida secretary of state Richard Stone, and Mayor George C. Tsourakis in front of the Florida historical marker dedicated to the Tarpon Springs sponge industry in April 1973. The young boy with glasses is future congressman Gus Bilirakis. The marker provides a succinct history of the sponge industry and notes, "Tarpon Springs Sponge Exchange has continued to serve as a focal point for the Greek community." (Photograph by Dick Kemp, courtesy of the *Tampa Tribune*.)

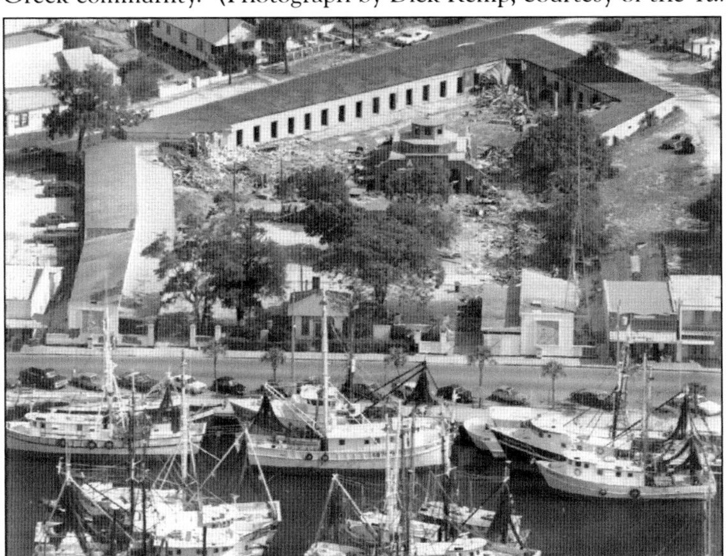

At left is an aerial view of the demolition of the Sponge Exchange in 1981. The Sponge Exchange was sold to new private owners who wanted to create a shopping complex. Although many members of the Greek community and preservationists from the Florida Department of State/Division of Historical Resources opposed the demolition, they were unable to stop it. (Photograph by Morris of Selbypic, courtesy of the *Tampa Tribune*.)

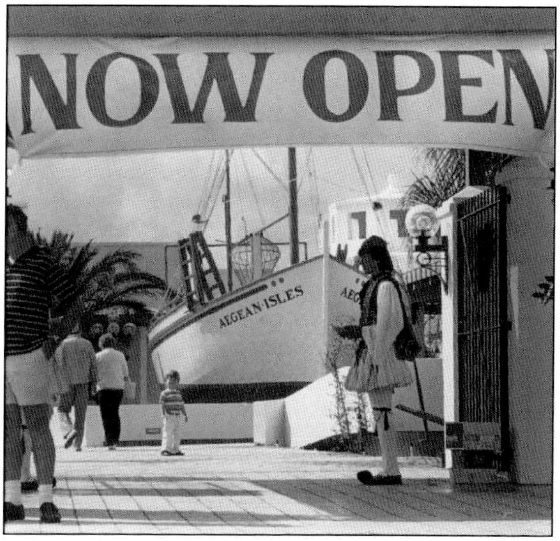

On the old Sponge Exchange site, a complex of shops designed with faux Cyclades architecture opened on March 16, 1983. Several *klouves* on the north side were retained, originally intended for use by sponge fisherman. To highlight local heritage, the owners bought, restored, and displayed the sponge boat *Apalachicola*, renamed *Aegean Isles*. Nick Anargiou built the boat in Apalachicola in the late 1920s for Capt. James Tsalichis of Tarpon Springs. It was sold to Miltiadis Galanos in the 1940s and served as a rescue boat during World War II before returning to the sponge business. (Photograph by Bob Westenhouse, courtesy of the *Tampa Tribune*.)

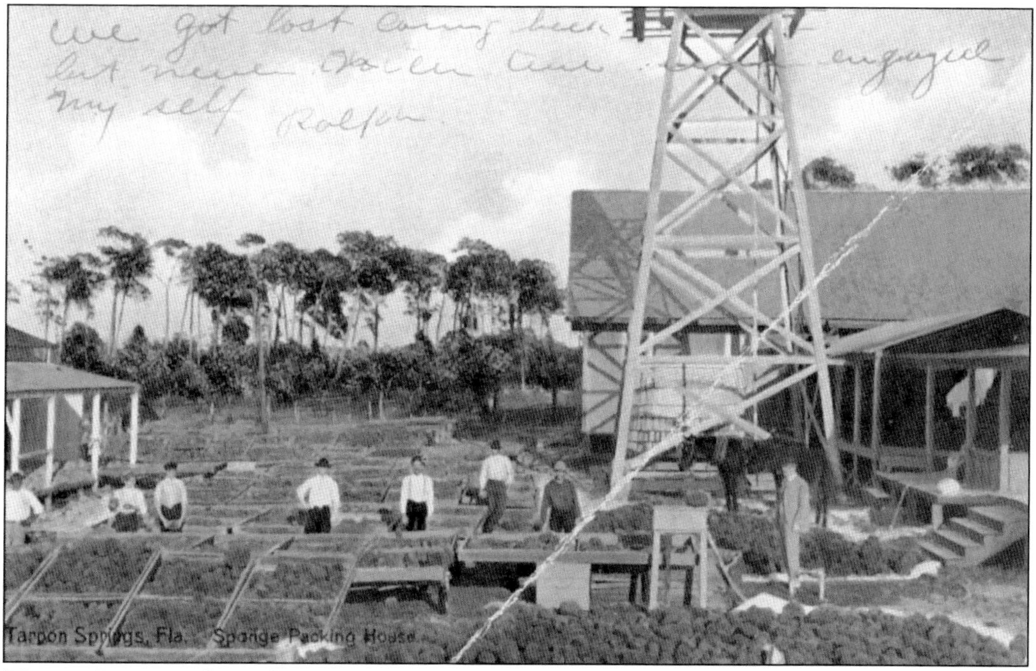

This early image from the Hampton Dunn Collection of Florida Postcards shows a sponge packinghouse associated with Trefon Constantinou. Many sponge merchants belong to families who have worked in the business for generations. In their warehouses, sponges are processed or cut according to order specifications. Some are sold in their natural state, and others are bleached yellow in successive chemical baths. They are trimmed to a size appropriate to their intended function, compacted into bales by a sponge press, sold, and shipped. (Courtesy of Special Collections Department, Tampa Library, University of South Florida.)

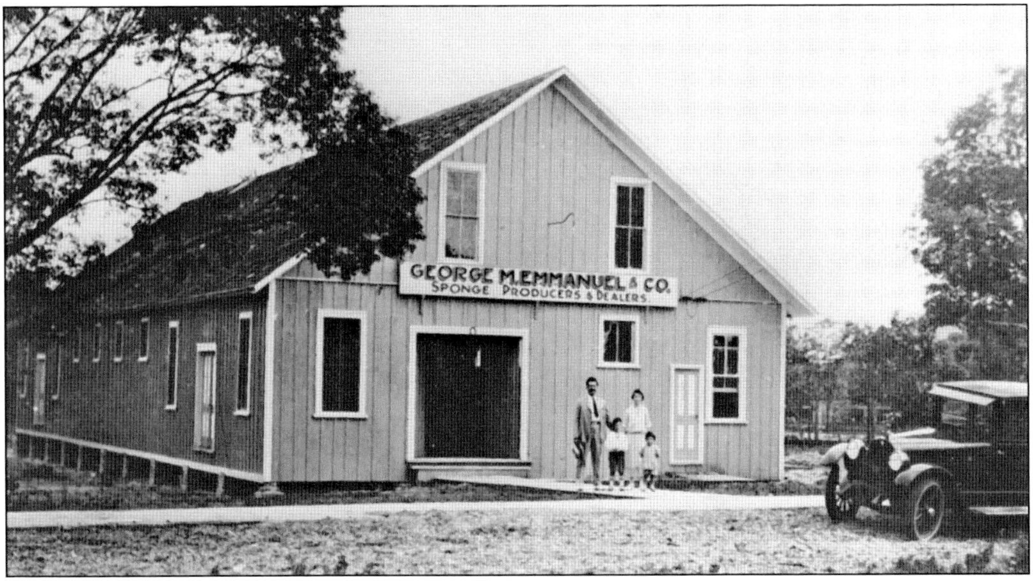

Sponge merchant George Emmanuel (1887–1968) is pictured with his wife, Alexandra, and children Michel and Helen outside their warehouse on North Safford Avenue. George was the son of Michalis Emmanuel, who was employed by British sponge merchants in Aegina before emigrating to Tarpon Springs with his son in 1906. There, Michalis founded a sponge company. Upon his father's death in 1913, George took over the business and went on to become a respected community leader. (Courtesy of the Tarpon Springs Area Historical Society.)

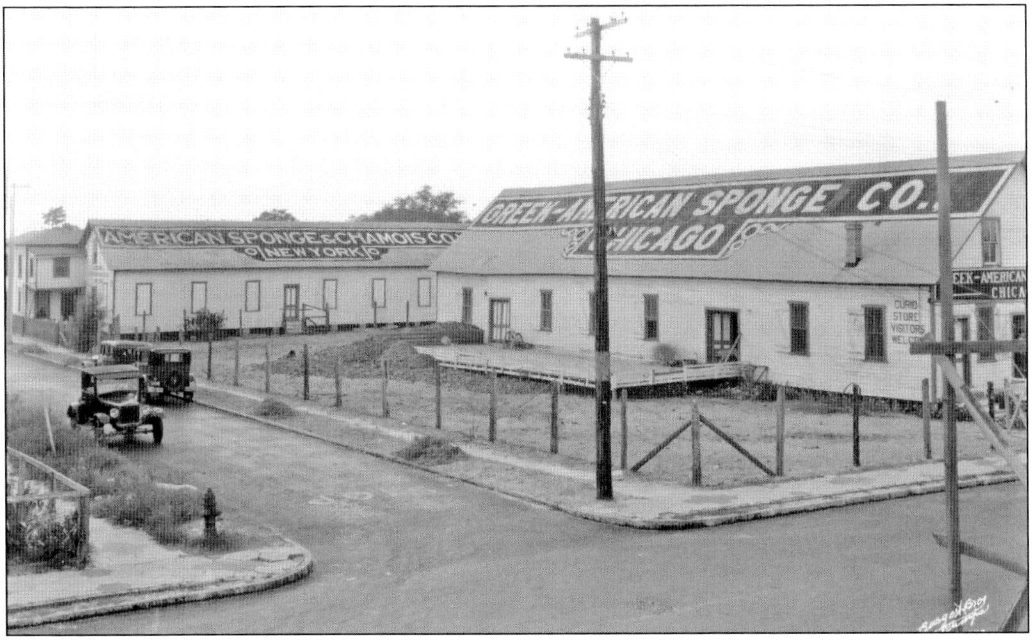

Sponge warehouses of the Greek-American Sponge Company of Chicago and the American Sponge & Chamois Company of New York are pictured in October 1932. In the past, there were many independent local sponge buyers, as well as agents of larger international merchant houses. (Photograph by Burgert Brothers, courtesy of the Tampa-Hillsborough County Public Library System.)

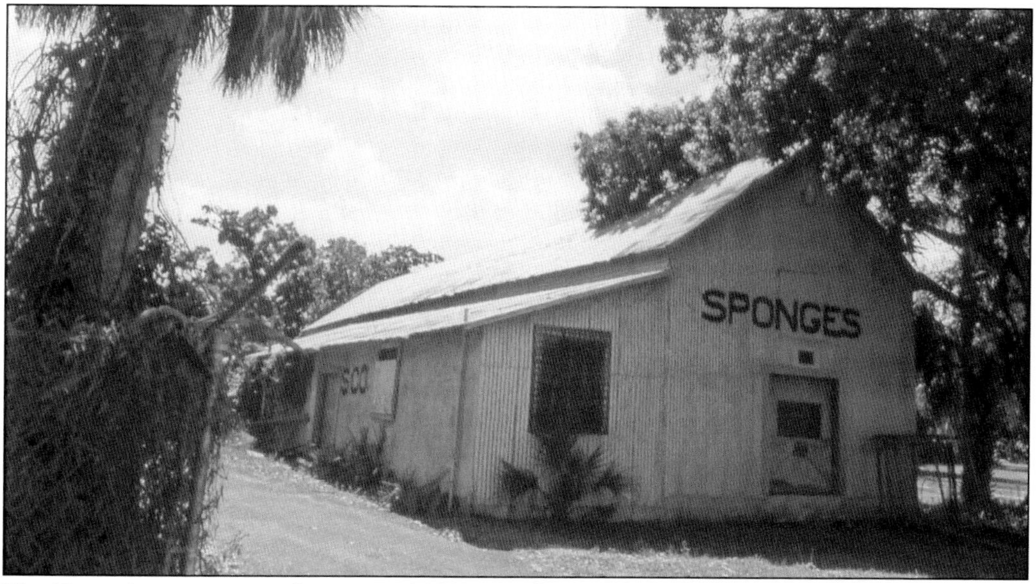

The Tsourakis sponge warehouse at 106 West Park Street was originally the E.R. Meres Sponge Packing House. Constructed about 1905, this wood-frame structure is the oldest extant example of a sponge packing plant in Tarpon Springs that was recently in operation. At the height of sponge industry activity in the 1920s, there were nearly two dozen such packinghouses. Listed in the National Register of Historic Places in 1991, this industrial vernacular building was most likely constructed without formal plans and assembled by area carpenters. (Photograph by Robert L. Stone, courtesy of State Archives of Florida, Florida Memory.)

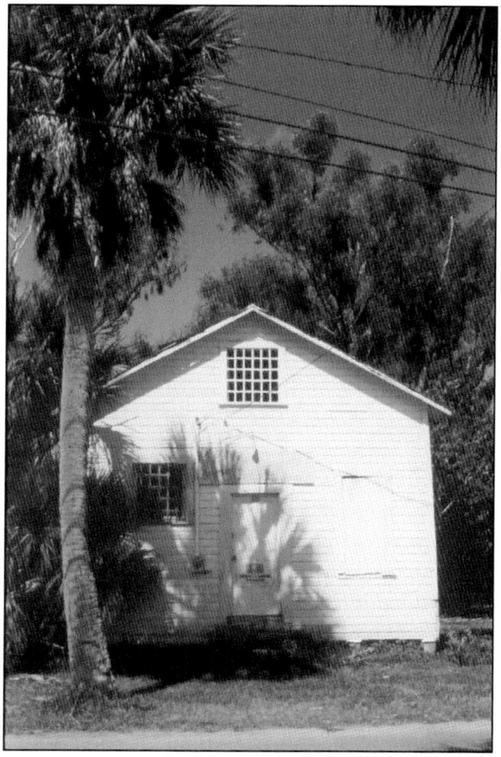

The Gulf of Mexico Sponge Company warehouse was built at 122 Roosevelt Boulevard around 1930 by Drosos Alahuzos, who arrived in the United States in 1916. Drosos ran the family sponge business out of Philadelphia but spent some of his time in Tarpon Springs, where his brothers Michael and Emmanuel had a warehouse. Michael Kousaleos and his father, George, had a sponge business in Pittsburgh and Philadelphia. After Droso's death in 1955, they purchased the sponge warehouse and operated the Gulf of Mexico Sponge Company until 1972. The Kousaleos family also helped bring new divers from Kalymnos. In 2004, Michael Kousaleos donated the warehouse to Heritage Village, Pinellas County's living history museum in Largo. (Photograph by the author.)

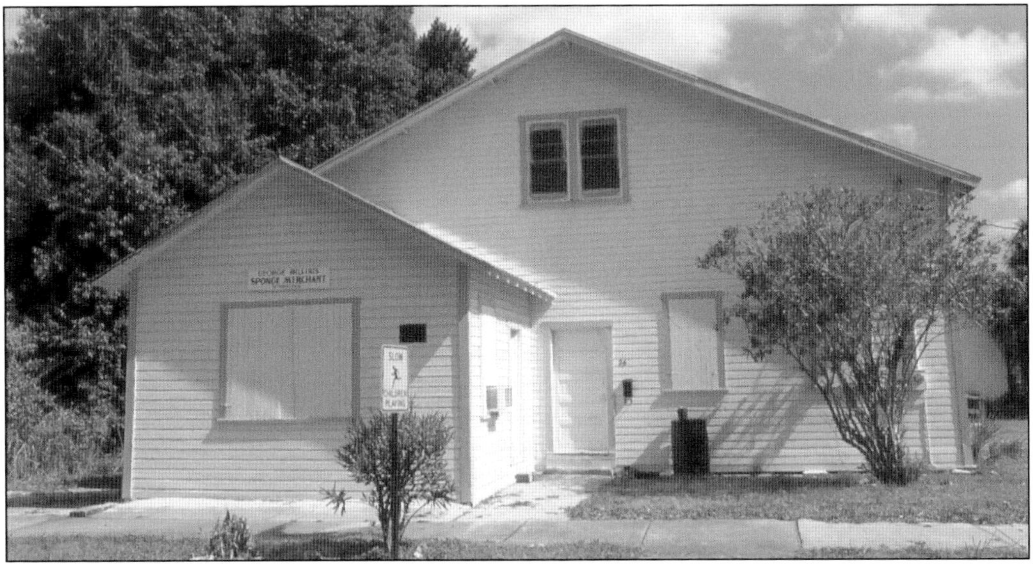

The historic N.G. Arfaras Sponge Packing Plant at 23 West Park Street is a one-story wood-frame building that was listed in the National Register of Historic Places in 1991. It was among the last of the sponge packing plants erected in Tarpon Springs before the decline of the commercial sponge industry in the late 1940s. It was in operation until recently, and the interior is arranged to serve the various steps involved with processing natural sponges. (Photograph by the author.)

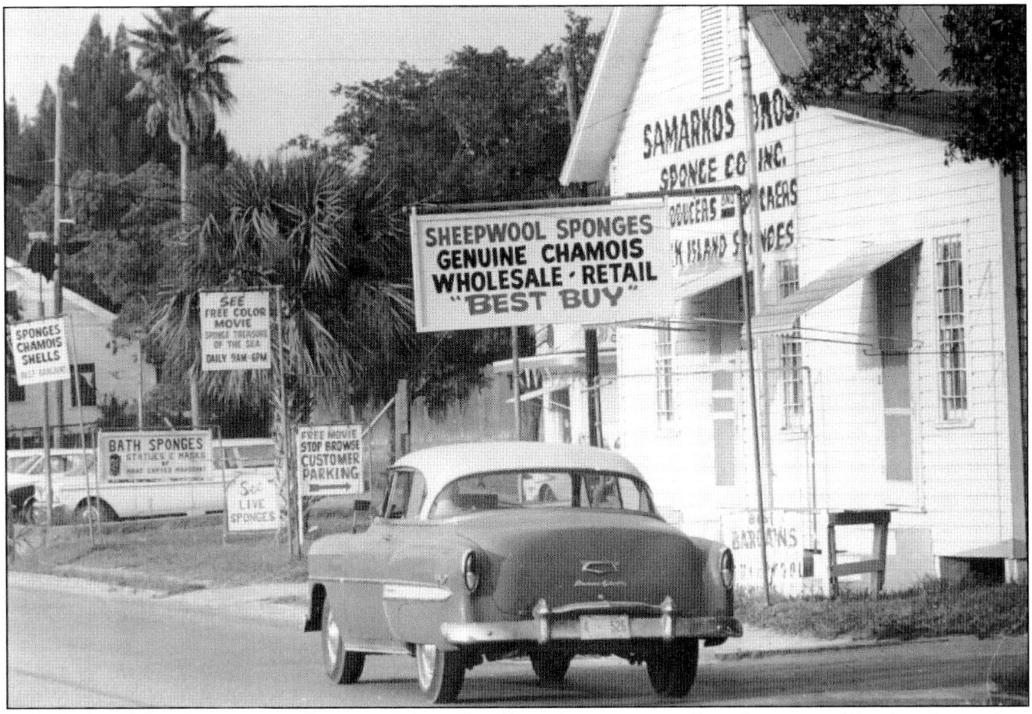

The Samarkos Sponge Warehouse on Pinellas Avenue was owned and operated by the Samarkos family, many of whom were active as captains, divers, and merchants in the sponge industry. Signs in this image from November 26, 1972, indicate that it sold tourist items in addition to sponges. It remained in business until about 2010. (Courtesy of the *Tampa Tribune*.)

Five

SHOPS, OFFICES, AND TOURISM

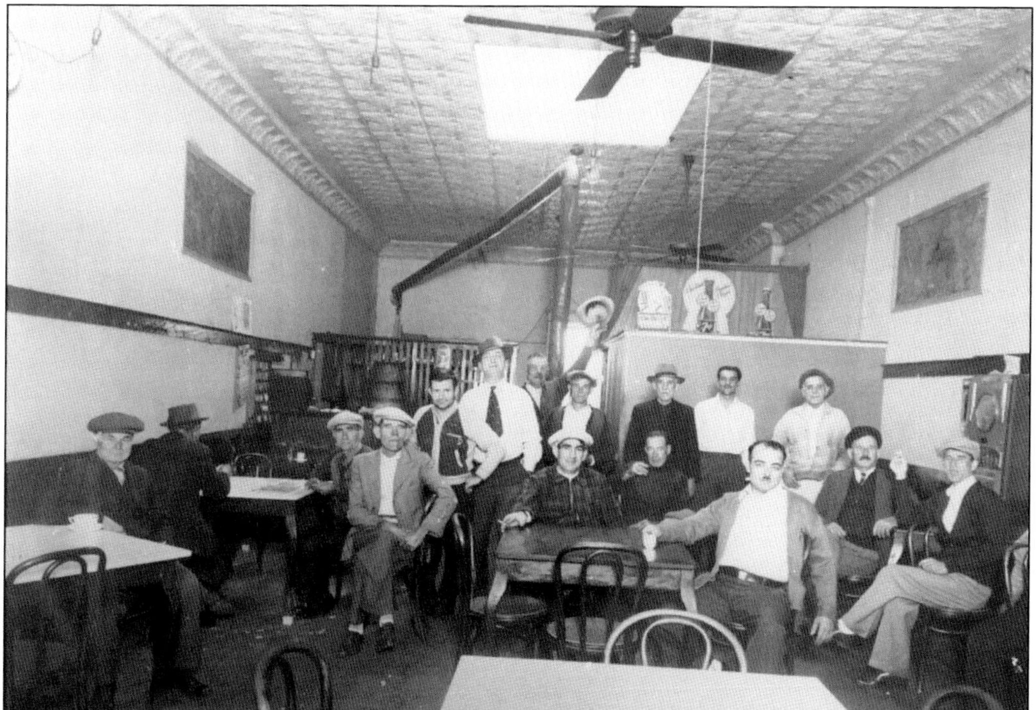

The *kafeneia* (men's coffeehouses) are located on West Athens Street. Their lengthy existence testifies to the long-standing, conservative tradition of Greek men spending their free time at these establishments. Today, as in the past, dozens of Greek men continue to frequent the *kafeneia*, sipping coffee, watching and commenting on passersby, sharing local information, and solving world problems. (Courtesy of Dr. Themistocles J. Diamandis.)

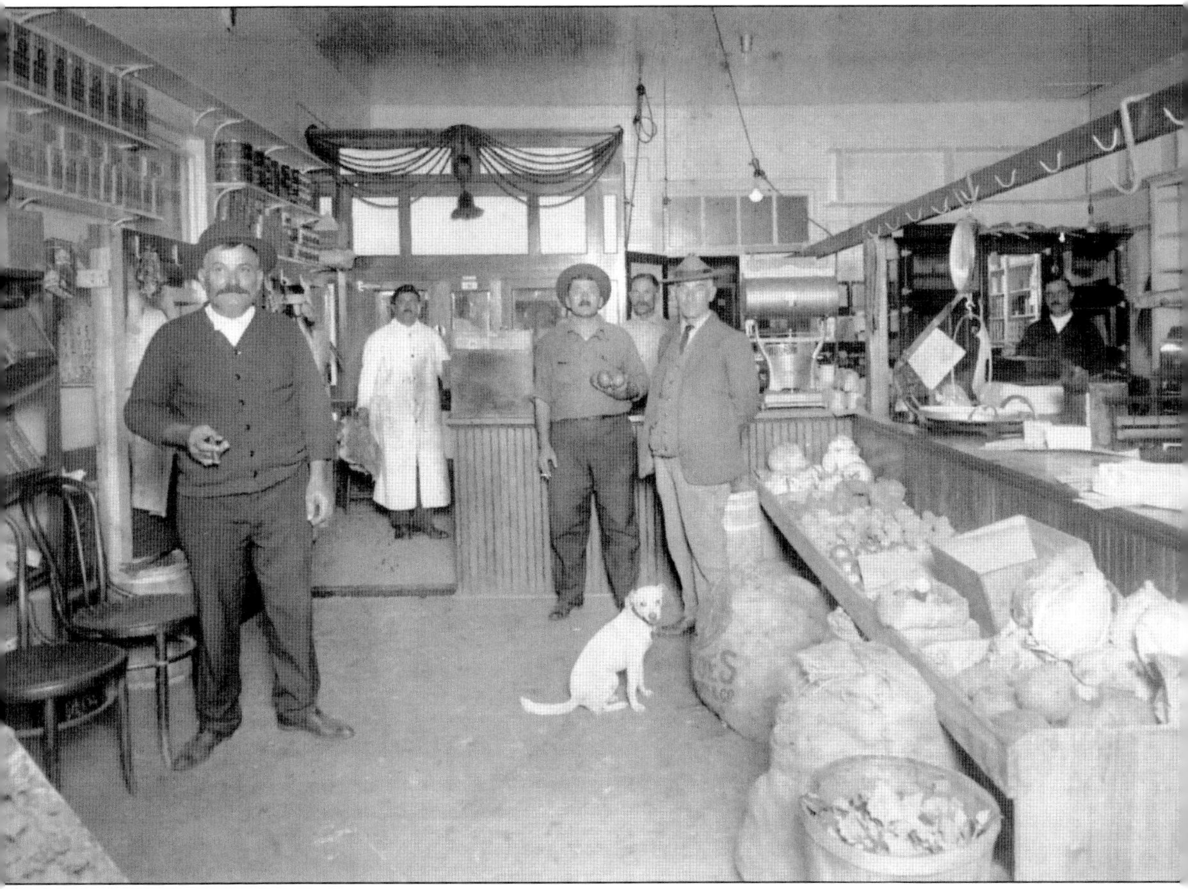

This is the Angel Market on Athens Street, where the National Bakery is now located. George Nikolaou Angeliniadis, the owner of the store, is seen at far right behind the counter. At left toward the front is Manuel Alahouzos. The original Angel Market was across the street where Halki Market later operated. (Courtesy of George Mandalou.)

Thelma Karavokiros Papafotis stocks the shelves in the Angel Market on Athens Street in the 1940s. In addition to canned goods, produce, and staples, customers could purchase freshly butchered meats. (Courtesy of Nickollet Tsourakis Henderson.)

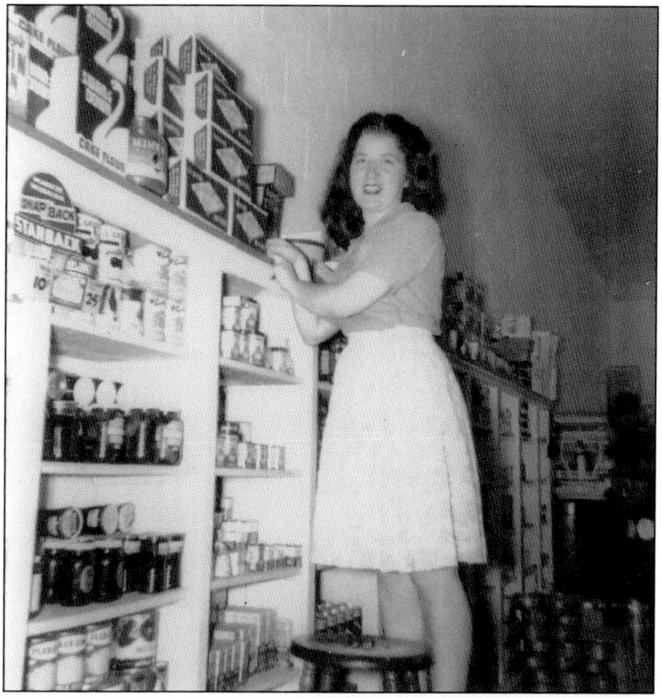

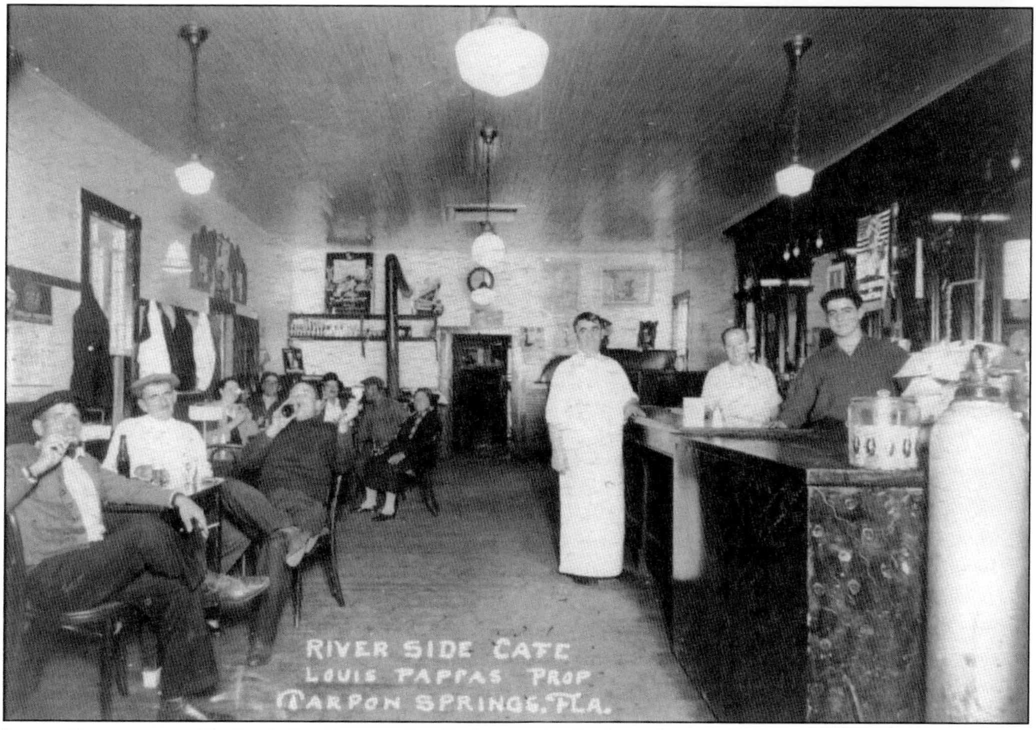

Louis Pappas established the Riverside Café in 1925 when he settled in Tarpon Springs after serving as Gen. John J. Pershing's cook during World War I. The café began by serving Greek men in the sponge industry and other community members, but it gradually became a regional icon of Greek cuisine. (Courtesy of the Tarpon Springs Area Historical Society.)

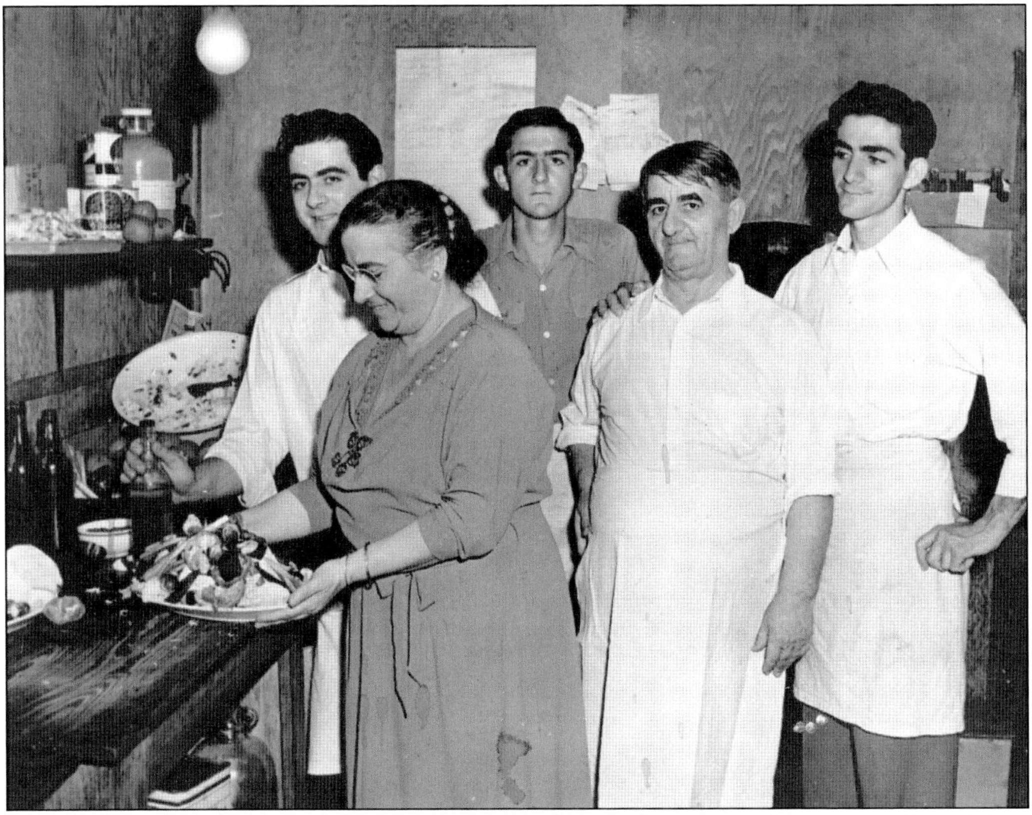

Flora Pappas prepares food in the company of her husband, Louis, and their sons, from left to right, Mike, Jack, and Lukas, in the 1940s. The Pappas family established the Riverside Café in 1925, and it gradually became a highly successful local landmark. Although the main restaurant closed a decade ago, some family members have opened other eating establishments. (Courtesy of the Tarpon Springs Area Historical Society.)

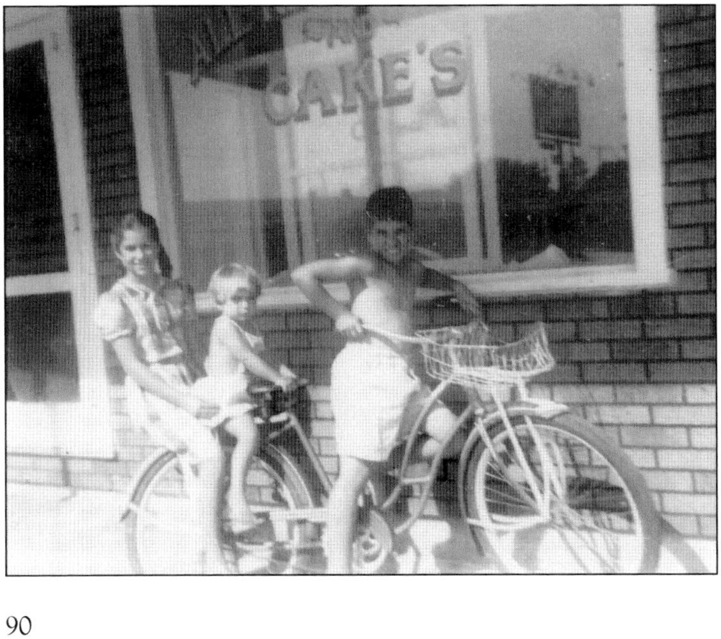

Evelyn Miaoulis Billirakis (left) and Kaliope Miaoulis Harvard are sitting on the back of a bike driven by their brother Nicholas Miaoulis in the 1940s. They are making a stop at the Greek American bakery on what is now Pinellas Avenue, which was owned and operated by the related Miaoulis and Lulias families. (Courtesy of John Lulias.)

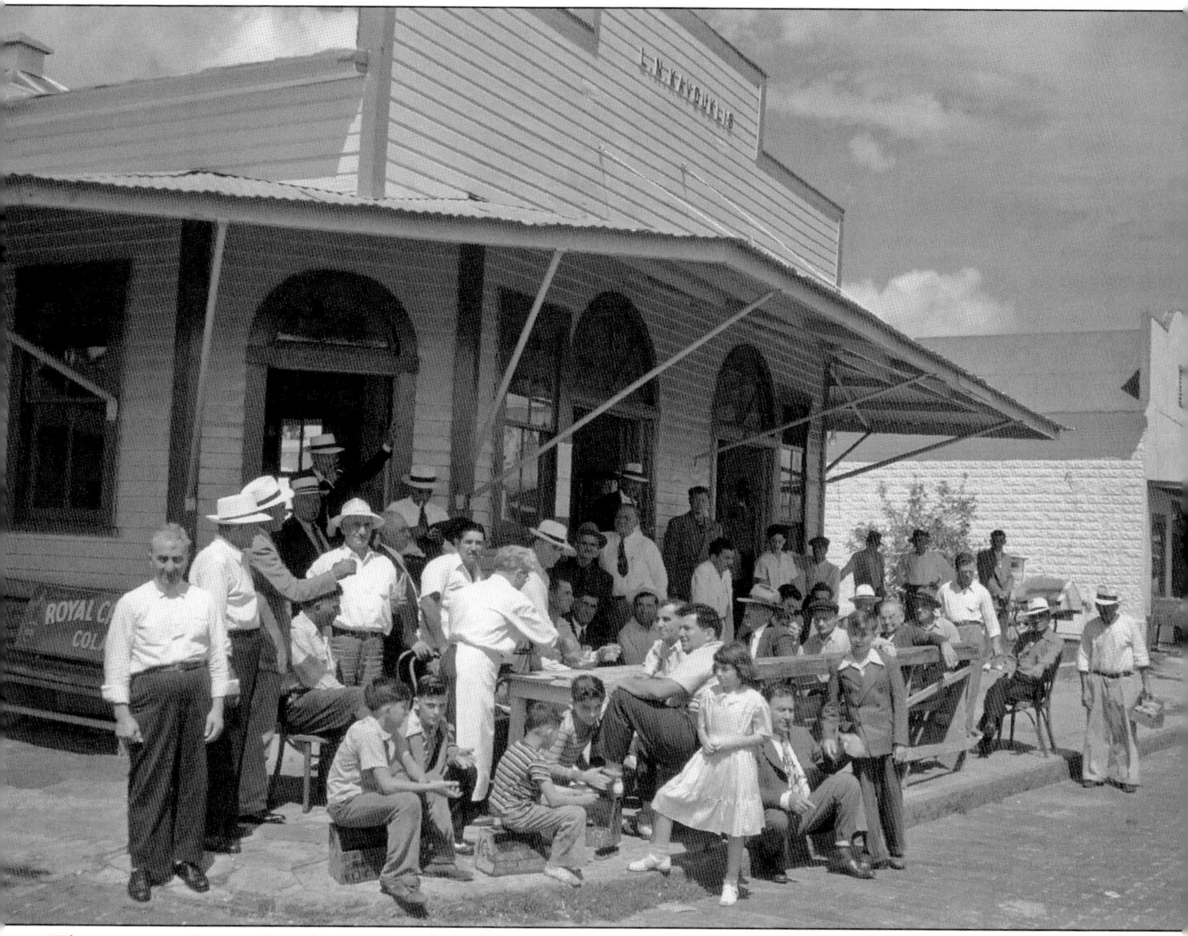

This image shows Greeks gathered in front of the Lazaros Coffee Shop on Athens Street on April 13, 1947. At the time, the establishment was owned by Lazaros Kavouklis. (Photograph by Joseph Janney Steinmetz, courtesy of State Archives of Florida, Florida Memory.)

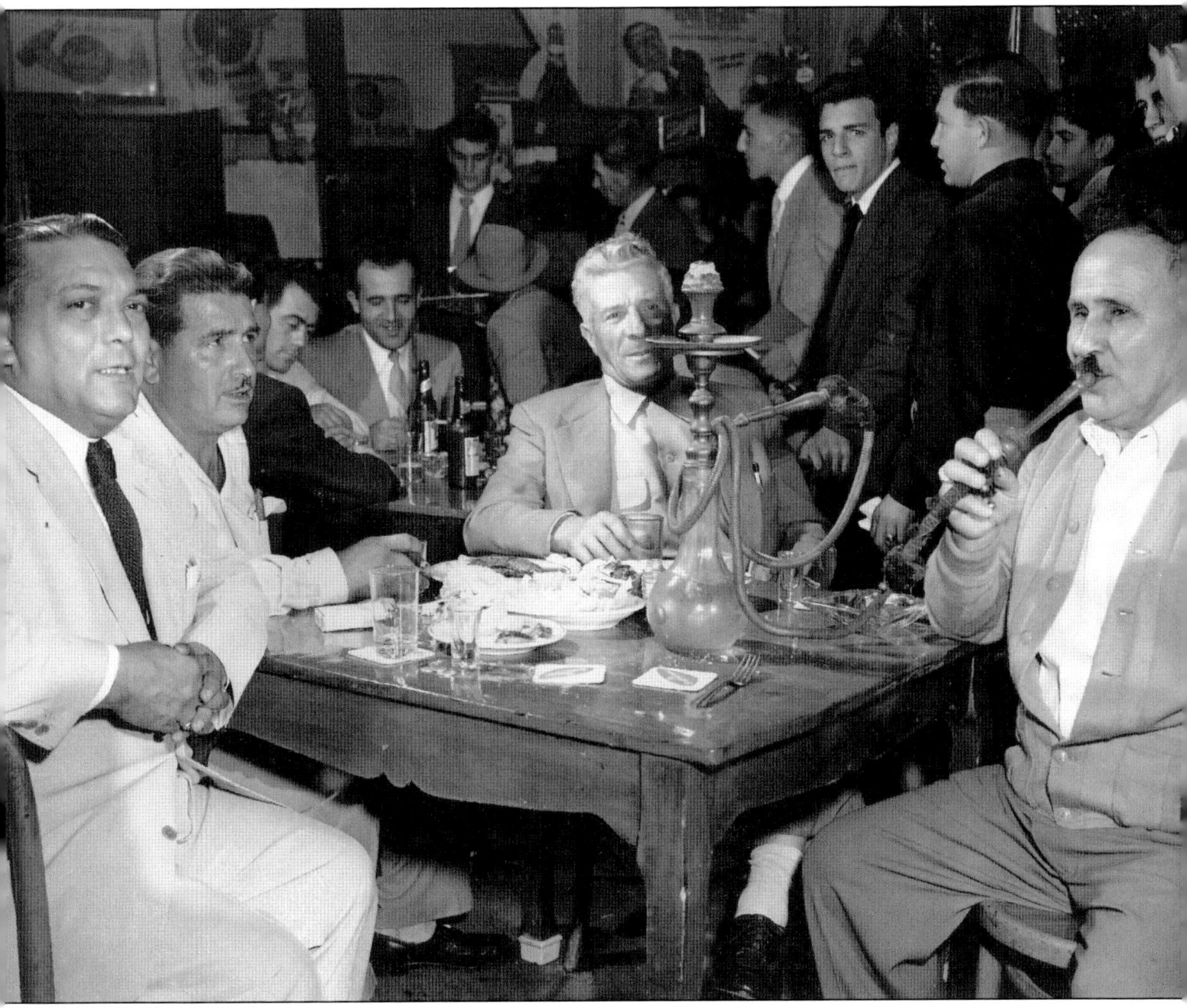

Men gather at the Samarkos Coffee House on Athens Street after the cross-diving on Epiphany 1945. From left to right are (front seated) unidentified, Michael Manias, Peter Mastrovasilis, and John A. Samarkos, smoking a *nargiles*; (back seated) George Kindinis and Nicholas Pantelis; (standing) Konstantinos Moutsatsos, unidentified, Steve Peterson, Bill Paskalakis, and Anthony Samarkos. The rest are unidentified. Moutsatsos, who retrieved the cross, is holding the tray that the cross divers traditionally take around town to collect donations for the church. (Courtesy of Anna Tsoukalas Billiris.)

Helen Samarkos Tsoukalas holds baby Anna Tsoukalas atop a sign for the Seven Seas Restaurant, owned by the Samarkos family. For many years, the Halki Market on Athens Street, owned and operated by Costas Paskalakis, was an important source of foodstuffs for neighborhood tables. At the Halki Market, housewives could purchase their Easter lambs, as well as special cuts that were necessary for dishes like *patsa* or *kokoretsi*. (Courtesy of Anna Tsoukalas Billiris.)

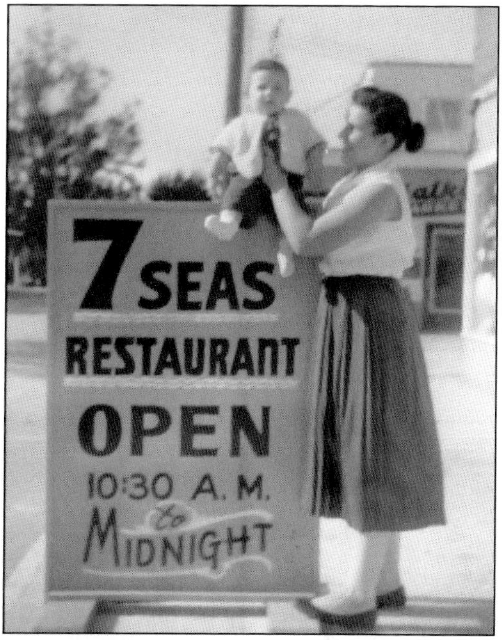

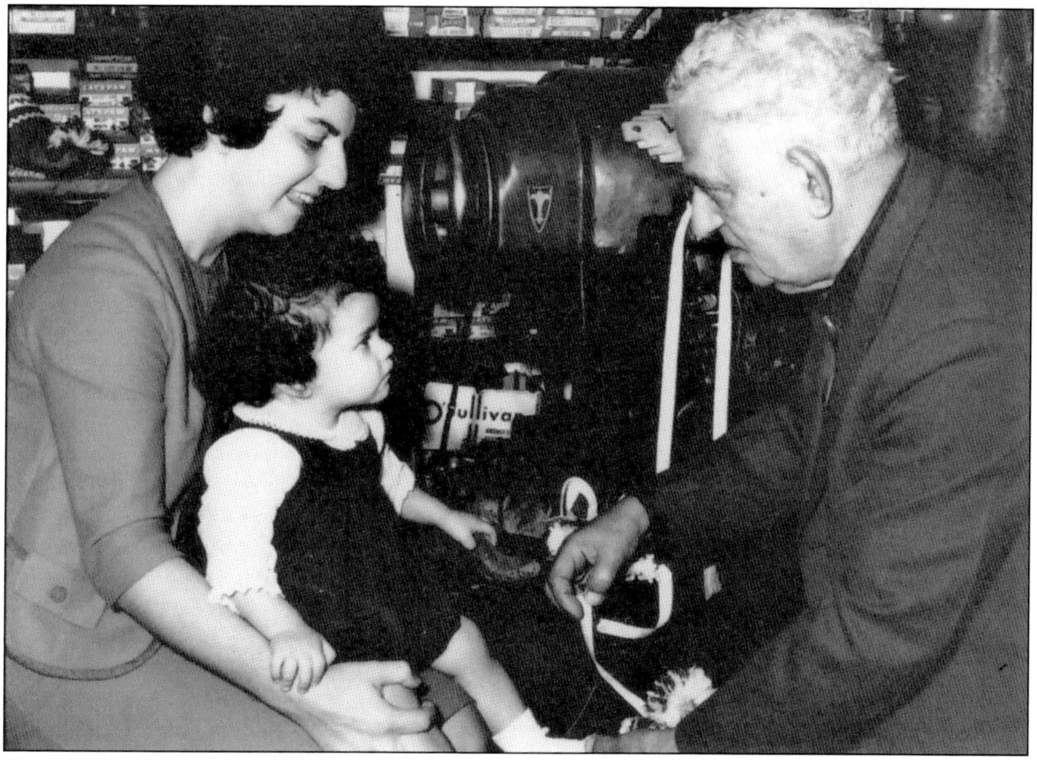

Vasile Faklis fits his granddaughter Andea Faklis Kopacz with a shoe as her mother, Katie Faklis, watches in 1966. Faklis' Department Store & Shoe Repair specialized then, as today, in shoes that are both stylish and healthy. The store still displays some of Vasile's original shoemaker tools, as well as a pair of weighted sponge diver's boots with his handwork in the leather coverings. (Courtesy of the Faklis family.)

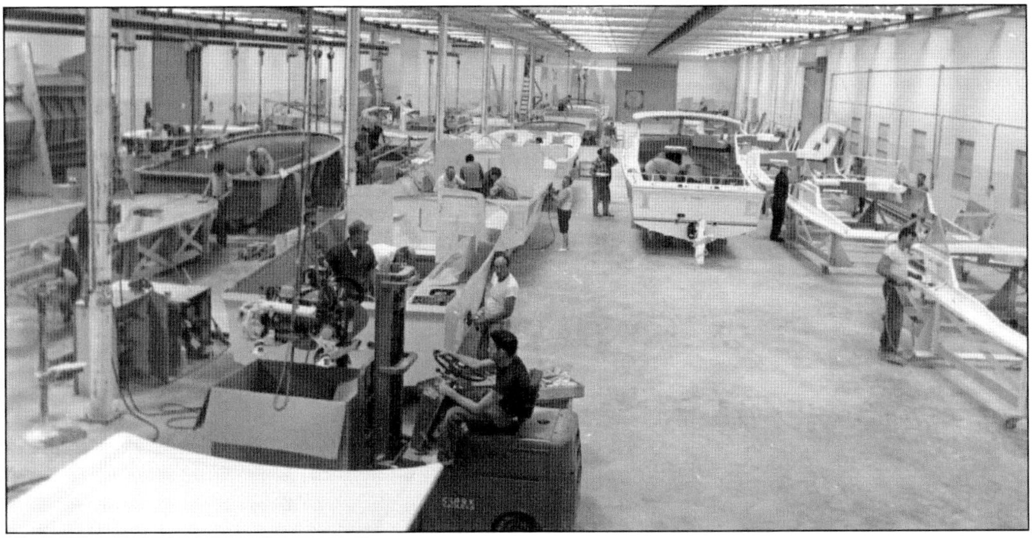

Stamas Boat Company employees make recreational boats in a newly built facility on March 21, 1967. As boys, Peter and Nicholas Stamas learned wooden boatbuilding from traditional Greek craftsmen. While still at Tarpon Springs High School in the late 1930s, they received a first prize at the Florida State Fair for a 22-foot wooden cruiser that they had constructed. Initially, they built commercial and deep-sea charter fishing boats. After World War II, the brothers started building boats regularly; they established their company in 1952. By the late 1950s, the Stamas brothers had recognized the potential of fiberglass and pioneered its use in boat construction. They switched entirely from wood to fiberglass in 1959. Today, Stamas is one of the oldest family-owned-and-operated boat companies in the nation. Many features that are now industry standards were originally Stamas innovations. (Photograph by Flash Jarocki, courtesy of the *Tampa Tribune*.)

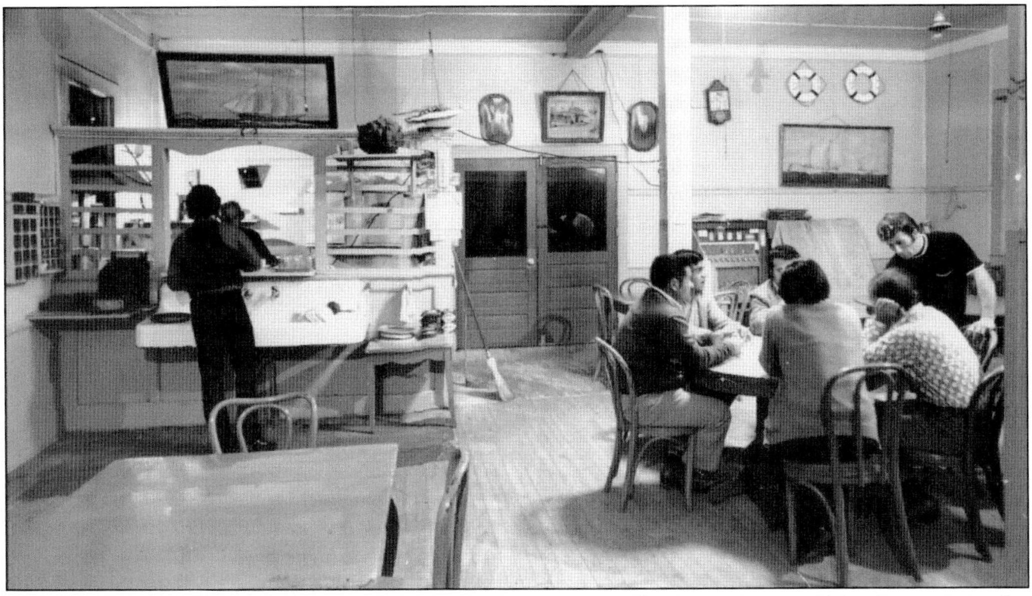

Inside a *kafeneion* during the 1970s, a waiter picks up a coffee from the small kitchen while the men take a break from playing cards to discuss a serious matter. For the last 110 years, Greek men have sat inside and outside the *kafeneia* from early in the morning until late at night. (Courtesy of Eleni Christopoulos-Lekkas.)

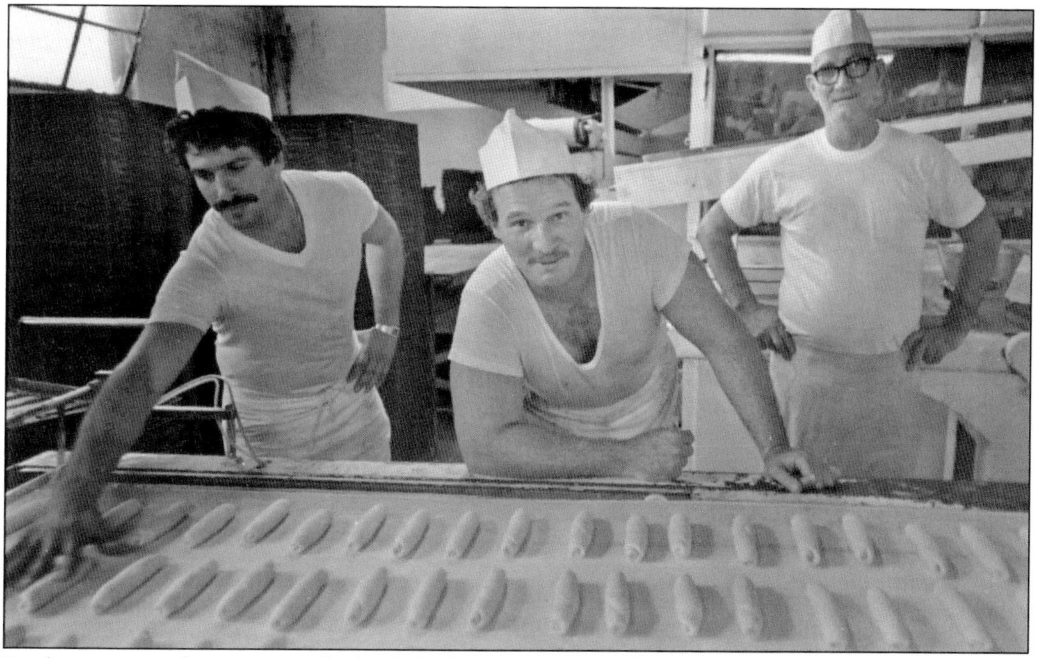

In this image taken on March 6, 1987, Roger Smirlis is flanked by employees Zach Marazos (left) and Junior Baxter. Smirlis baked all varieties of European and American breads, as did his grandfather dating back to the early 20th century. (Courtesy of the *Tampa Tribune*.)

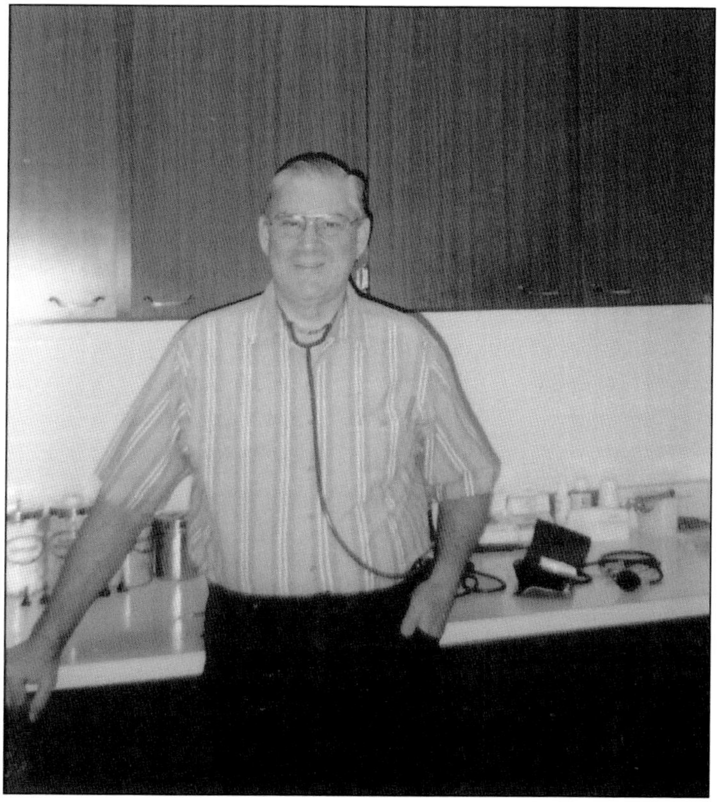

Dr. Themistocles J. Diamandis, known as "Dr. D," was a beloved doctor in Tarpon Springs for 47 years until he retired. After attending medical school at the University of Miami, he returned to Tarpon Springs to work in the hospital where he was born. He opened a private practice in 1970. Dr. Diamandis was known for making house calls, regardless of time or payment. He was also a student of local history and developed a large collection of historical photographs and articles. (Courtesy of Alyce Diamandis.)

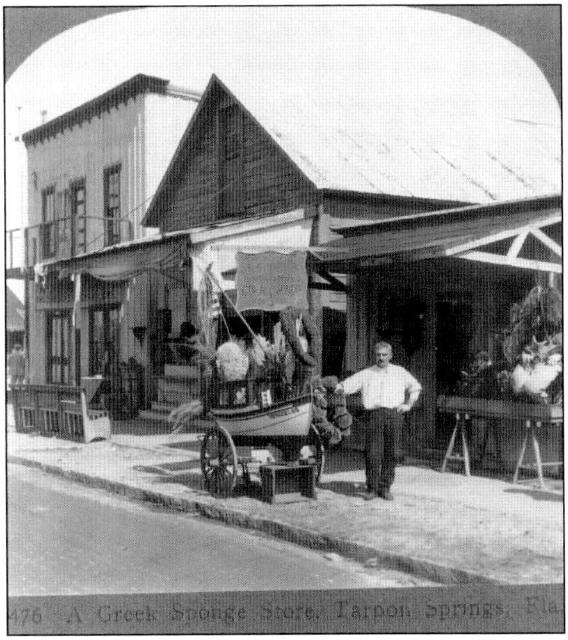

A man stands next to the Sea Curiosities from Gulf of Mexico tourist display on January 30, 1928. Note the dinghy named for Greek prime minister Eleftherios Venizelos, as well as the shop to the left, which is a ship's chandlery. Mass tourism boomed after World War I as the middle class expanded. The influx of Greeks coincided with growing interest in cultural tourism. Since the 1920s and 1930s, it has been the biggest attraction for tourists visiting Tarpon Springs. (Courtesy of State Archives of Florida, Florida Memory.)

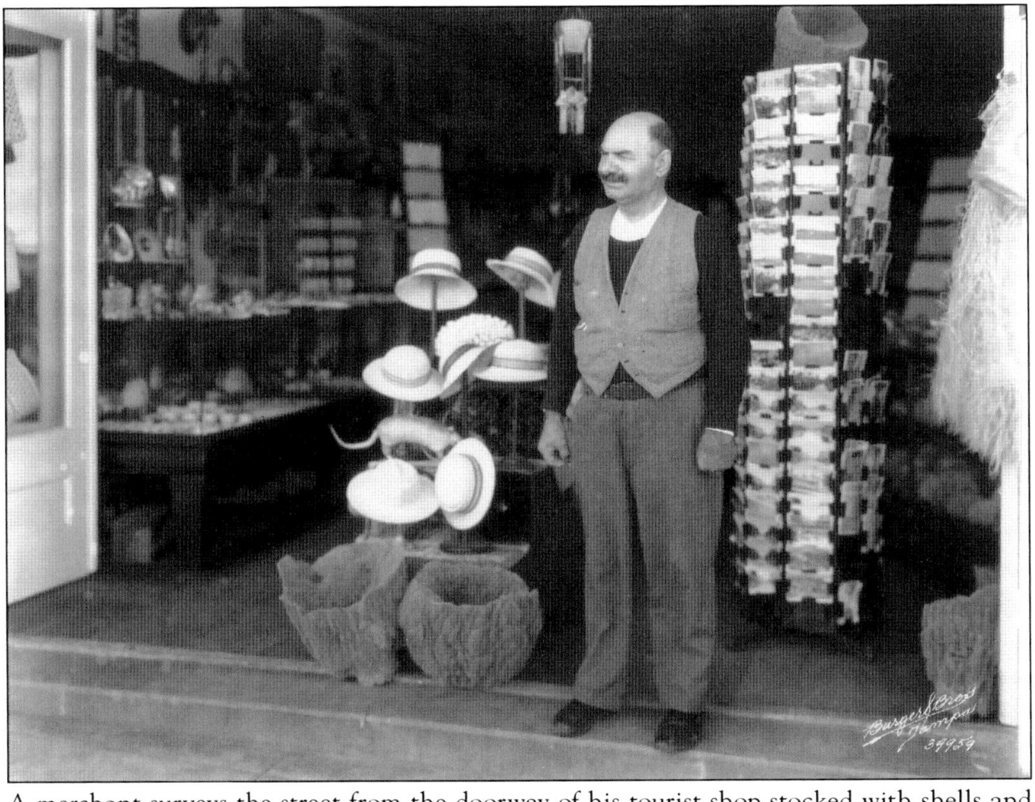

A merchant surveys the street from the doorway of his tourist shop stocked with shells and sponges in 1936. In decades past, tourist shops near the Sponge Docks marketed items such as sponges, shells, curios, and Greek vases. (Photograph by Burgert Brothers, courtesy of the Tampa-Hillsborough County Public Library System.)

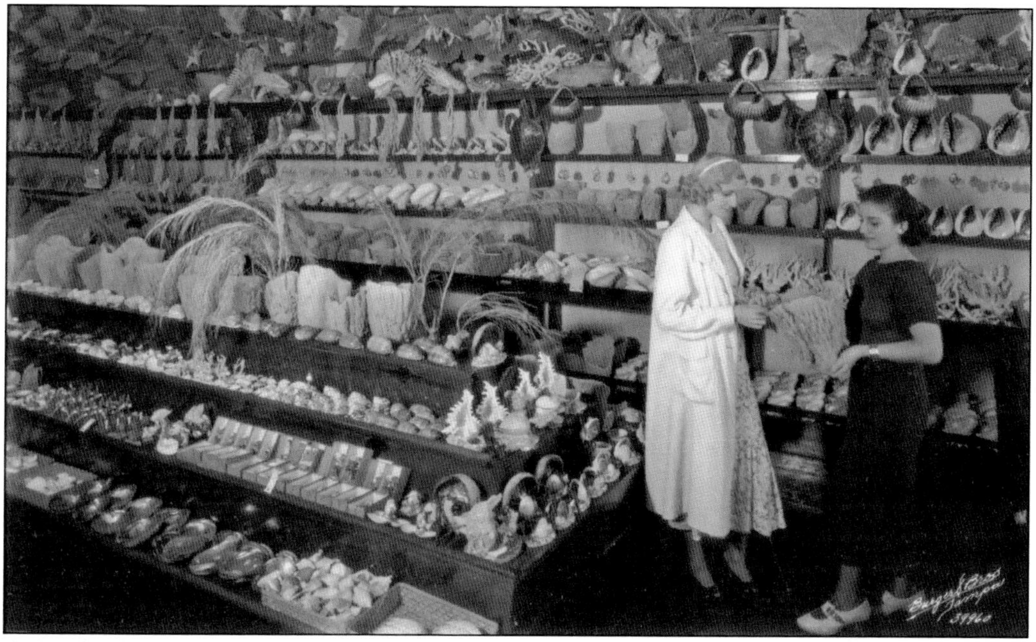

A Greek saleswoman explains the properties of a vase sponge inside a tourist store near the Sponge Docks in 1936. Shops very similar to this one remain today. (Photograph by Burgert Brothers, courtesy of the Tampa-Hillsborough County Public Library System.)

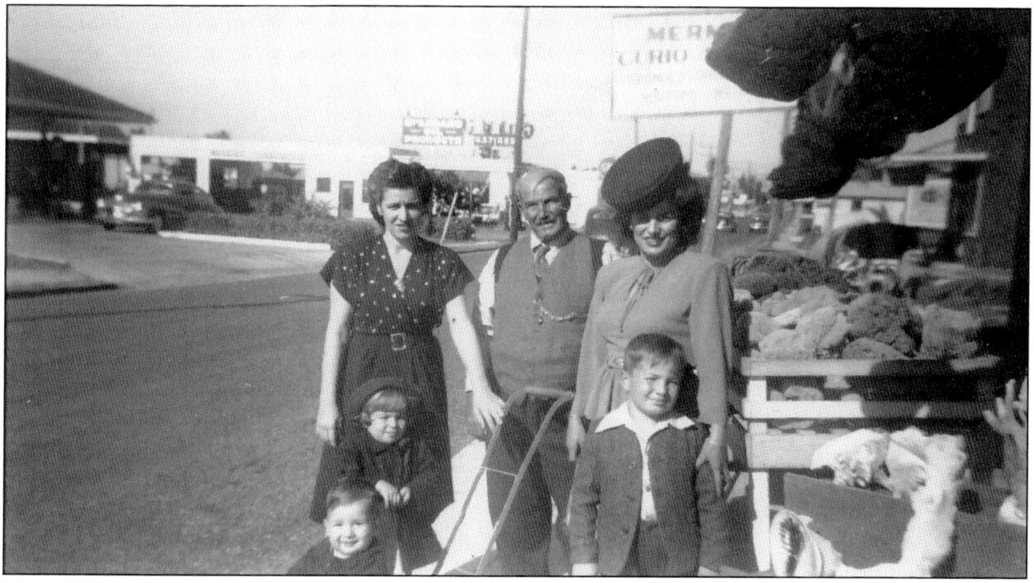

Outside their gift store on Pinellas Avenue in 1948 are, from left to right, children Costas Pappas and Fanitsa and Theodosios Frantzis and adults Katherine Esfakis Pappas, her father-in-law Costas George Pappas, and her sister-in-law Zula Pappas Frantzis. Katherine was raised in the Greek community of the Bahamas, which has maintained close personal and commercial ties with Tarpon Springs Greeks for the last century. She moved to Tarpon Springs and married George Pappas. His father, Costas, was nicknamed "the Iron Man" because he was the diver who would stay down the longest. He and his three brothers arrived with the original 500 spongers in 1905. (Courtesy of Joyce Pappas.)

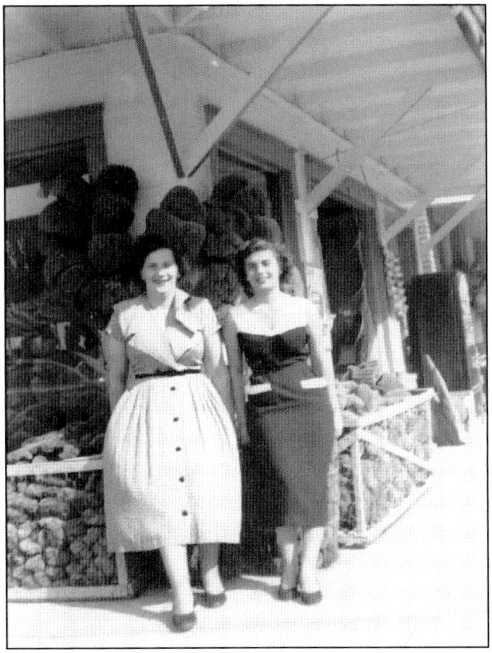

Sylvia Billiris (left) owned the gift shop where Anna Smolios Kouskoutis Ioannidis (right) worked in the 1950s. With the decline of the sponge business in the late 1940s and early 1950s, tourism based on Greek culture and the sponge industry became the biggest source of income for Tarpon Springs. (Courtesy of Eleni Christopoulos-Lekkas.)

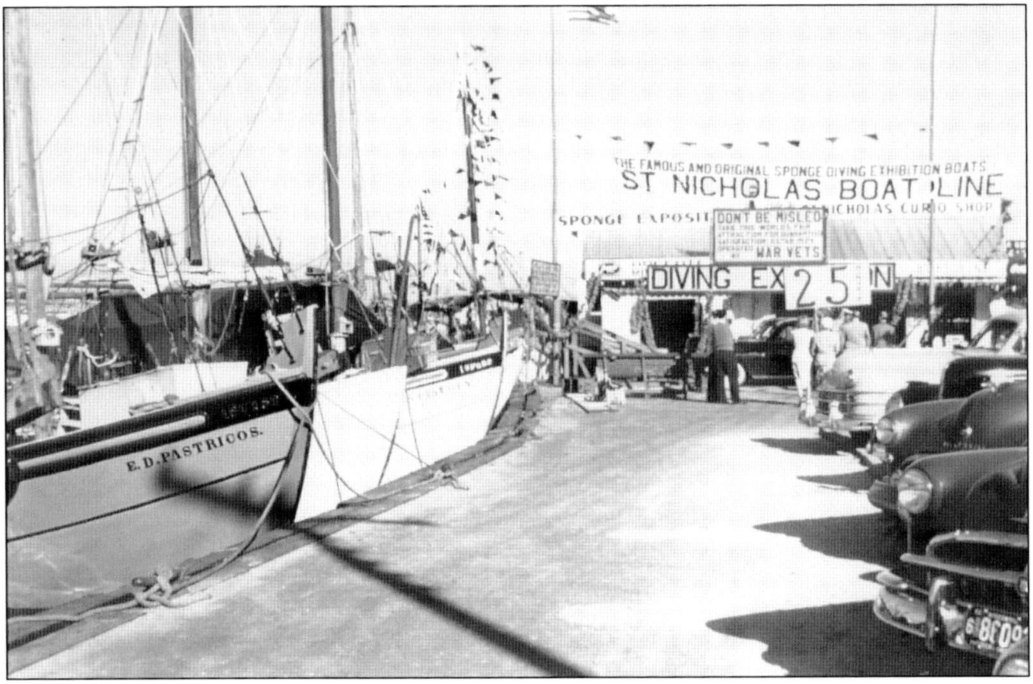

In 1924, the Billiris family created one of the early sponge industry attractions. St. Nicholas Boat Line Sponge Diving Exhibition still functions as a cruise up the Anclote River from the Sponge Docks that incorporates an exhibition of hard hat diving. The family started the business because weather prevented the divers from working during the winter, when the tourists visited. But even during the off-season, the captain was responsible for the well-being of his crews and their families. This 1950s image shows the entrance to St. Nicholas Boat Line at the end of the Sponge Docks on Dodecanese Avenue. (Courtesy of State Archives of Florida, Florida Memory.)

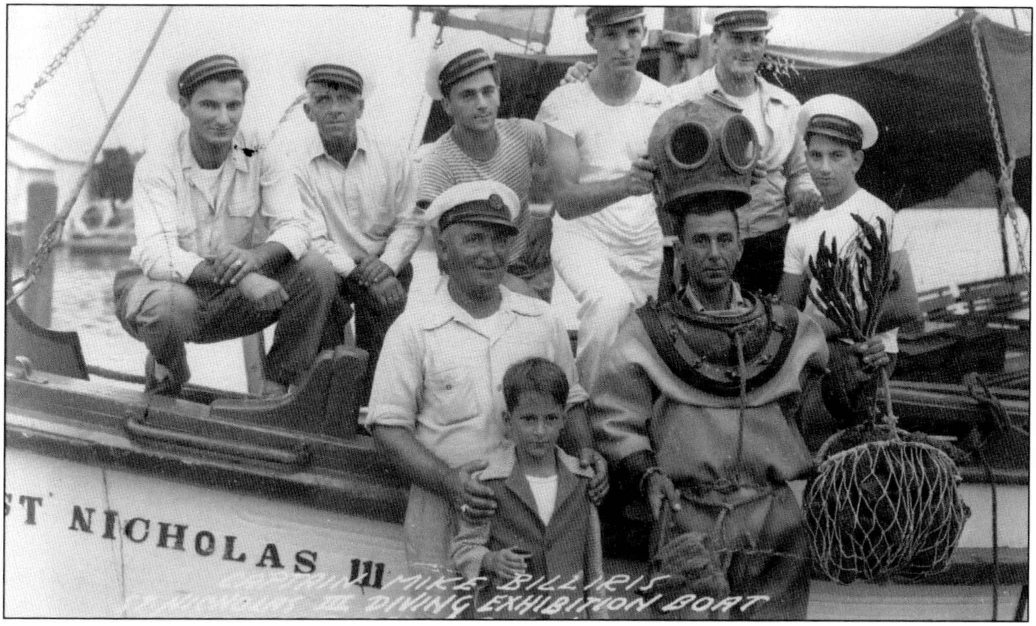

The crew of the tourist boat *St. Nicholas III* poses for a photograph. From left to right are (on the dock) Capt. Michael J. Billiris, Angelo V. Billiris, and unidentified; (on the boat) George M. Billiris, Theodore J. Billiris, unidentified, Ted M. Billiris, John M. Billiris, and Mike E. Tsongranis. The St. Nicholas Boat Line often employed younger divers and crew during the winter tourist season and older divers during the summer when sponging was at its best. Thus, tourism became an important local economic strategy. (Courtesy of Eleni Christopoulos-Lekkas.)

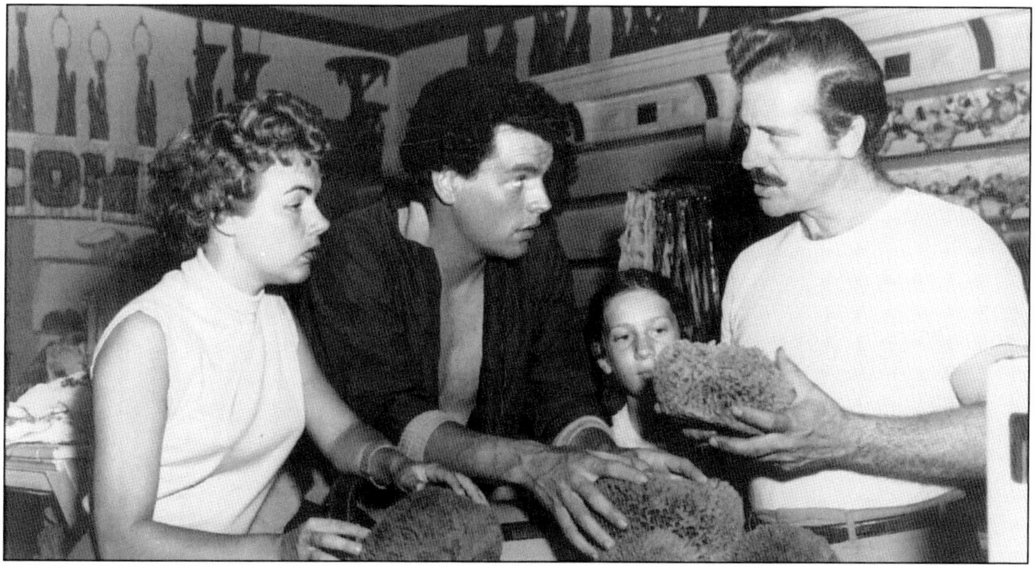

While in Tarpon Springs to film *Beneath the 12-Mile Reef* (1953), Terry Moore (left) and Robert Wagner (second from left) talk with John Gonatos in his family's Olympic tourist shop. Gonatos plays a Conch sponger in *Beneath the 12-Mile Reef*, appears in diving scenes for *16 Fathoms Deep*, acts in several other Hollywood films (including two directed by his friend Elia Kazan), and also gave diving lessons to Lloyd Bridges before he filmed the television series *Sea Hunt*. (Courtesy of Dr. Themistocles J. Diamandis.)

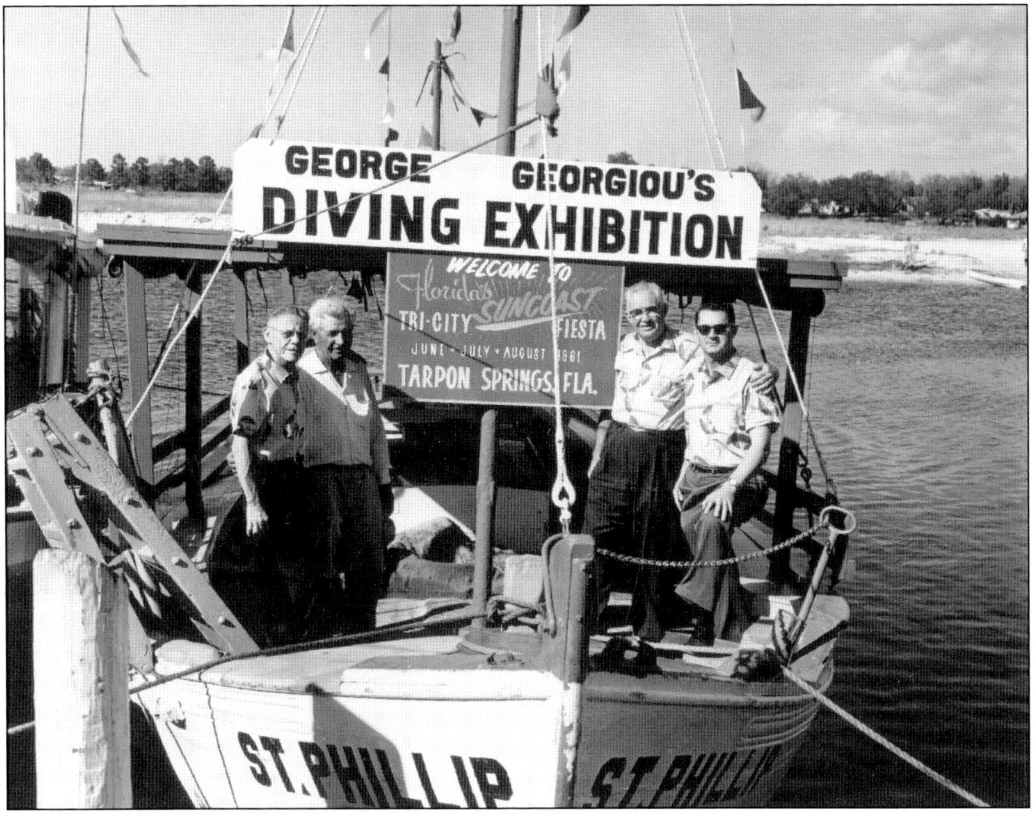

Four men are pictured aboard George Georgiou's Diving Exhibition boat at the Tri-City Suncoast Fiesta in 1961. John Georgiou operated his first sponge boat, the *Plastiras*, from 1947 to 1952. He then began to charter his second boat, the *Aspasia*, and gave sponge diving exhibitions with the *Plastiras* while the *Aspasia* was in the Gulf. His son George later became involved in the family business. (Photograph by Jim Stokes, courtesy of State Archives of Florida, Florida Memory.)

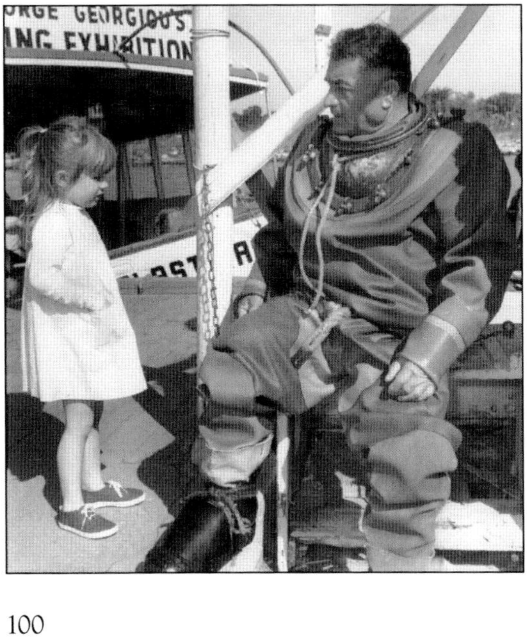

Mike Renios is suited up for George Georgiou's Diving Exhibition on the *Plastiras* on February 10, 1969. The tourist exhibition boats often provided employment for divers in the off-season or for those who were not able to spend weeks out in the Gulf of Mexico. (Courtesy of the *Tampa Tribune*.)

Six

Family Life and Diversions

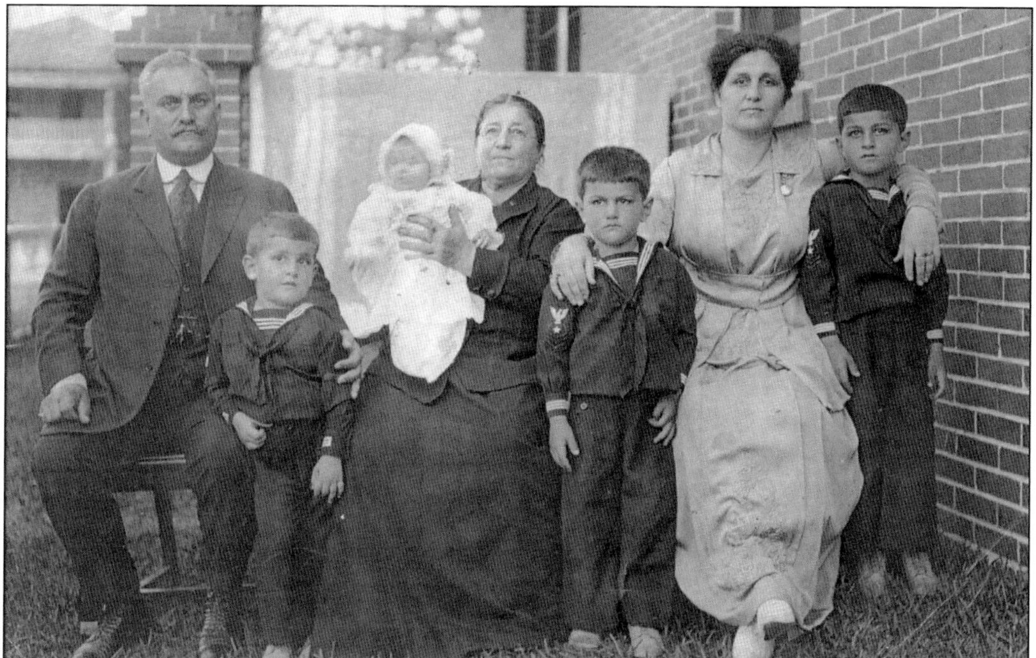

The Alissandratos family gathers together outside their home in 1920. From left to right are Demosthenes, Tako, baby Katherine, Athena Kamvisis (mother of Asimoula), Andrew, Asimoula, and Alexander. The Alissandratos family has remained in the same house on Tarpon Avenue since it was built in 1916. Katherine attended college, then taught at Tarpon Springs High School, where she met her future husband, music teacher Henry Kelly. (Courtesy of Katherine Alissandratos Kelly.)

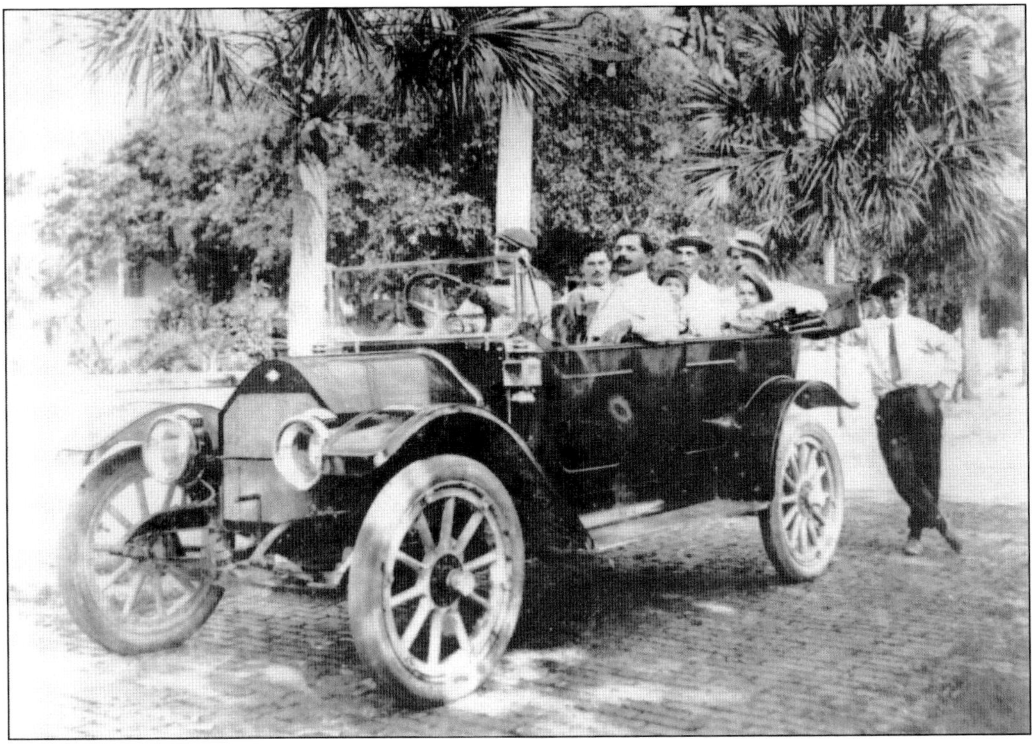

On a beautiful day in 1924, the Tulumaris family is ready to venture out for a drive in their car. Before strip malls and extensive development, Tarpon Springs was considered a place of great natural beauty, attracting artists and wealthy snowbirds in the winter. (Courtesy of the City of Tarpon Springs.)

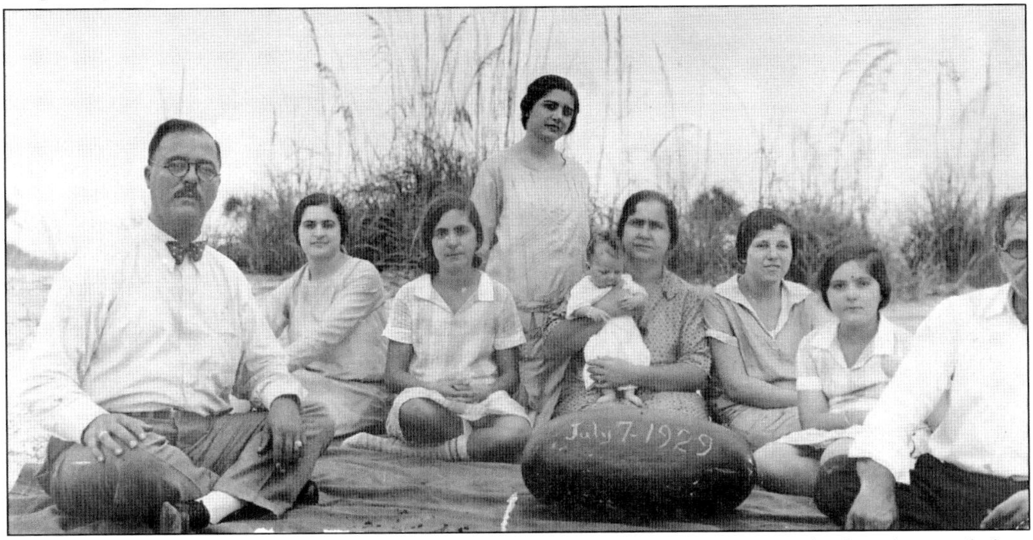

The Angel (originally Angeliniadis) family often had holiday picnics on the beach—and they remember them today with great fondness. This one took place on July 7, 1929—the date carved in the watermelon. From left to right are George Angel, unidentified, Katina Angel, Cleo Kapitanis, Themelina Alahouzos Angel holding baby Mikelo Kapetanis, Kaliope Alahouzos Kapetanis, Maria Angel, and George Kapetanis. (Courtesy of George Mandalou.)

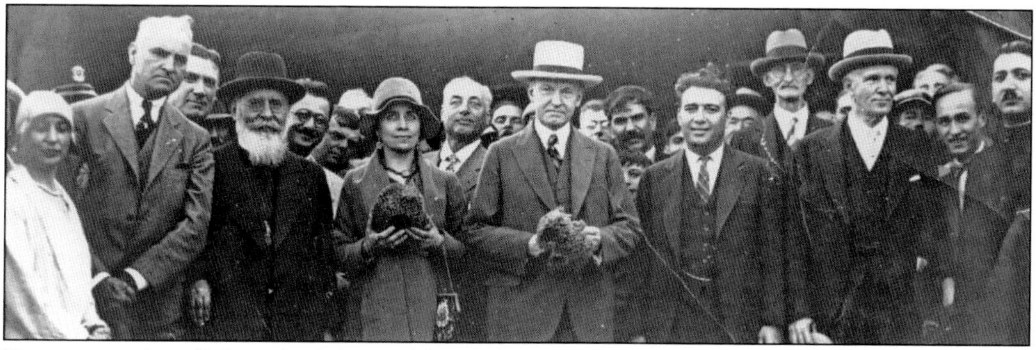

Former president Calvin Coolidge and first lady Grace Coolidge (center) visit Tarpon Springs in January 1930, shortly after his presidency and only three years before he died of a heart attack. Not only are the Coolidges seen here with souvenir sponges in hand, but they also boarded a sponge boat. Many Tarponites, including members of the Greek community, are seen accompanying the couple. (Courtesy of the Tarpon Springs Area Historical Society.)

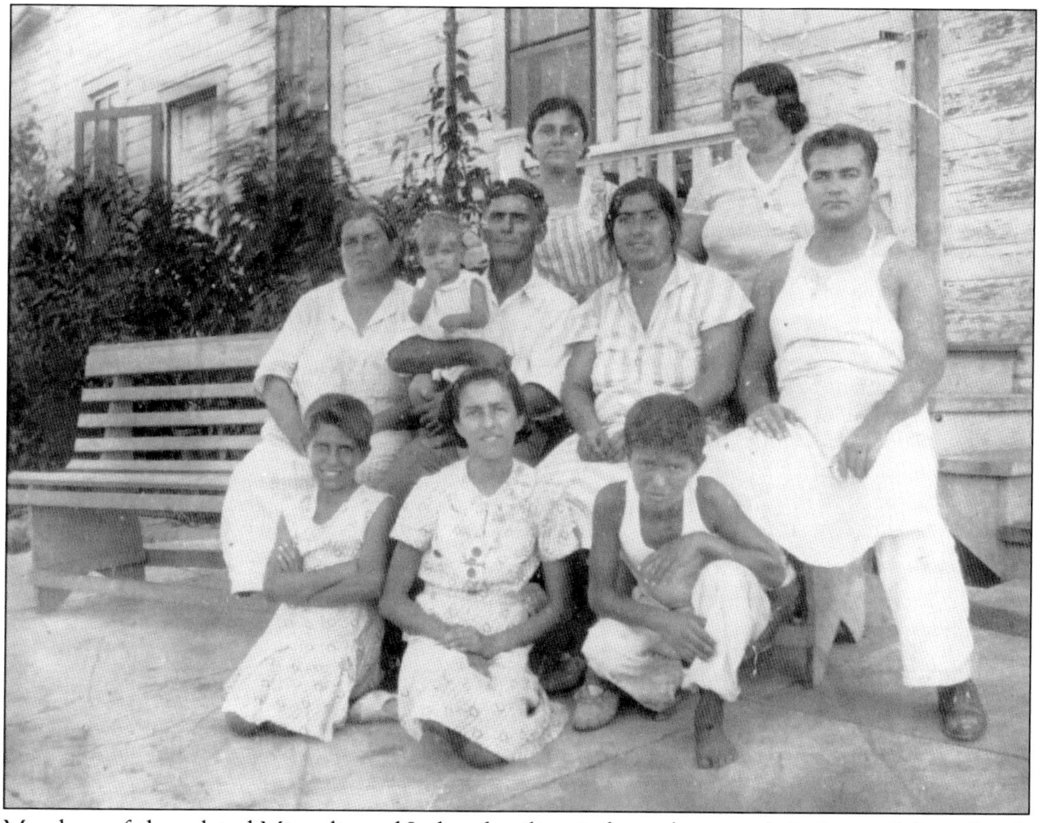

Members of the related Miaoulis and Lulias families sit for a photograph in front of their Greek American Bakery in the 1940s. From left to right are (first row) Kaliope Manias Lulias, Irene Manias Lelekis, and Nick Manias; (second row) Evdokia Manias, Nikitas Manias holding Evelyn Miaoulis Bilirakis, Maria Manias Miaoulis, and Kosta Miaoulis; (third row) Irene Koulianos and Kalotina Zervos. (Courtesy of Evelyn Miaoulis Bilirakis.)

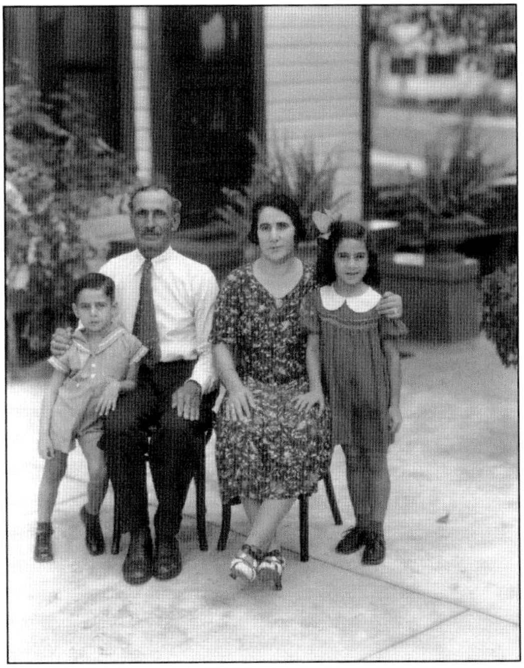

The family of a sponge fisherman poses for a photograph in front of their home on November 16, 1936. Although the talented Burgert Brothers photographers from Tampa found intriguing subjects in Tarpon Springs, they did not always record the names of those they photographed. (Photograph by Burgert Brothers, courtesy of the Tampa-Hillsborough County Public Library System.)

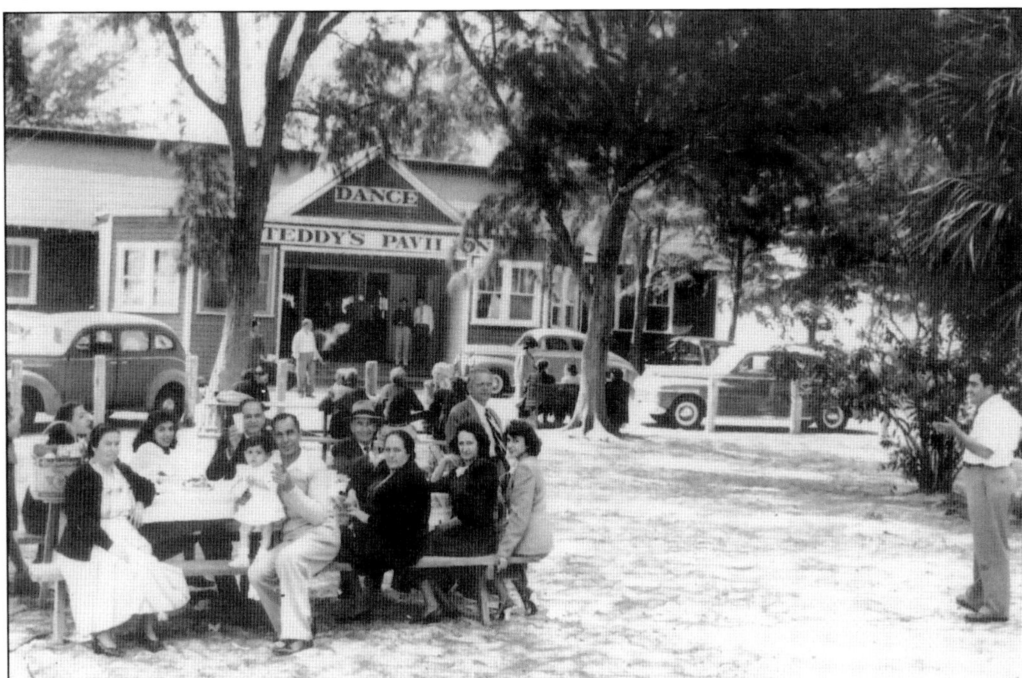

Family and friends, including members of the Tsalichis, Mastorides, and Megaloudis families, gather at a picnic table outside Teddy's Pavilion on Sunset Beach in the 1940s. For many years, Teddy's Pavilion was a popular local establishment for entertainment and social gatherings, with both open-air and enclosed spaces. A jitney ran from town to the pier, and many would go to swim and have picnics. Bands played for evening events or wedding receptions and baptisms, and there was also a jukebox inside. (Courtesy of Goldie Tsalichis Parr.)

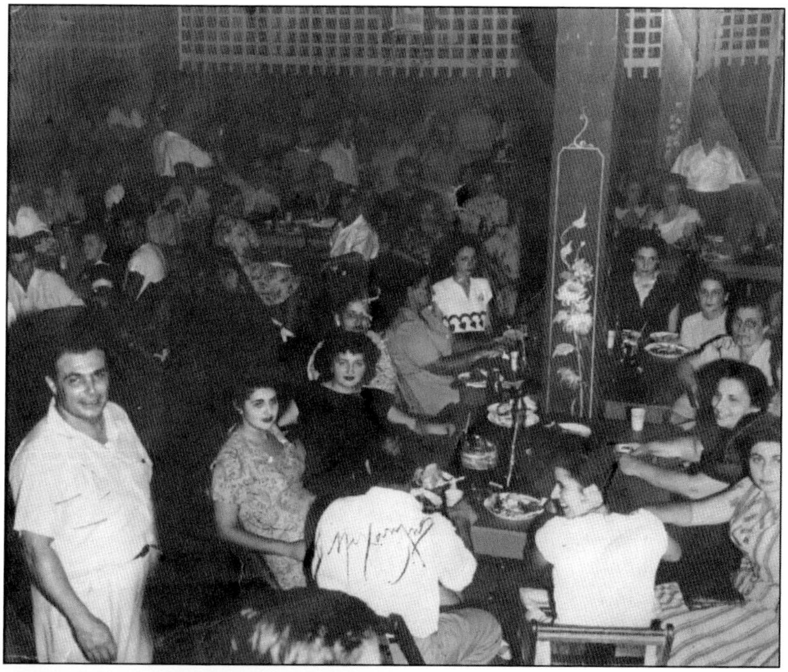

A large crowd gathers inside Teddy's Pavilion for a festive occasion at Sunset Beach in the 1940s. George Pappas stands in the left foreground. (Courtesy of Joyce Pappas.)

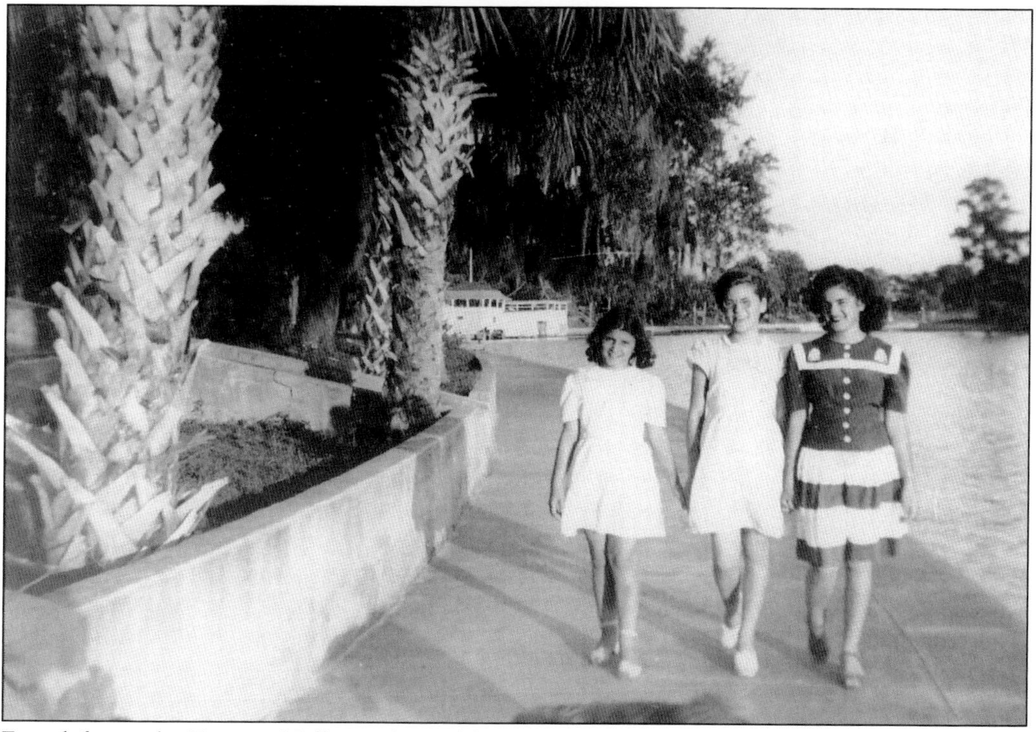

From left to right, Frances, Nellie, and Magdaline Peronis stroll around Spring Bayou on a beautiful spring day in the 1940s. Nellie and Magdaline married the Tiliakos brothers, who were shrimp boat builders in Fernandina Beach, and Frances moved to Indiana—but none of the sisters forgot their family and friends in Tarpon Springs. (Courtesy of Magdaline Peronis Tiliakos and Nellie Peronis Tiliakos.)

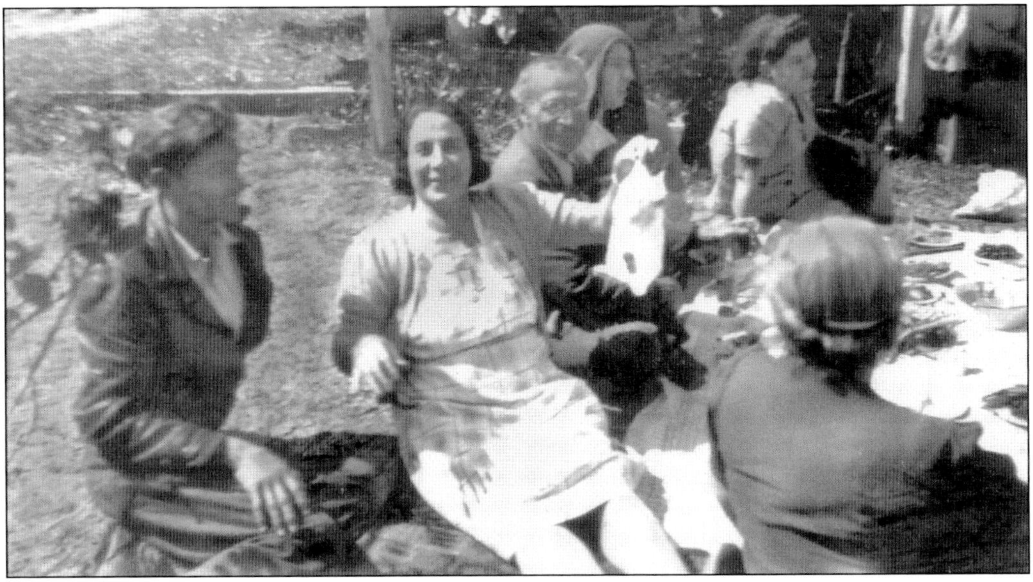

The Tsalichis family enjoys a picnic on Kathara Deftera/Καθαρά Δευτέρα (Clean Monday) in 1941. Anna Karagiannis Kotis looks surprised and perplexed because her nephew Michael Tsalichis (left) has just handed her a live rabbit. Kathara Deftera is the first day of Great Lent at the beginning of the seventh week before Easter. It is a day to make a new beginning spiritually by observing the Lenten fast in which the faithful abstain from meat, dairy, oil, and other foods. It is not a somber day, but instead is celebrated with outdoor picnics, flying kites, merriment, and delicious Lenten dishes. (Courtesy of Goldie Tsalichis Parr.)

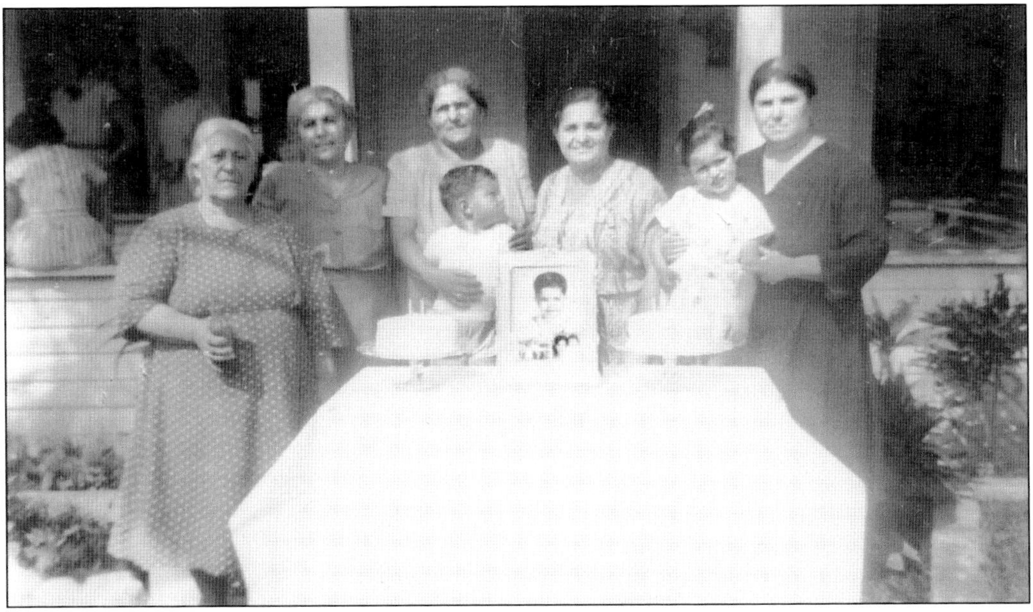

There is a birthday party in progress among a group of friends and neighbors on Mill Street, near Athens Street, in the 1940s. Standing around two cakes and a photograph of birthday boy Jack Gombos are, from left to right, Maria Athanason, Sevasti Georgiadis, Nikki Ergas holding Michael Kouremetis, Maria Fotakis, and Maria Karavokiros holding Nancy Miradakis. (Courtesy of Nickollet Tsourakis Henderson.)

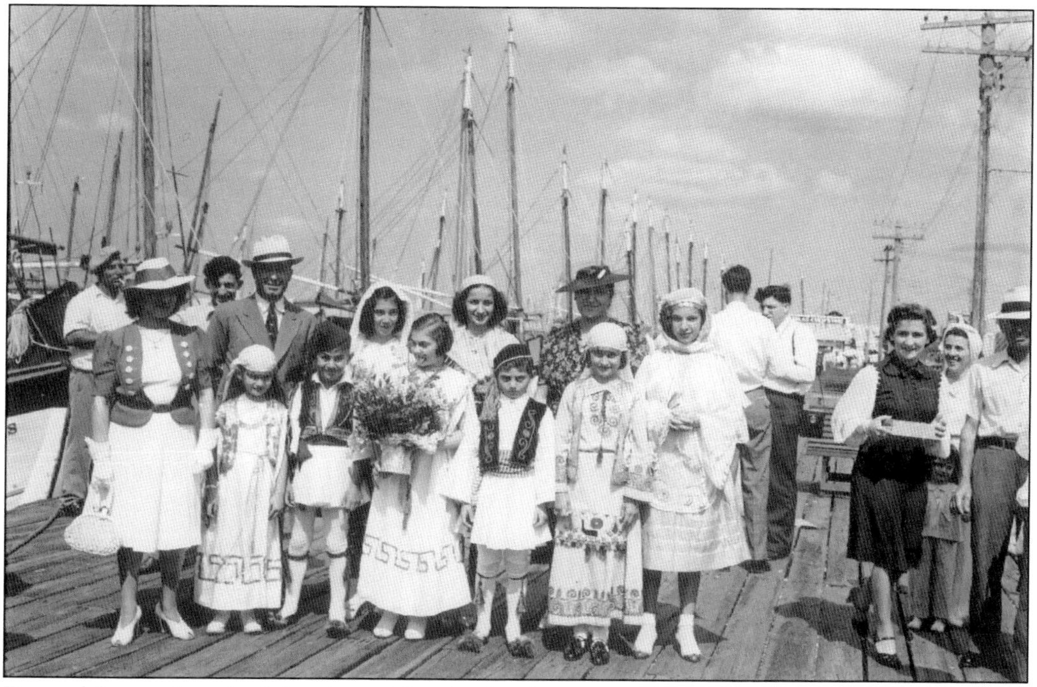

Dressed for a cultural celebration, a Greek school group poses on the Sponge Docks during the 1940s. The two sponge divers at left behind them are Emmanuel Mehas (left) and John Maillis. Those identified in the first row are teacher Irene Giannaras (left), Kalliope Simeon (fourth from right), Nick Faklis (third from right), and Mary Stavropoulos (right); in the second row are, from left to right, Theodore Frantzis, Fanny Ipsilantis, Irene Tittas, and teacher Fanny Alahouzos. The woman at right in the scarf is Nikki Pandakos, with her young daughter Alice. (Photograph by Robertson and Fresh, courtesy of Special Collections Department, Tampa Library, University of South Florida.)

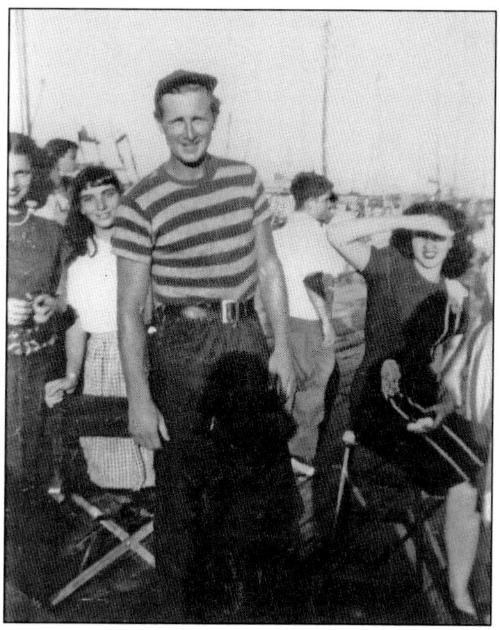

Actor Lloyd Bridges poses with townspeople at the Sponge Docks during the filming of *16 Fathoms Deep* (1948) in Tarpon Springs. During the late 1940s and early 1950s, both this film and *Beneath the 12-Mile Reef* (1953) created a romantic aura around the sponge industry and publicized Tarpon Springs. Since parts of the films were shot in Tarpon Springs, locals sometimes worked as extras, and they often visited the Sponge Docks area to watch the filming. (Courtesy of Nellie Peronis Tiliakos and Magdaline Peronis Tiliakos.)

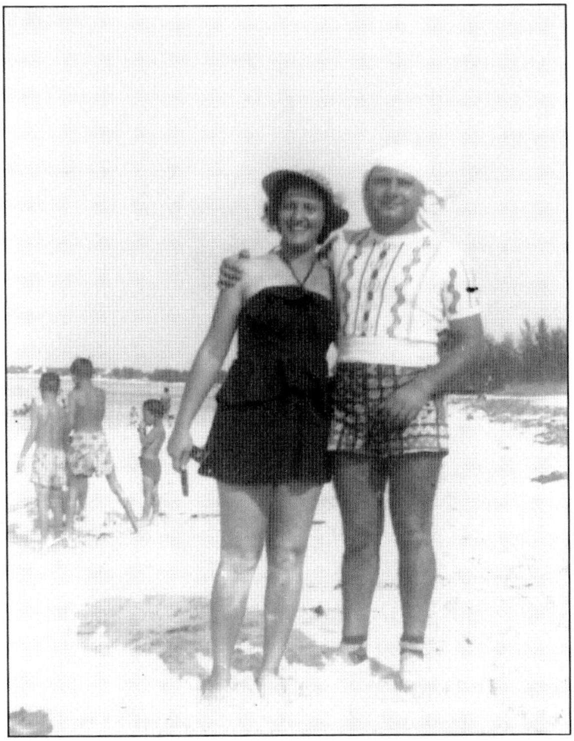

Duchess Giallourakis Arfaras and Michel Arfaras enjoy the beach on their honeymoon in 1951. The Giallourakis family was involved in the sponge industry, and it was through them that Duchess was introduced to her future husband, Tunisian Greek sponge merchant Arfaras. She became very involved in local business activities, owned Duchess Curio Shop, and served as president of the Sponge Merchants Association. (Courtesy of Duchess Giallourakis Arfaras.)

During the filming of *Beneath the 12-Mile Reef* (1953), the sponge boat *Eleni* was painted to look as though it had been burned by the rival Key West Conch sponge fishermen. After the filming ended, the boat was restored to its original condition. Nickolas Lerios is at the back—he worked as a stunt diver for the production. (Courtesy of Kaliope Lerios George.)

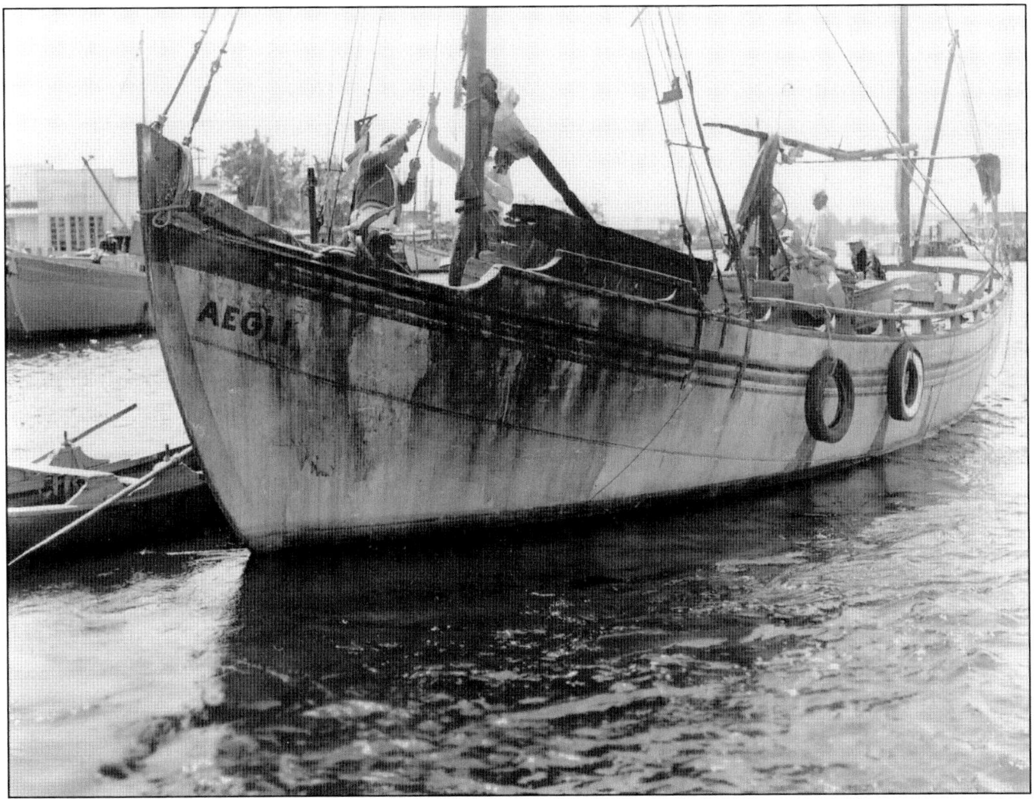

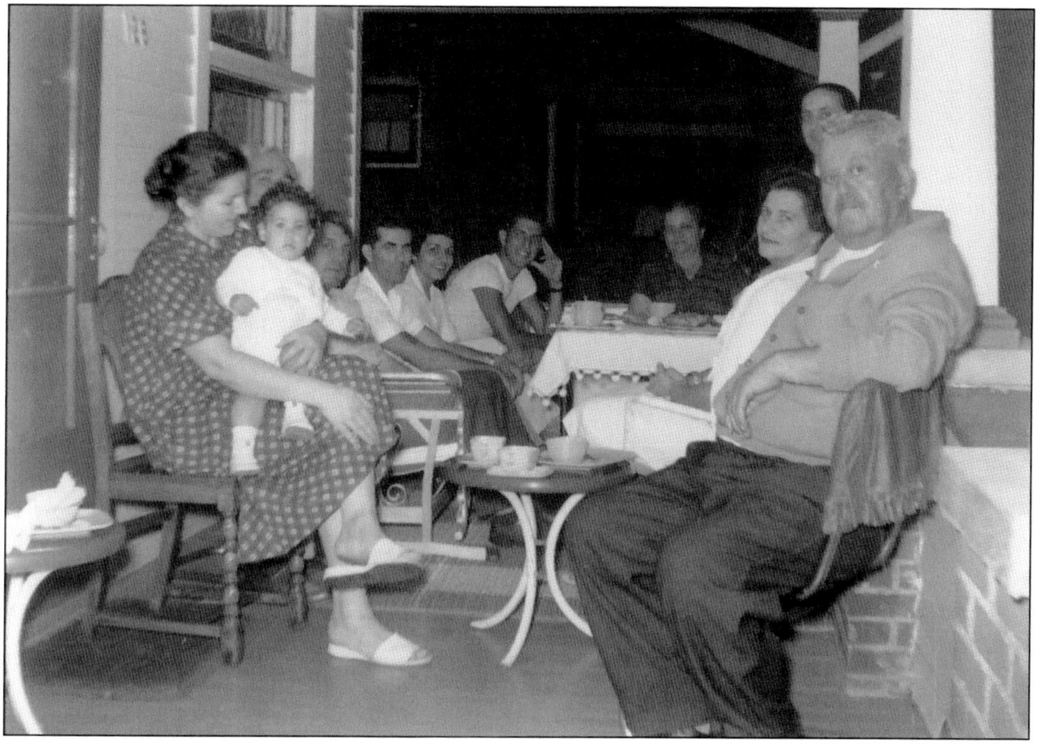

Family and friends enjoy the evening breezes on their porch in August 1958. The woman at left with a child on her lap is Sophie Pavlos Tsongranis, the wife of the Reverend Father George Tsongranis. At right, Sylvia Billiris sits behind the unidentified man in front, and standing behind her is Nellie Pavlos, the sister of Sophie. Before air-conditioning became widespread in Florida during the 1960s, people frequently gathered on their porches to enjoy companionship and the relative coolness of the evening. Most of the houses in the Greektown area were built with front porches that facilitated this kind of social gathering. (Courtesy of Eleni Christopoulos-Lekkas.)

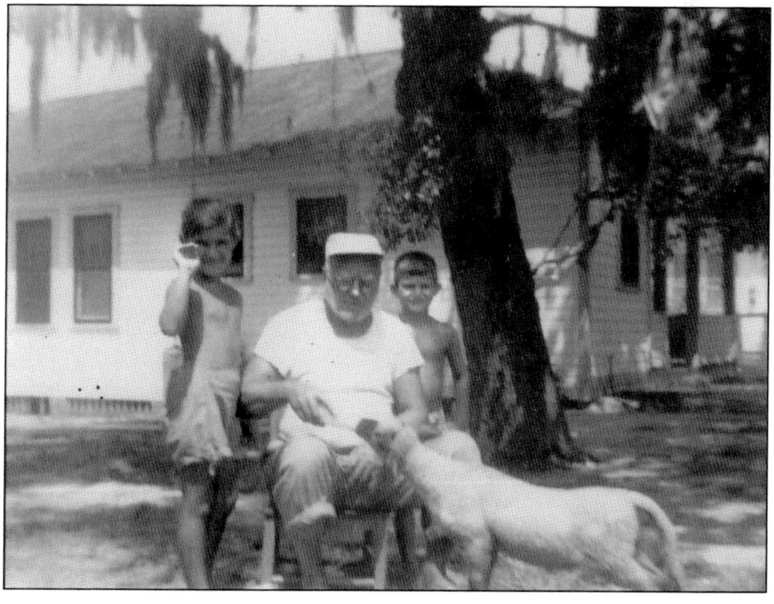

Jordan Kindinis and his grandchildren Colleen and Jerry Kindinis feed their pet lamb, Kitso, on Hope Street in 1960. Jordan, originally from Kalymnos, worked for many years on sponge boats as a lifeline tender and a cook. (Photograph by Flash Jarocki, courtesy of Colleen Kindinis.)

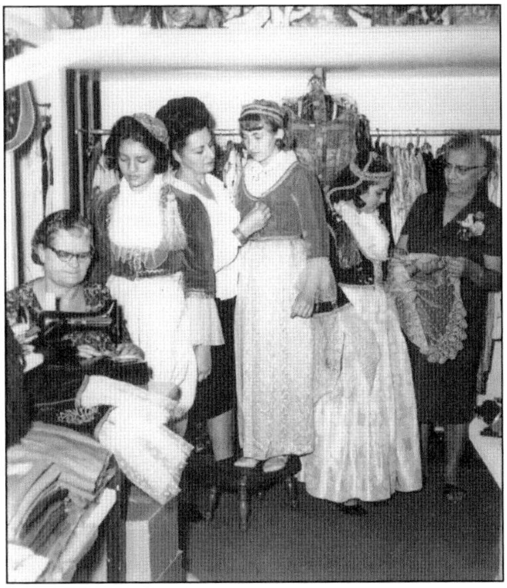

Greek girls traditionally learned needlework to make clothing or linens for their dowry. Few create these beautiful items today, but some local needlework experts create regional dress with intricate details for dance groups or community events. Those working on Epiphany costumes in 1965 are, from left to right, seamstresses Katina Dede, Bertha Houllis, and Flora Pappas and girls Irene Arfaras, Maguerite Smirlis, and Olympia Pappas. (Photograph by Flash Janarcki, courtesy of the Tarpon Springs Area Historical Society.)

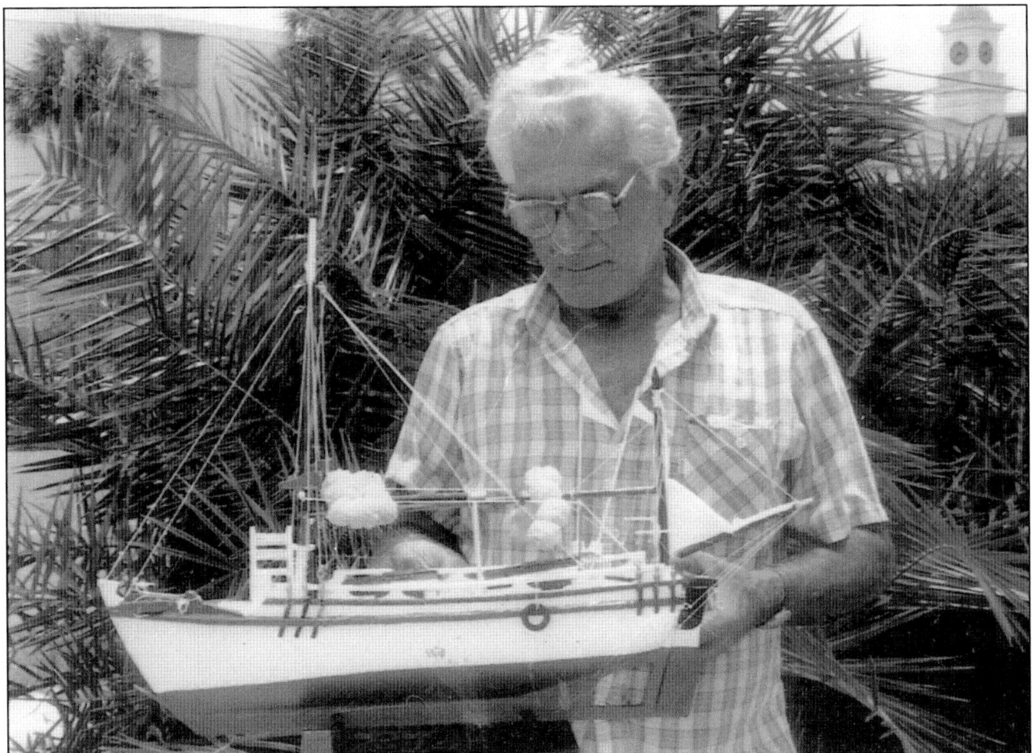

The son of a diver and hook boat captain, Costa John Tsataros (1926–2001) also became a sponge diver. While at sea, he often whittled, creating beautiful sponge boats from blocks of wood. Today, his sons John and Steve continue his father's tradition. It was not uncommon for the men who built or worked on the sponge boats to make elaborate model boats in their leisure time. Most models are exact replicas, produced in much the same way as real boats. They often painted them white like working sponge boats, with a few red, black, and/or yellow horizontal stripes along the sides or with a black base and blue trim. (Courtesy of the City of Tarpon Springs.)

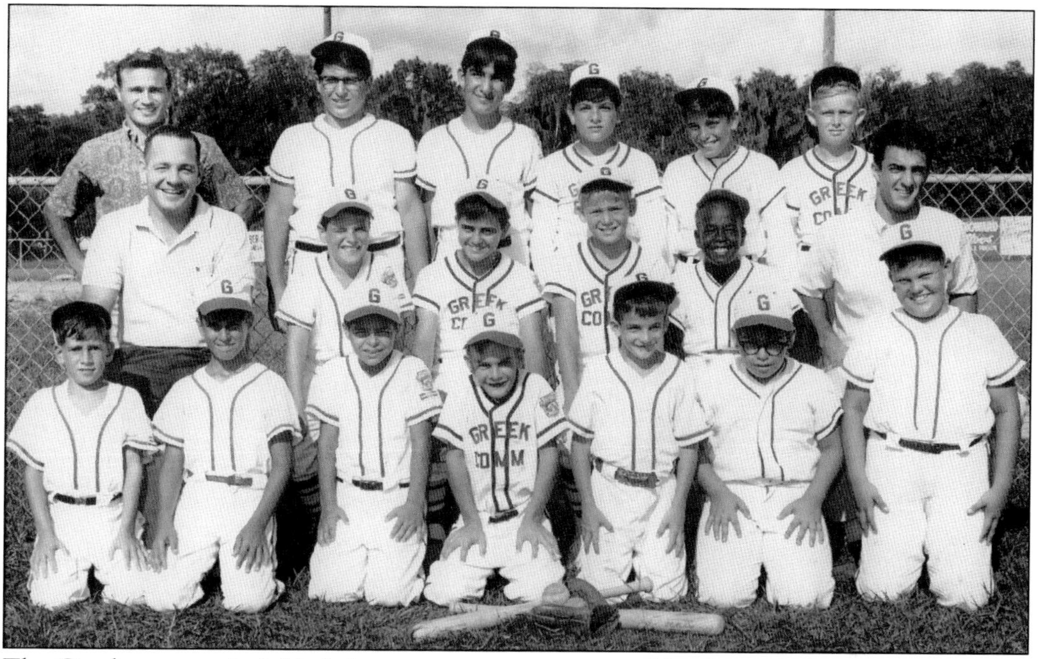

The Greek community's Little League team was sponsored by St. Nicholas Greek Orthodox Cathedral. The 1966 team photograph includes, from left to right, (first row) Theo Karaphillis, Nick Karaphillis, Nick Faklis, Cam Gause, Garrett Gause, George Lontakos, and Steve Koulias; (second row) coach Mike Theodosis, David Dagenhardt, Wade Karakas, David Bartelt, Nelson Joaquin, and coach Peter Kolianos; (third row) unidentified, Nick Toth, Angelo Lontakos, Angelo Danapas, unidentified, and Ronnie Ammons. (Courtesy of Mary Lerios Toth.)

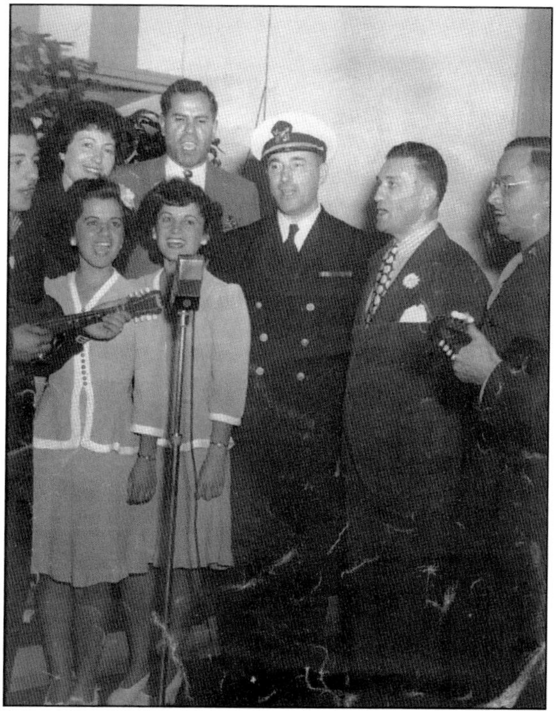

In 1939 and 1940, scholars from the WPA's Joint Committee on Folk Arts made 60 sound recordings in Tarpon Springs that preserved the musicians and music of the era. On August 25, 1939, Robert Cook, Stetson Kennedy, and Alton C. Morris recorded this group singing Greek songs. In the first row are high school students Katherine Kavouklis Arvanitis (left) and Maggie Kavouklis Nichols; those identified in the second row are Michael Kousaleous (left, playing mandolin), Michael Samarkos (third from left), and Michael Nicholis (second from right). (Courtesy of Maggie Kavouklis Nichols.)

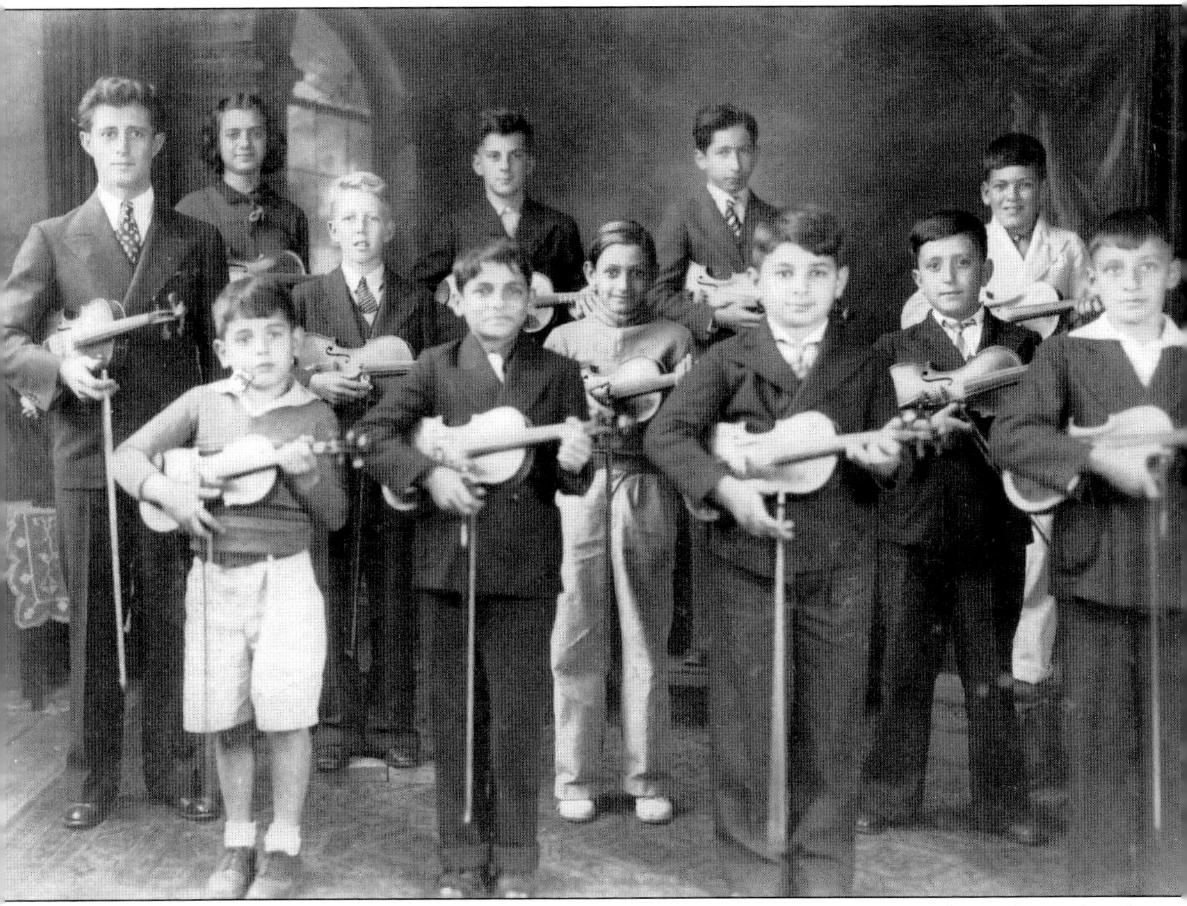

Sotirios "Sam" Bessis (far left), who studied at the University of Tampa, taught violin to local students. Taken around 1939, this images shows Bessis with some of his students, including Katherine Kavouklis Arvanitis (behind him) and, from left to right, (first row) unidentified, Mike Faklis, Mike Lontakos, and unidentified; (second row) unidentified, Mike Tsalichis, and Steve Kotis; (third row) unidentified, Pete Krouskos, and Andrew Malisses. (Courtesy of Goldie Tsalichis Parr.)

Helen Samarkos Tsoukalas was elected Miss Calymnos in 1953. She is wearing the traditional woman's dress for the island of Kalymnos, called a *kavadi*. It usually consists of a robe-like silk dress over a white underdress and tied with a multicolored belt. On her head, she wears a *tsemberi* (head scarf). (Courtesy of Anna Tsoukalas Billiris.)

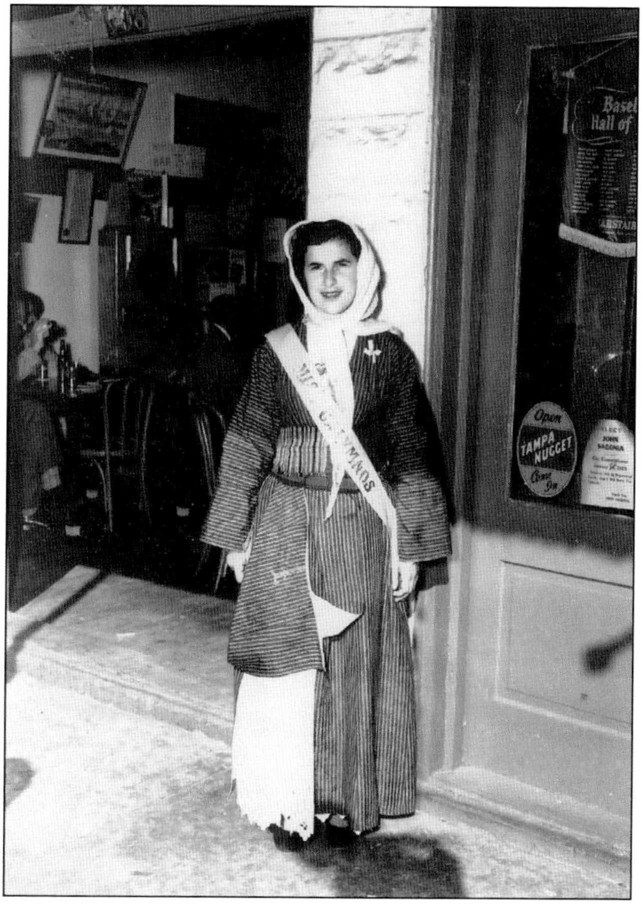

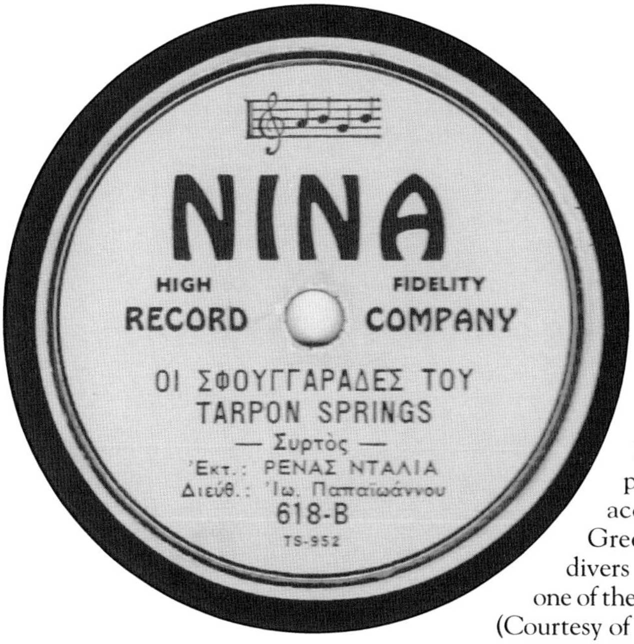

"Οι Σφουγγαραδες Του Tarpon Springs" ("The Sponge Divers of Tarpon Springs"), produced by Nina Records around 1955, was written by Greek music great Ioannis Papaioannou. It is performed by popular vocalist Rena Dalia, who is accompanied by Papaioannou. Many Greek songs were written about sponge divers and the sponge business, but this is one of the few specifically about Tarpon Springs. (Courtesy of Meletios Pouliopoulos.)

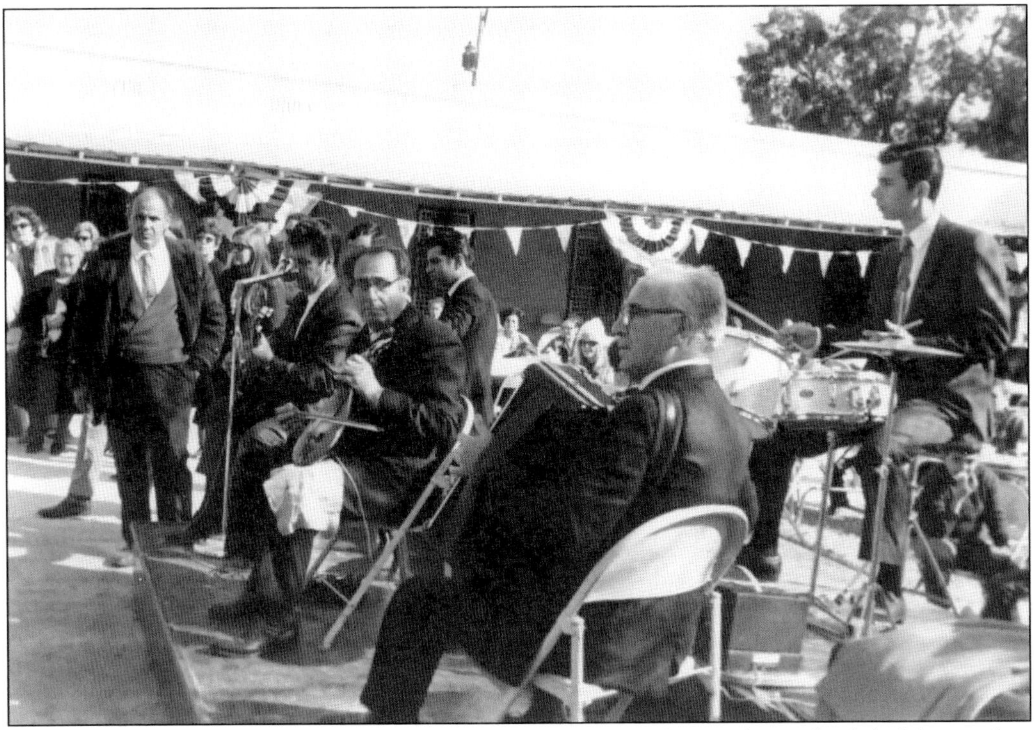

John K. Gianaros (1904–1998) plays accordion with a band at the Epiphany *glendi* (celebration) in the Sponge Exchange, possibly during the early 1960s. Another band member is Pete Keramides, on bouzouki. For almost 40 years, Gianaros performed with bands in California, Miami, New York, and elsewhere at parties, hotels, and *cafés aman* (Greek clubs). From the 1930s to the 1950s, he regularly recorded with Liberty, Kalos Diskos, Metropolitan, and Mastertone labels. After retirement, he continued to perform traditional music and his own compositions in Tarpon Springs. Gianaros received a 1994 Florida Folk Heritage Award. (Courtesy of the Tarpon Springs Area Historical Society.)

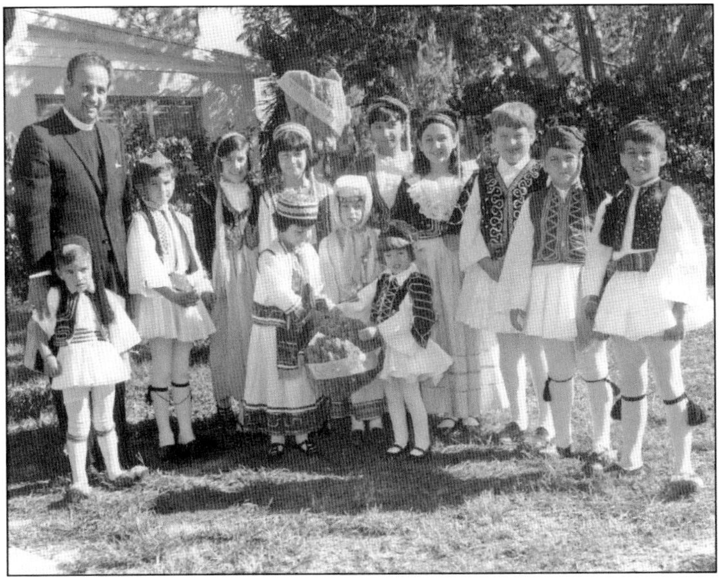

Members of a dance group wait with the Reverend Father Kalariotes to see vice presidential candidate Spiro Agnew on October 31, 1968. St. Nicholas Greek Orthodox Cathedral has long taught and sponsored Greek dance groups composed of church youth as part of its ministry. Such groups have demonstrated at local, national, and international events. (Photograph by Connie Standish, courtesy of the *Tampa Tribune*.)

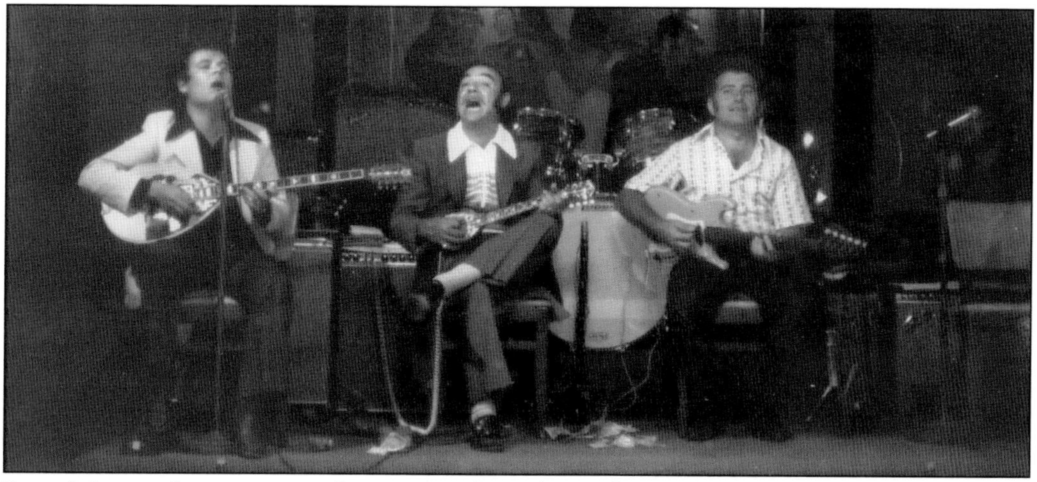

From left to right, musicians George Aggelopoulos on bouzouki, Dimitris "Jimmy" Tzaras on *baglamas*, Niko on drums, and Pete Patides on guitar perform at Zorba's on Athens Street in the 1970s. Zorba's was an important community entertainment institution from the 1960s until it was closed after a fire in 2015. Before it was christened Zorba's by Nicholas and Kalli Patides in 1969, it was called Port Said by owner Nick Dris. Over the years and through many owners, it was part of the national circuit of Greek clubs played by many outstanding musicians. (Courtesy of Eleni Christopoulos-Lekkas.)

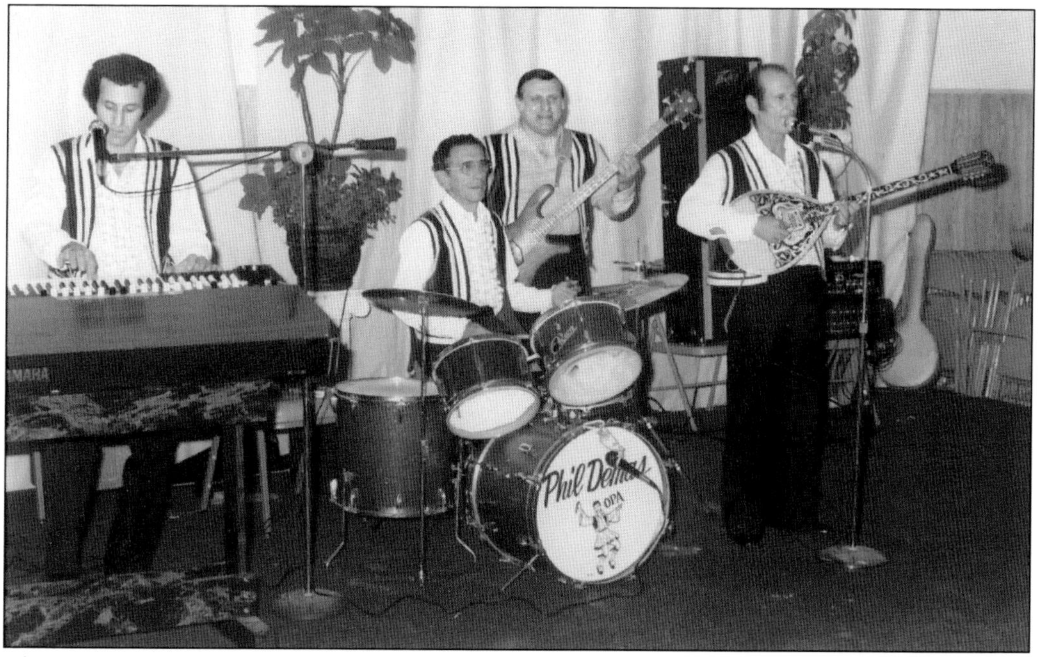

The Phil Demos Band includes, from left to right, Ted Tsangarinos on keyboard, Phil Demas on drums, an unidentified guitarist, and Spiro Skordilis on bouzouki. The band frequently played popular Greek music at community events in the late 1970s or early 1980s. Skordilis had been a popular musician and composer in Greece before he came to the United States, where he eventually settled in Tarpon Springs. The Greek community has always maintained regional, religious, and popular musical traditions performed by individuals and groups in homes, churches, clubs, and social organizations. (Courtesy of Kay Skordilis.)

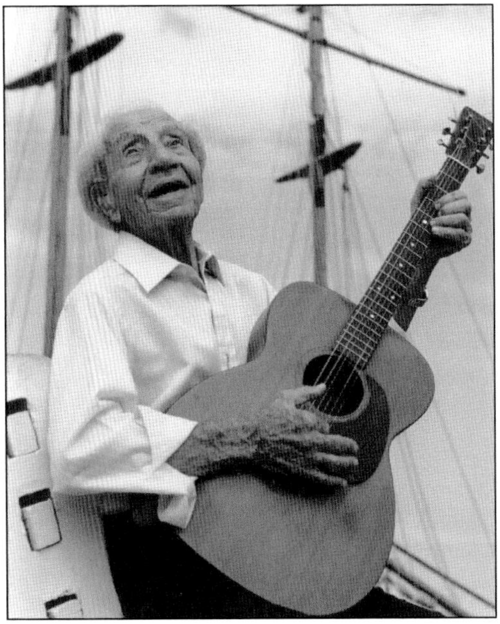

George Katsaros (1888–1997) was one of the most widely respected Greek musicians of the 20th century. Born on Amorgos, he arrived in New York in 1913. For more than 80 years, his strong voice and unique style were heard in Greek restaurants, ballrooms, hotels, clubs, concert halls, and ships throughout the United States. By the 1920s, he had become so popular that he signed contracts with major record companies and many of his compositions were favorites in Greece and diasporic communities. Katsaros was a longtime resident of Tarpon Springs, where he played at festivals and community events until the end of his life. (Courtesy of the City of Tarpon Springs.)

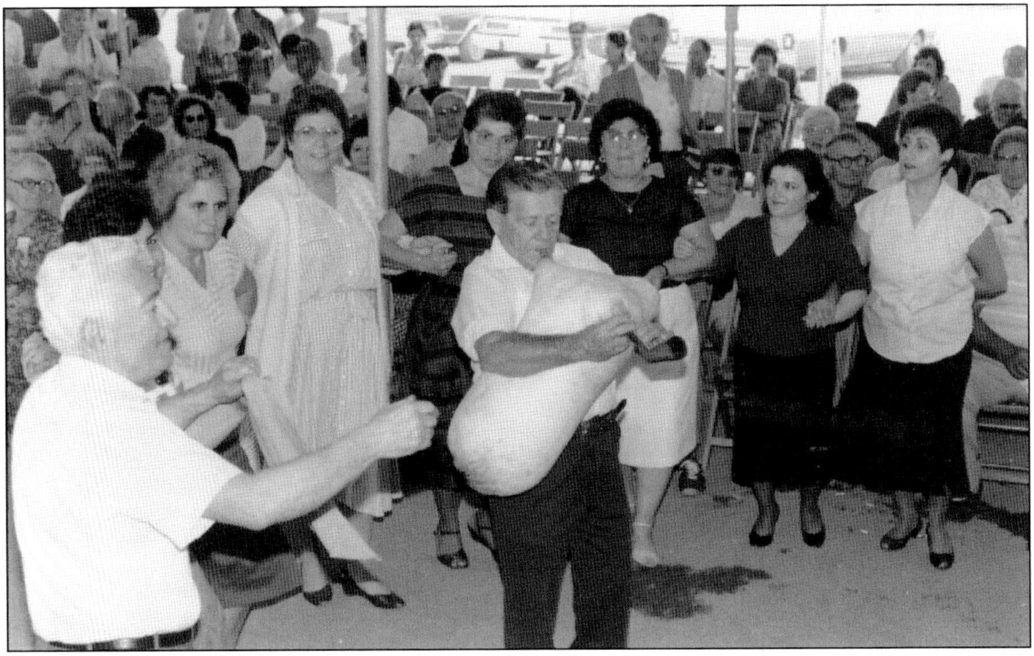

Nikitas Tsimouris (1924–2001) plays complex rhythm patterns on the *tsabouna*, a type of island bagpipe. Born on Kalymnos, he arrived in Tarpon Springs in 1968. Tsimouris worked on sponge boats, in restaurants and the stucco trade, and as custodian of St. Nicholas. He performed Kalymnian music for numerous family and community events, as well as the Florida Folk Festival. Family members, including his wife, Nomiki, and his sisters, Nomiki, Focaina, and Maria Elena, often sang and danced. Tsimouris received the National Heritage Fellowship in 1991. Dancers pictured include, from left to right, unidentified, Kaliope Saroukos, unidentified, Maria Pantelis, Popi Peppas, unidentified, Popi Saroukos, and Sevasti Skandaliavis. (Photograph by Scott Keeler, courtesy of the City of Tarpon Springs.)

Seven

RECENT TIMES

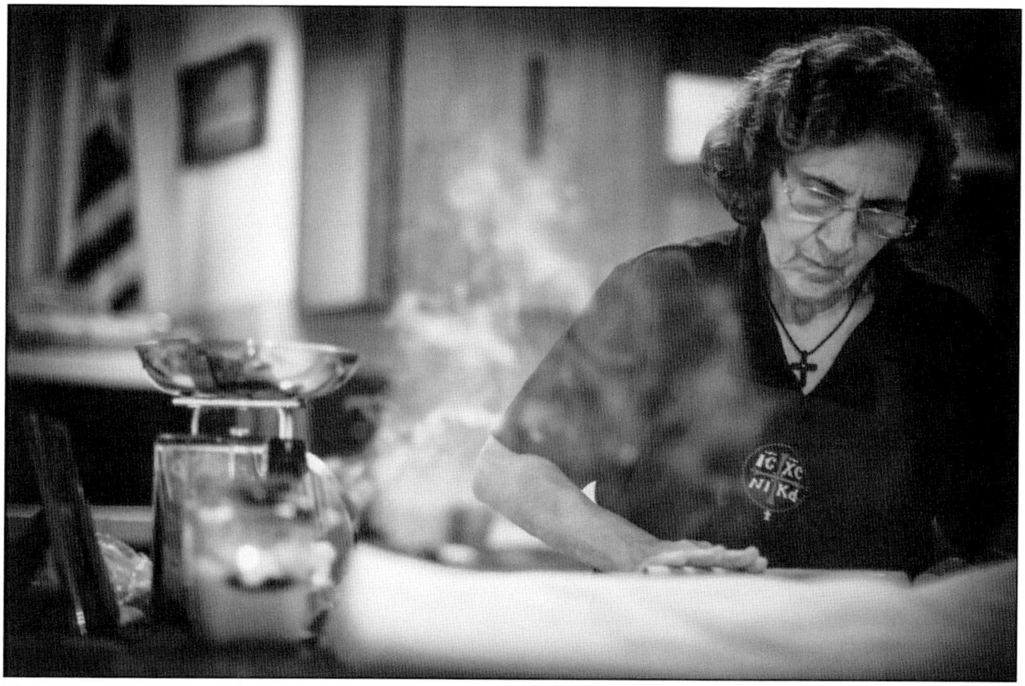

Katerina Zaronias is shown making *prosforo*, the bread used in Greek Orthodox services. Like the bread of earlier times, it is made with the simplest ingredients: flour, yeast, water, and salt. Each loaf is stamped with a *sfragida*, a wooden seal carved with religious symbols. Community women periodically bake and contribute prosforo as an offering to the church, along with wine, oil, and lists of the living and deceased for whom they wish to have prayers said. (Photograph by Eleni Christopoulos-Lekkas.)

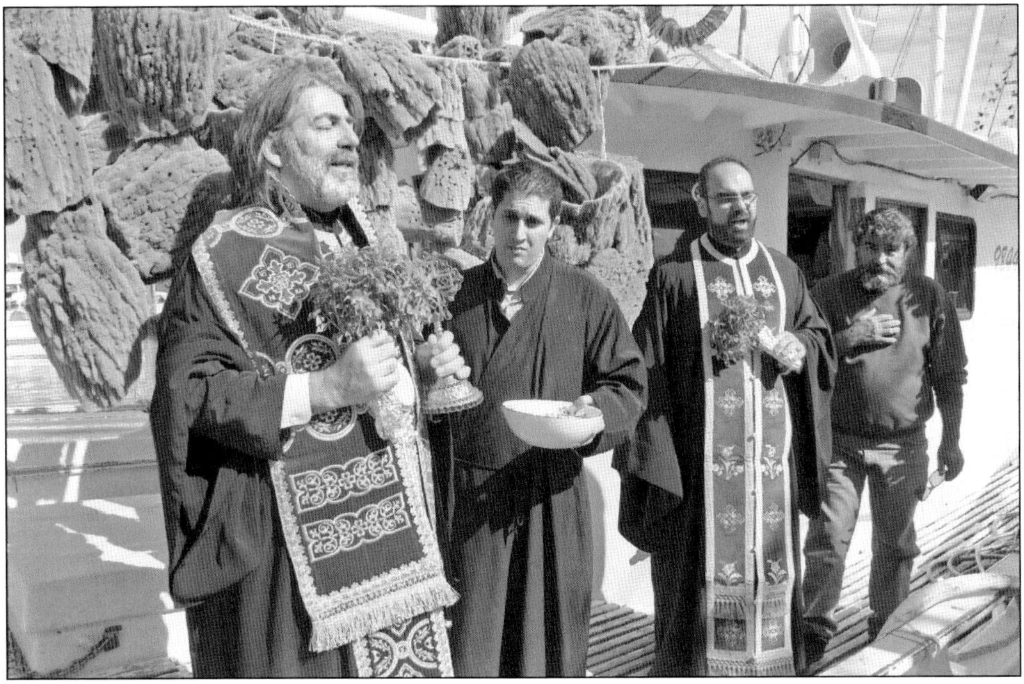

On January 5, 2012, Metropolitan Nikitas Lulias of the Greek Orthodox church, a Tarpon Springs native, blesses the *Anastasi* sponge boat with the help of acolyte Valantis Kouros and the Reverend Father Vasileios Tsourlis as sponge boat captain and diver Anastasios Karistinos looks on. Metropolitan Nikitas revived the local custom of blessing the boats as well as the waters in 2003, after a lapse of almost 20 years. He frequently returns from his post in San Francisco to perform the Liturgy at St. Nicholas on important community occasions. A metropolitan is the equivalent of an archbishop. (Photograph by the author.)

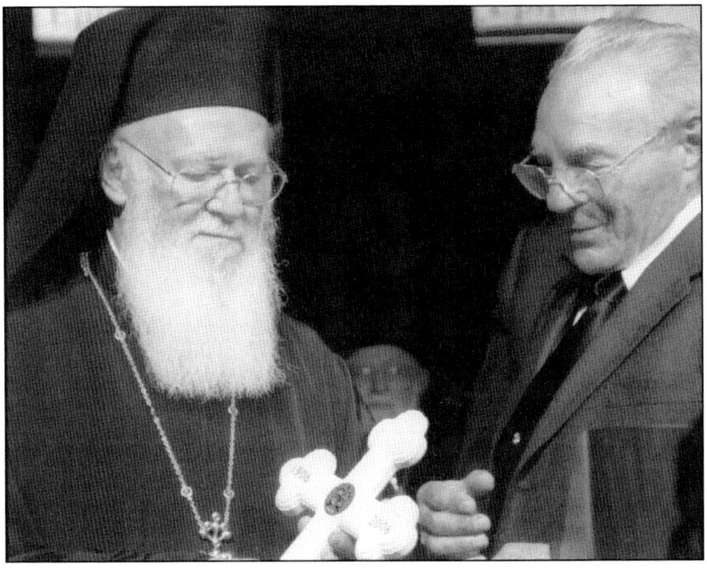

Ecumenical Patriarch Bartolomew of Constantinople (left) and Mercury "Bill" Paskalakis (1935–2010) inspect the cross made for the 100th anniversary of the Epiphany celebration in Tarpon Springs. Paskalakis taught shop classes at Tarpon High School and then at Tarpon Springs Middle School. In 1970, he began crafting 9-by-11-inch wooden crosses weighted with lead for use in the Epiphany dive. (Courtesy of Mercury Paskalakis.)

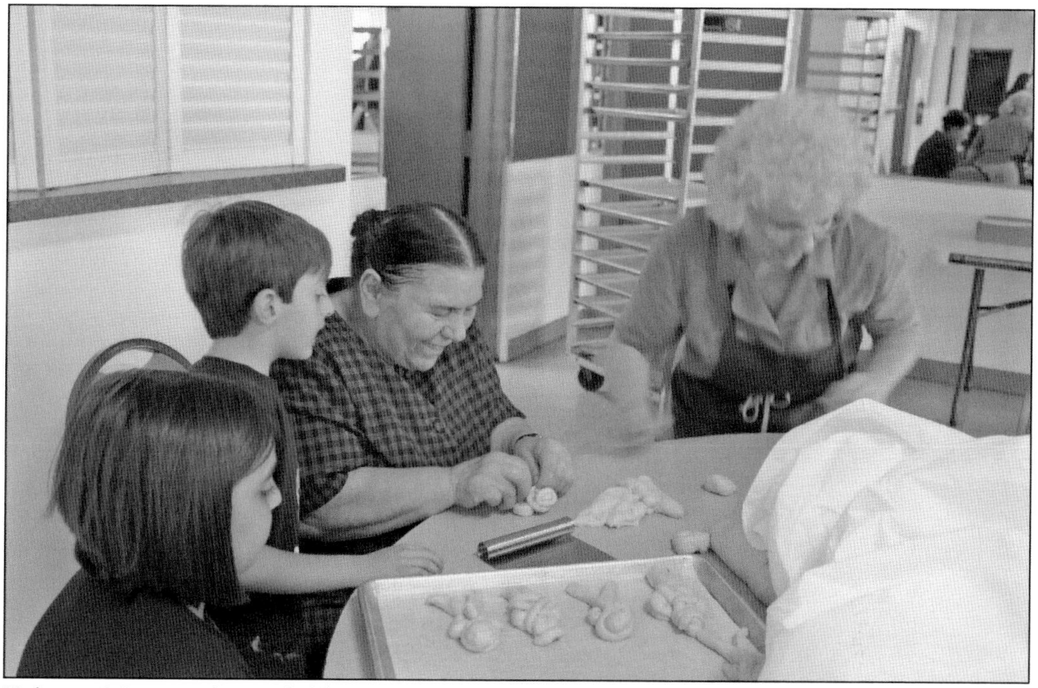

Kalotina Mougros shows children how to make *lazarakia* at St. Nicholas Cathedral's Father Tryfon Hall in 2009. People bake lazarakia, small spice breads in the form of Lazarus, on the Saturday before Holy Week to commemorate Christ raising Lazarus from the dead. In compliance with Lenten restrictions, they lack eggs or dairy. (Photograph by author, courtesy of the City of Tarpon Springs.)

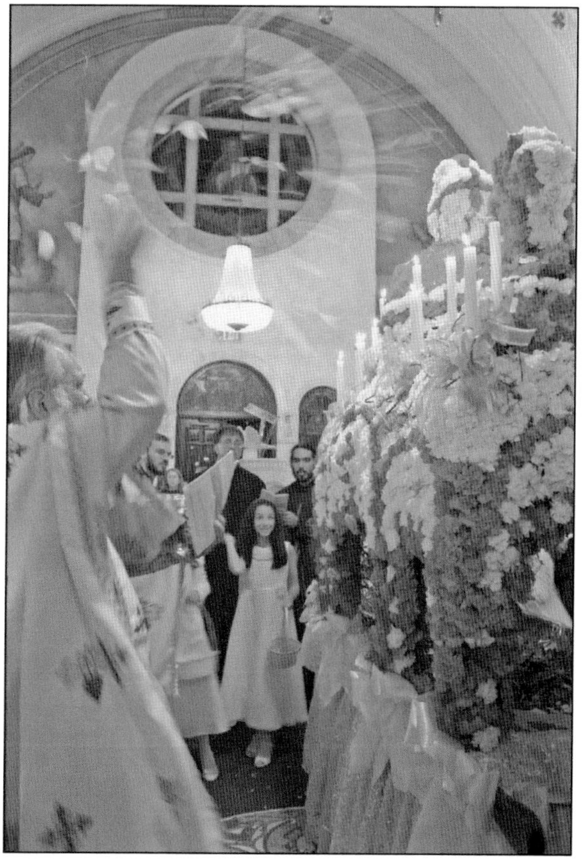

The Reverend Father Michael Eaccarino, protopresbyter, blesses the *kouvouklion* (tomb) of Christ during the singing of the Lamentations at the Matins Service of Holy Friday at St. Nicholas Greek Orthodox Cathedral in 2009. Earlier in the day, young women of the parish had decorated it. After being blessed, it was carried outside the church in procession around the neighborhood, followed by hundreds of parishioners. (Photograph by the author.)

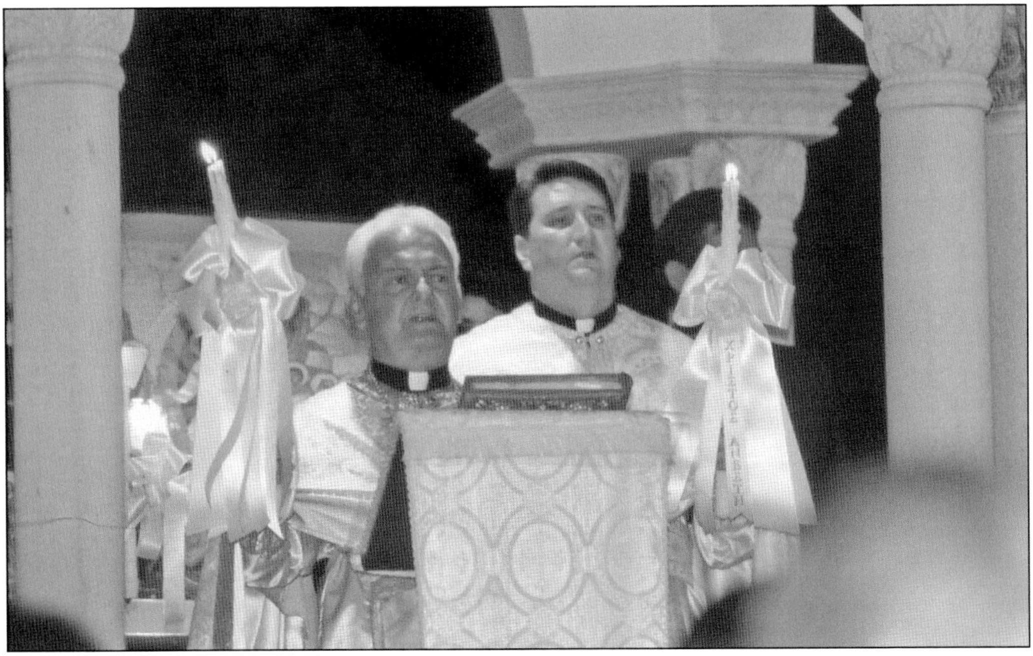

The Reverend Father Tryfon Theophilopoulos (left) celebrates Easter with the Reverend Father Constantine Simeonides at St. Nicholas in 2004. Tryfon (1935–2005) was assigned to St. Nicholas in December 1975. He was loved by the community, whom he served with wisdom and devotion for 30 years. The resurrection is celebrated with a late Saturday-night Liturgy during which the lights are extinguished and the priest brings out a single candle whose flame is passed to the candles of the worshippers. Guarding the flame, they return home to break the strict 40-day Lenten fast with *magiritsa* or *patsa* soups. (Photograph by Eleni Christopoulos-Lekkas.)

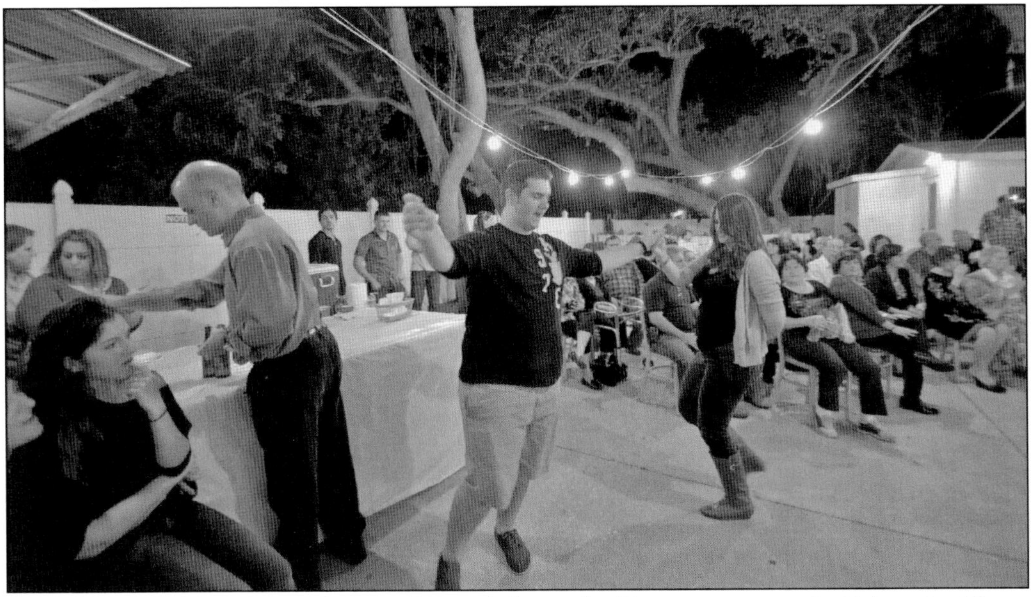

Mikés Kambourakis dances with Stacey Kontodiakos at the *Xenitia* concert at the Kalymnian House on November 11, 2013. Other members of the Kalymnian Society are seated and enjoying the music, which focused on songs about immigration. (Photograph by Eleni Christopoulos-Lekkas.)

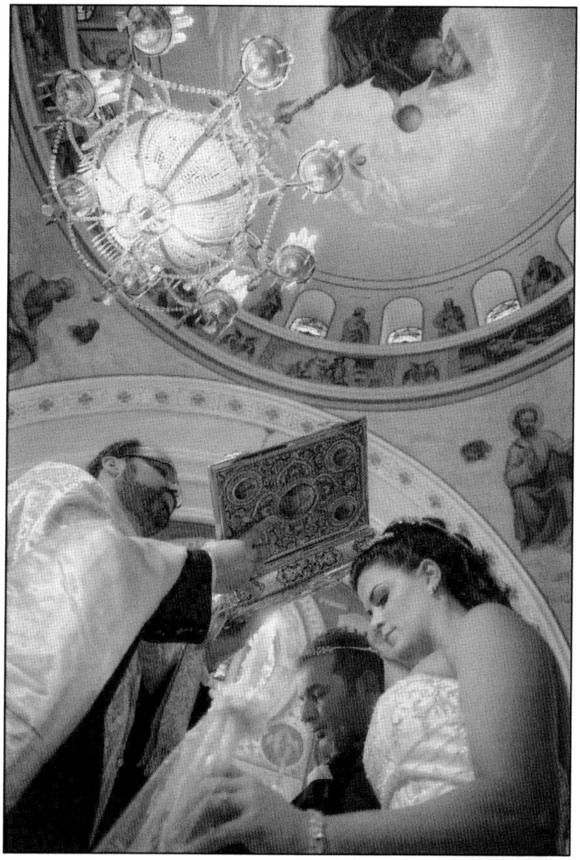

Wearing their *stefana* (wedding crowns) and holding their candles, Pete and Renee Korfiatis kneel as the Reverend Father Vasileios Tsourlis marries them in St. Nicholas Greek Orthodox Cathedral. (Photograph by Eleni Christopoulos-Lekkas.)

Goldie Tsalichis Parr stands in front of St. Michael Archangel Shrine. The sister of Steve Tsalichis, who was afflicted with an incurable brain tumor as a child, Goldie lives in a house on the family property and now takes most of the responsibility for the daily functions of the shrine. (Photograph by Eleni Christopoulos-Lekkas.)

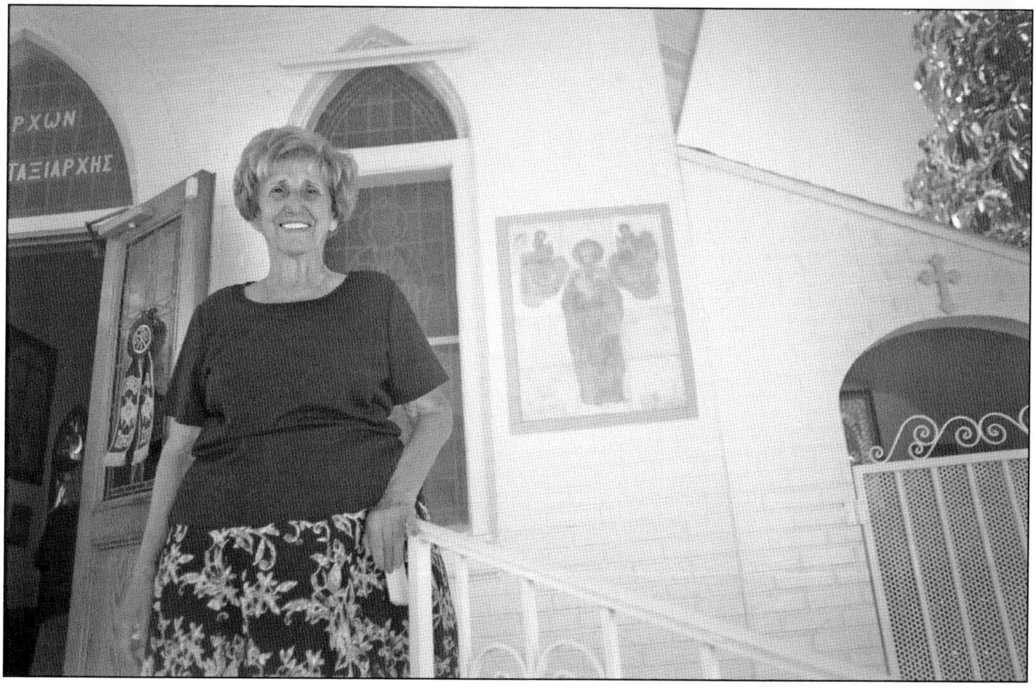

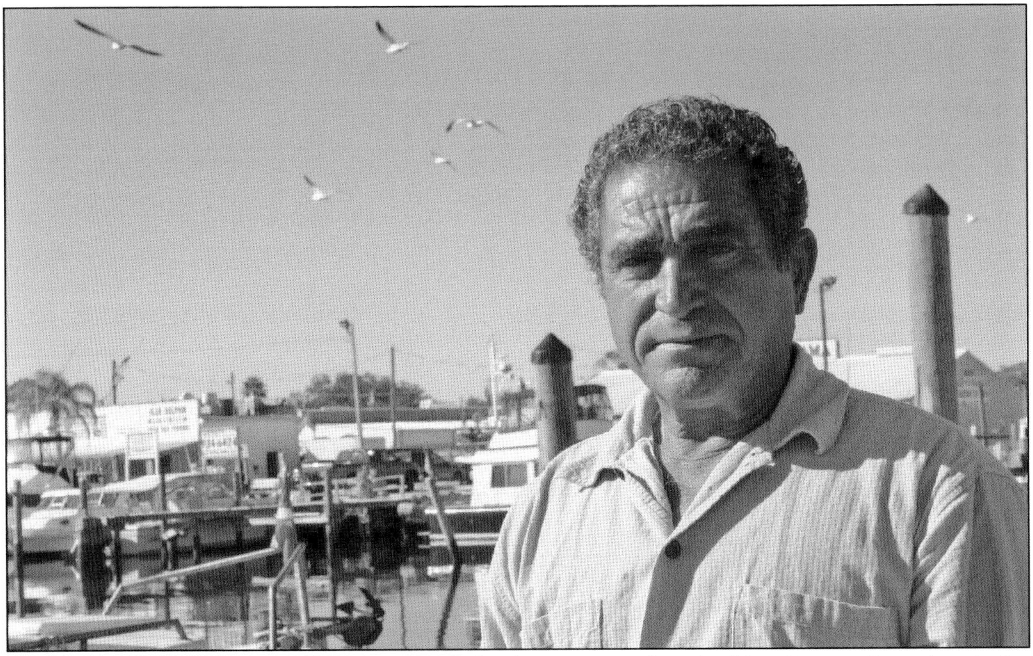

Florida Folk Heritage Award recipient and third-generation boatbuilder George Saroukos is the last master builder of Greek sponge boats. During the first half of the 20th century, hundreds of *achtarmas*-style sponge boats were built in Tarpon Springs. (Photograph by the author.)

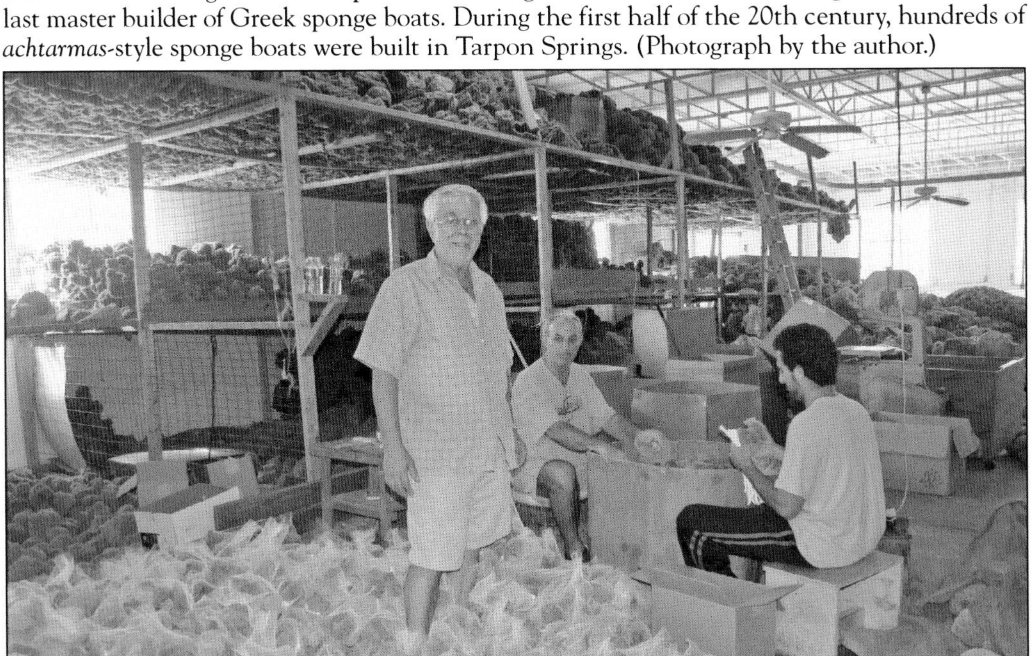

One of Tarpon Springs' largest sponge merchants was Michail Koutouzis (1942–2013), standing amid sponges being packaged for sale in his sponge warehouse in April 2008. Originally from Kalymnos, Koutouzis and his brothers were all sponge merchants, first in business together and then separately. Two of the brothers left for the United States while the other remained in Greece, but they maintained close business and personal ties. Koutouzis first went to the Chicago area before settling in Tarpon Springs, where his family remains in the business. (Photograph by the author.)

Anthony "Curly" Spanolios is seen here trimming sponges near the Sponge Docks. When he was young, his family owned a woodyard on Athens Street, where he helped his father make charcoal for the sponge boats and private residences. Curly later worked for his uncle as a diver and deckhand. Although he is long past retirement age, Curly continues to enjoy the companionship he shares with others working with sponge commerce and tourism on the Sponge Docks. (Photograph by the author.)

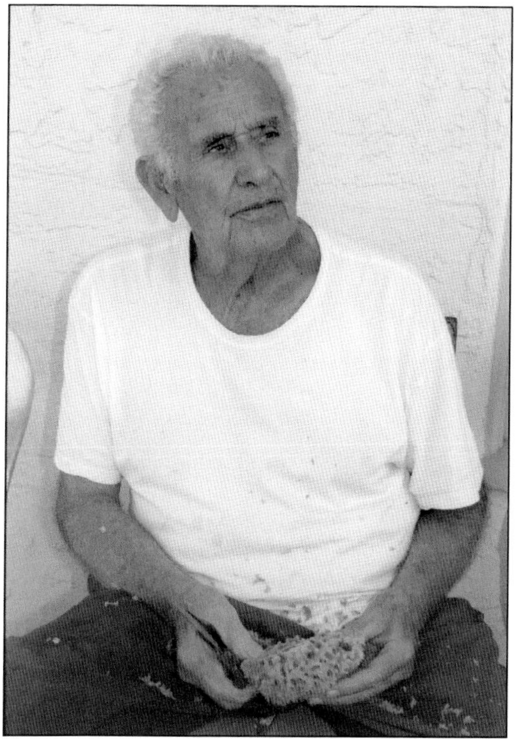

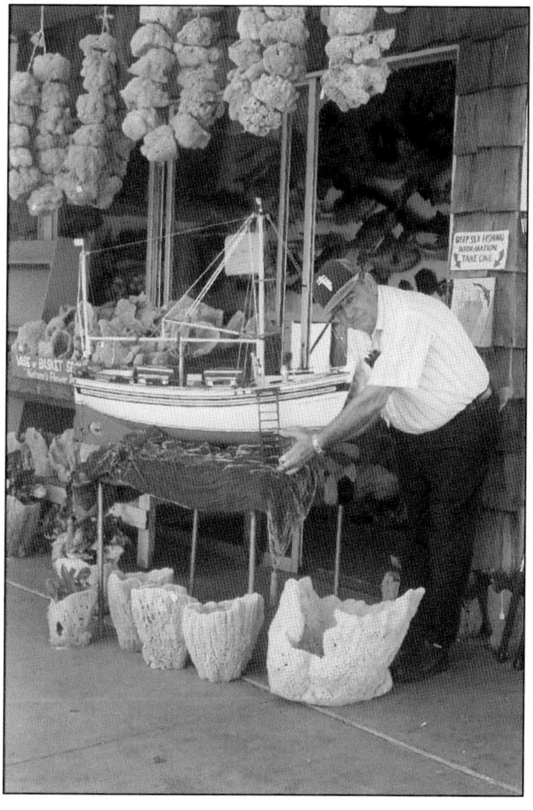

During his later years, Steve Stavrakis (1928–2012) made model sponge boats that he gifted to family members. When his father came from Halki around 1918, he first moved to Tampa, then to Tarpon Springs, where he owned a ship's chandlery for a time. While in high school, Stavrakis spent a summer working in Apalachicola with his great-uncle Nicholas Anargirou, a master boatbuilder from Halki. Anargirou also built model sponge boats; Stavrakis studied their design and made rigging for one of them. Stavrakis also spent two summers working as a deckhand on sponge boats. Reproduced in a one-inch to one-foot scale, the models he created are exact replicas of the boats he worked on, including many of the blocks, brackets, lanterns, and other items. (Photograph by Bud Lee, courtesy of the University of Central Florida.)

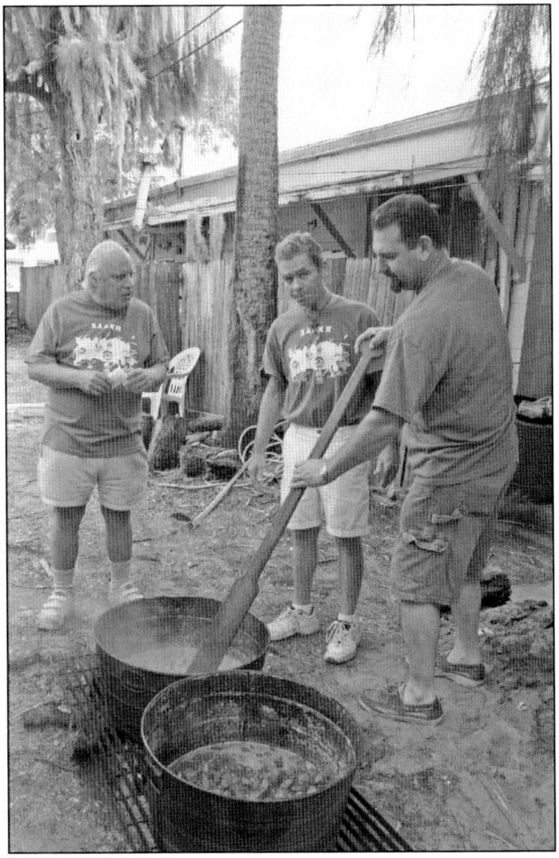

From left to right, Steve Tsalickis, Todd Paskalakis, and George Hourdas make *kavourmas* for the annual luncheon of the Halki Society in October 2012. They use the traditional cooking utensils consisting of a washtub and paddle. Although spongers now have refrigerators on board and no longer need to prepare it, some residents still make *kavourmas* on special occasions or to teach others about the tradition. (Photograph by author, courtesy of the City of Tarpon Springs.)

Mikés Koursiotis works alongside his mother, Maria, at their traditional Greek restaurant, Mama Maria's. In 1959, sponge diver John "Sfeeka" Koursiotis left Kalymnos for Tarpon Springs. Unfortunately, in 1978, his diving career was cut short by the bends, the crippling decompression sickness suffered by many divers. To help support the family, his wife opened a successful restaurant with home-style Greek cooking, and three children have followed in her footsteps. (Photograph by Eleni Christopoulos-Lekkas.)

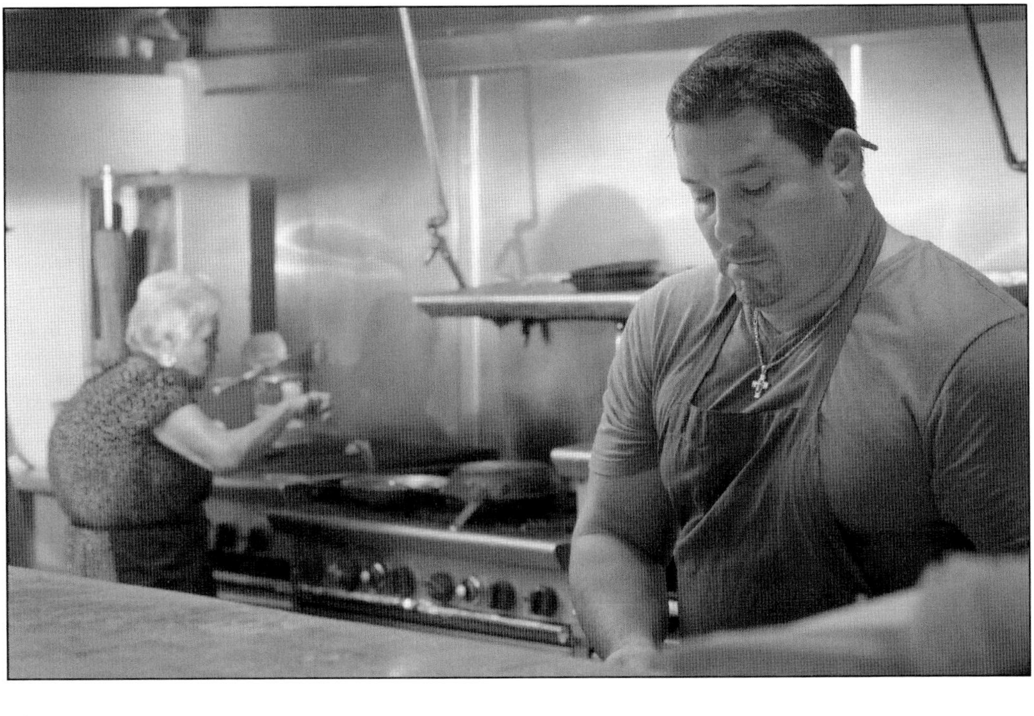

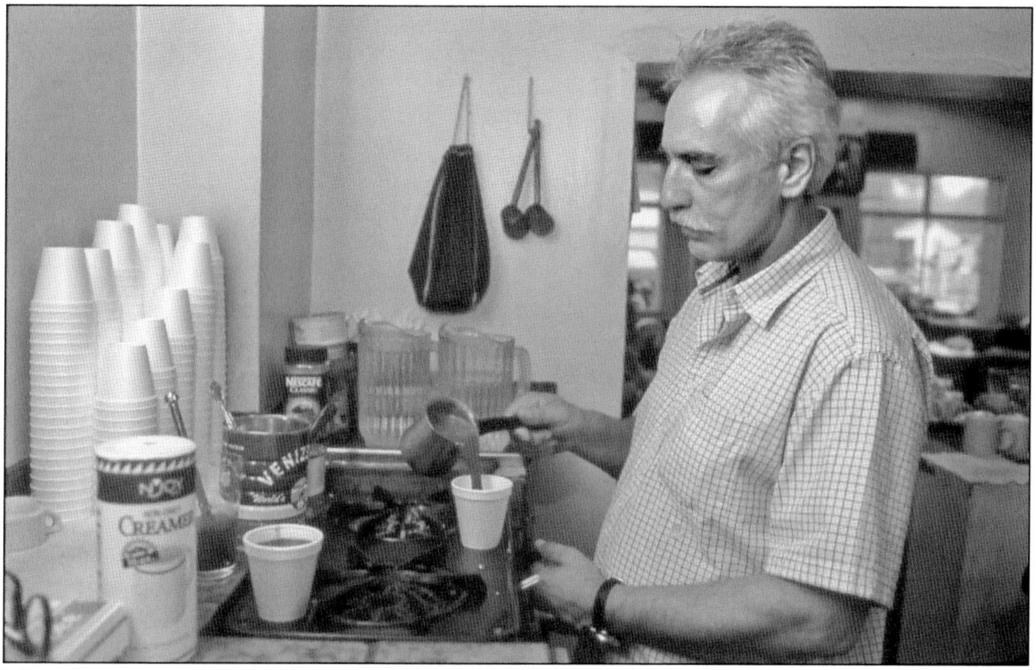

John Klonaris makes Greek coffee for customers at Angel's (formerly Lazaros Coffee Shop) on Athens Street on April 25, 2003. Three traditional men's coffeehouses on Athens Street continue to do a brisk business from early in the morning until late at night. (Photograph by Robert L. Stone, courtesy of State Archives of Florida, Florida Memory.)

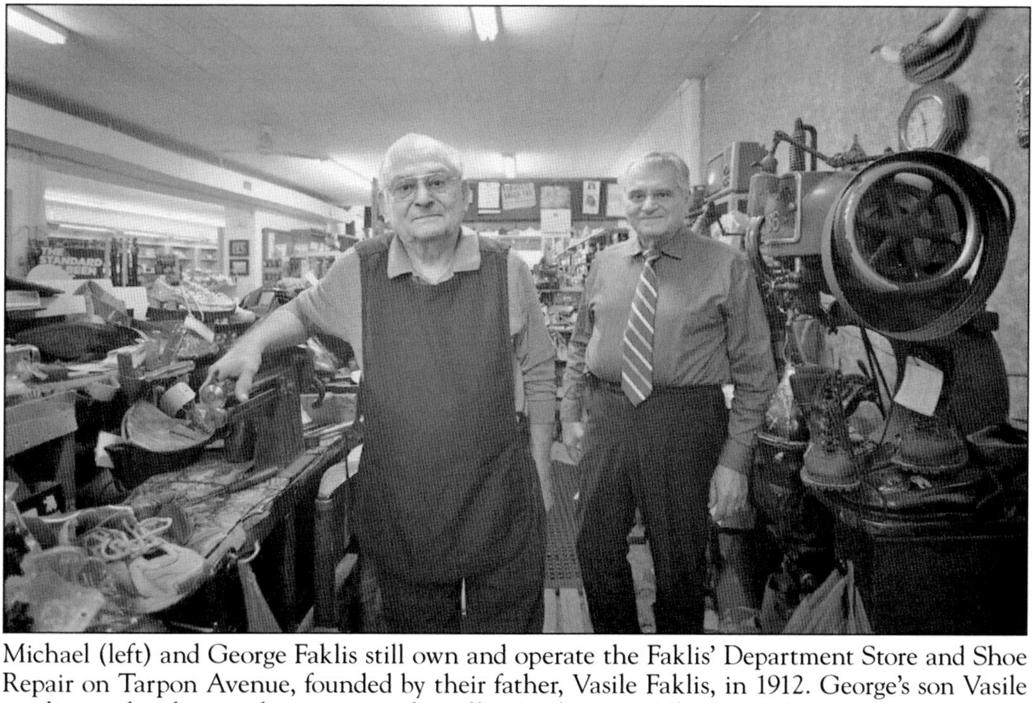

Michael (left) and George Faklis still own and operate the Faklis' Department Store and Shoe Repair on Tarpon Avenue, founded by their father, Vasile Faklis, in 1912. George's son Vasile is a licensed orthotist who maintains his office in the store. The entire family remains actively involved in the Symian Society. (Photograph by Eleni Christopoulos-Lekkas.)

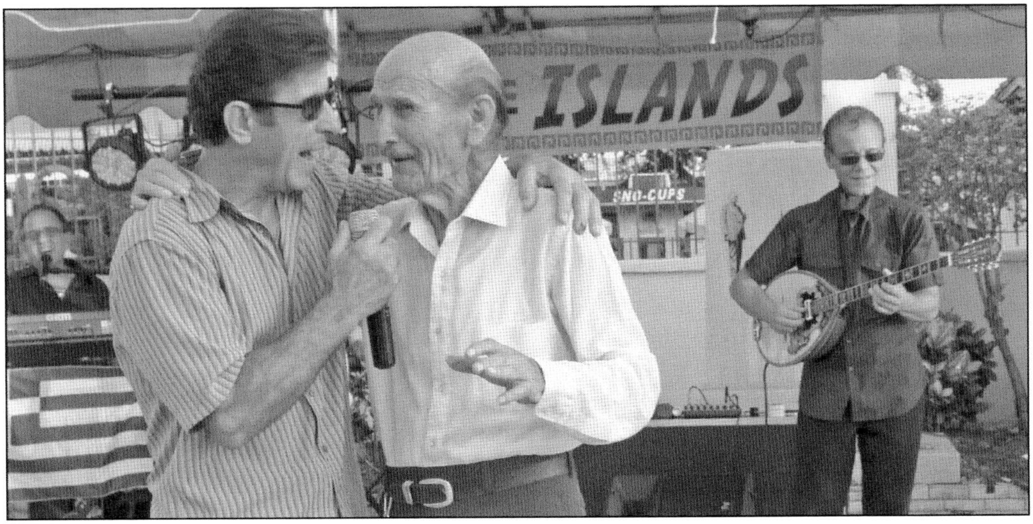

Spiros Skordilis (front right) joins vocalist Elias Poulos of Ellada to sing one of his own compositions at the Night in the Islands event held at the Sponge Docks on August 6, 2011. Other Ellada members are keyboard player Dino Theofilos (far left) and bouzouki player George Soffos (far right). With its Greek music, social dancing, and outdoor dining, many residents feel that Night in the Islands has brought some of the feeling of the old celebrations back to the Sponge Docks. (Photograph by the author.)

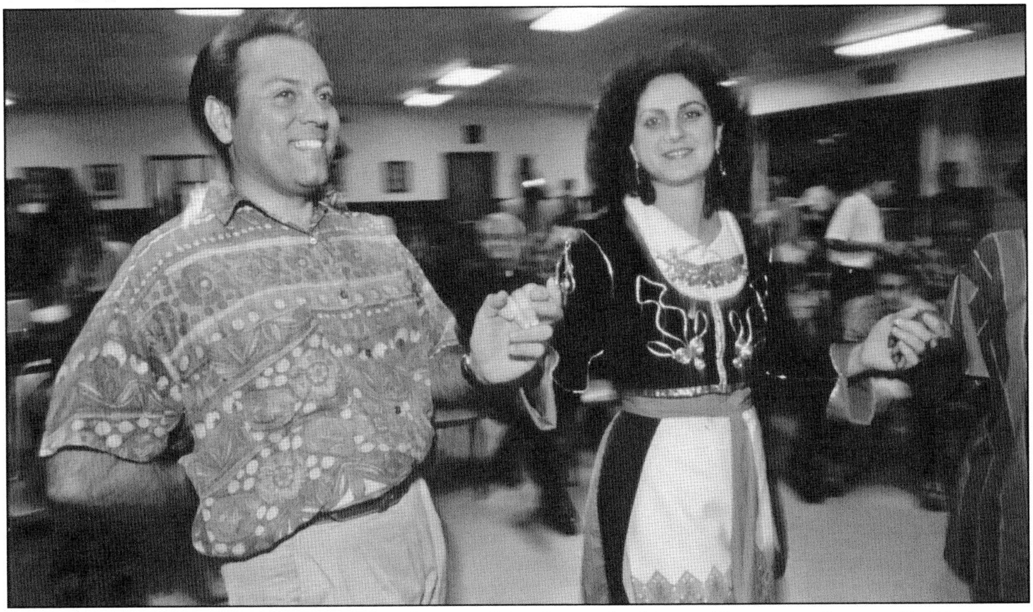

John Lulias and Maria Karavokiros Kouskoutis of the Levendia Dance Troupe perform at St. Nicholas. In 1979, Lulias formed Levendia and developed it into one of the premier Greek folk dance troupes in the United States. He directed the group for more than 25 years. At times, there were over 200 dancers, with an adult performing group numbering over 45. The group traveled domestically and internationally, promoting, perpetuating, and preserving Greek culture through song and dance. Lulias established the Winter Dance Conference in Tarpon Springs and often brought in outside expert instructors. Today, his former student Maria directs the Levendia Dance Troupe. (Photograph by Ron J. Bernard, courtesy of the *Tampa Tribune*.)

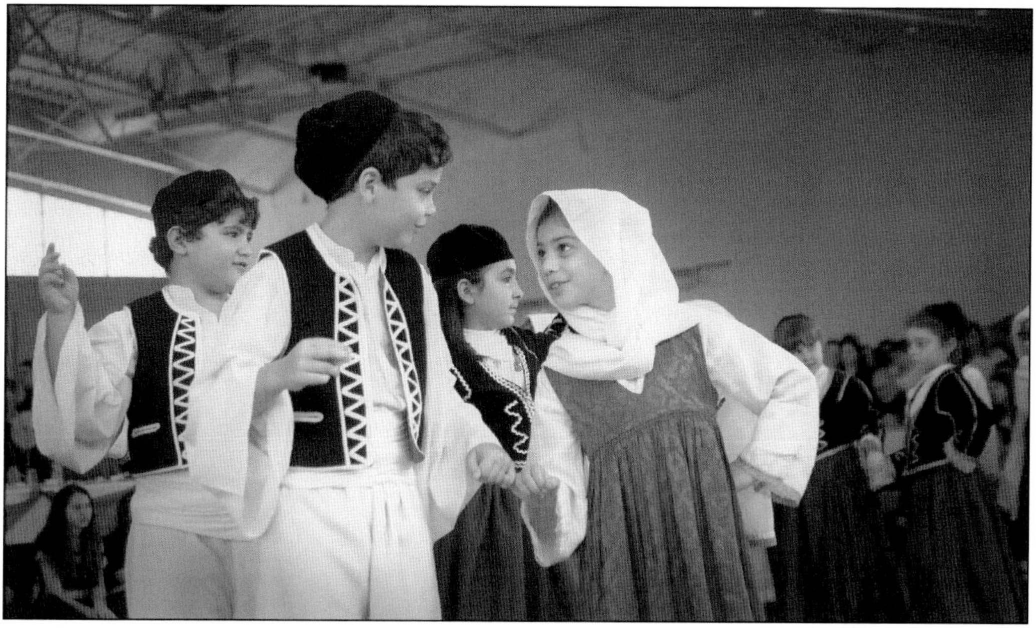

Members of the Sfoungarakia subgroup of Levendia perform for the 2013 Epiphany *glendi* (celebration) at the St. Nicholas Community Center. The young couple in front is Yianni Korfiatis and Efymia Trikilis, with George Lekkas and Katerina Lecourezos behind. They may not yet be aware of it, but these young dancers are preserving dance traditions brought by their grandparents and great-grandparents. (Photograph by Eleni Christopoulos-Lekkas.)

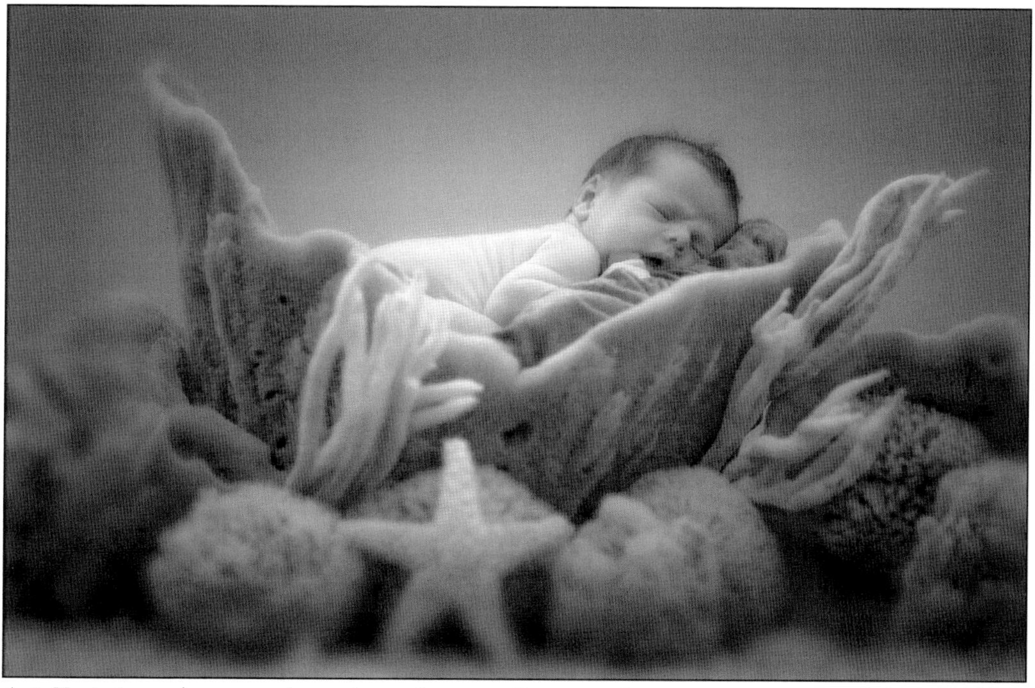

Aris Karistinos, the son and grandson of sponge divers, nestles in a vase sponge in September 2010. Like the baby in the sponge 100 years earlier, he will carry into the future the history and traditions of this community born from the sponge industry. (Photograph by Eleni Christopoulos-Lekkas.)